PERELANDRA
GARDEN WORKBOOK

A Complete Guide to Gardening
With Nature Intelligences

PERELANDRA

GARDEN WORKBOOK

SECOND EDITION

A COMPLETE GUIDE
TO GARDENING WITH
NATURE INTELLIGENCES

MACHAELLE SMALL WRIGHT

PERELANDRA, LTD.

CENTER FOR NATURE RESEARCH
JEFFERSONTON ✱ VIRGINIA

This book is manufactured in the United States of America.
Designed by James F. Brisson, Williamsville, VT 05362
Cover design by James F. Brisson
Copyedited by Elizabeth McHale, Williamsburg, MA 01096
Legwork, pasteup, computer technician, support and meals by Clarence N. Wright
Formatting, typesetting and computer wizardry by Machaelle Small Wright
This book was formatted, laid out and produced using the Xerox Ventura
Publisher software along with the Hewlett Packard Laser Jet 4 printer.
Published by Perelandra, Ltd., P.O. Box 3603, Warrenton, VA 20188

Library of Congress Card Catalog Number: 93-083705
Wright, Machaelle Small
Perelandra Garden Workbook:
A Complete Guide to Gardening with Nature Intelligences
Second Edition

Printed on paper with recycled content.

First hardcover printing: March 1987
ISBN 0-9617713-1-3
4 6 8 9 7 5 3
First softcover printing: May 1988
ISBN 0-9617713-2-1
6 8 9 7 5

Second edition printing: April 1993
ISBN 0-927978-12-1
8 9

To all the
devas and nature spirits
who have come together to
teach me, show me and work with me,
so that I could begin to understand
how their slice of reality
fits into the larger
whole.

My appreciation
and love for them is
beyond words.

TABLE OF CONTENTS

INTRODUCTION

When I published the first edition of the *Perelandra Garden Workbook* in 1987, I was the only person who had worked with the processes and procedures described in that book. As I wrote the book, I made every attempt to explain everything as fully as I possibly could, drawing on my own experiences, and giving all the hints and comments I could remember that might be helpful. To be honest, I wasn't sure how the book would be received. By necessity, the *Workbook* must be comprehensive. It must cover all the bases of a co-creative partnership with nature. The switch from traditional gardening methods to the co-creative method is not a small thing. I had visions of people getting the *Workbook*, looking at all the instructions and charts, and just stringing me up for writing something so "complex."

Well, I'm still alive and, much to my surprise, the *Workbook* has been well received. Thousands of people are using the first edition with amazing success and making the switch to co-creative gardening. What's even more amazing to me is how many people express that this book makes sense to them! Obviously, I'm not the only one in the world who is willing to think differently *and* follow up by doing whacky things.

Since 1987, I've received quite a bit of mail from *Workbook* readers. They tell me about their successes, and they talk about the difficulties they have with the book. Plus, at the Workbook Workshop at Perelandra I hear more. This second edition includes additional information that is in response to the reader/user reactions I've been getting. It also includes improvements in some of the processes due to the ongoing research with nature at Perelandra.

In the first edition's Introduction, I wrote,

> As I moved through the garden's annual cycle in this book, giving as many details as I possibly could about how and why I do what I do, I was joined by the individual devas and nature spirits involved, and they added their insight and information. In essence, I said to them, "If you had a chance to say something right now on this subject, what would you say?" For each session, I have identified the deva or nature spirit so that you'll be able to keep the players straight, and also so that you may begin to sense the differences between them. The word "you" in these sessions refers to you, the reader. I have functioned as merely the translator between you and nature....

In this second edition, I worked with the same nature team. We even "reopened" all the sessions for any changes and updates that nature wished. There is no conflict between what is presented in this edition and the first edition. None of the changes were negating. They are *upgrades*. So, if you have been using the first edition of the *Workbook*, you don't have to feel you've been steered "wrong" because you have discovered that in this second edition some of the processes have been changed. Again, the modifications are *improvements* and not fundamental changes. This is how nature wishes to work these processes with us now.

Another point: There are a handful of sessions that were done during the early years of research, and pertain to the understanding of specific processes as I was developing them. I have indicated them by giving the date they were translated in the paragraph just prior to the session. In these, the word "you" refers to me, for I functioned in the dual role of translator and recipient.

From listening to others, I have learned that some people can pick up the *Workbook* and integrate most of it in their gardening or farming literally within one or two growing seasons. It all makes sense to them and, from what I'm hearing, they just breeze right through the changes required to become a co-creative partner with nature. When I meet these people, I try to impress on them that it took me *ten years* of research and work to develop the processes in the *Workbook*, and I'd appreciate it if they wouldn't make me look like an idiot—slow down, make it look a little hard, for god's sake!

I've also heard from others who looked at the book when they first got it, become totally overwhelmed and put it on the shelf for a year or two before they mustered the courage to read it. Then they read little bits and pieces of it at a time, found out working it wasn't nearly as difficult as they anticipated, and began working with nature in co-creative partnership in their garden.

Still others felt overwhelmed when they saw the book, but didn't put it on the shelf for two years. They tell me they concentrated on one or two chapters each year, and integrated just those changes during the growing season. The next year they added another chapter or two. This sounds like a fine way to deal with the *Workbook* if you feel at all overwhelmed by it. Take it slow. You are changing not only how you garden but also how you think about gardening—and *life.*

So, my advice about this is to encourage you to find the approach to this book that feels comfortable to you, and then move forward at *your* pace as you develop your co-creative relationship with nature. The important thing is to begin working with nature in a new and direct way. It is *not* important that you fully integrate your gardening practices with the material in this book in one year. Nature will move along with you at your pace and in your timing.

I have included a glossary (Appendix A). If you are anything like me, you won't notice this until you finish reading the book and wonder what's on all those remaining pages. But in case you have difficulty with some of the terminology, be it horticultural or esoteric, I thought you might find the glossary helpful.

In the glossary section, I have also included *Co-Creative Definitions Dealing with Nature, Life, Science, the Universe and All Else.* In 1990, I asked nature to define ten terms that it has used a lot in the sessions we've had together. I had a feeling nature's definition of these terms and ours weren't exactly the same. Well, I was right. Nature's perception of words such as form, nature, consciousness, life vitality, energy and soul are quite

If you'd like some encouragement and moral support as you read and work the Workbook, *I suggest* Perelandra Voices, *our newsletter. The newsletter consists of articles and letters from folks who have been using the various Perelandra processes and wish to share their successes and difficulties with others. The newsletter is published annually, and because the information is not dated we continue to offer each year's newsletter. We have issues of* Voices *from 1991 to the current year available. Ordering information is in the back of the book.*

different from ours. I highly recommend that you read the *Co-Creative Definitions*—in them nature gives the foundation of the co-creative partnership and explains why it is so important.

This leads me to another point: I present the co-creative partnership within the context of a garden because the garden happens to be my laboratory where the principles and processes are worked out. There is a potential co-creative partnership in all natural settings. You do not have to have a garden to establish this partnership with nature. But you do need guidelines and processes, and this is what I give you in this book. If you would like to establish a co-creative partnership in forestry, landscaping, tree farming, regular farming, container planting, etc., all you need to do is the following: Read this book—sessions and all—and get a feel for how the partnership works in a garden context. Then retrofit the processes to your particular context. By this I mean that you will need to change the questions you ask, or use different lists that apply more to your specific area of interest.* You will *not* need to change the steps of the processes. In fact, I urge you not to change or drop any of the steps. The processes are complete and balanced as presented, and are what nature wishes to use when working with us. Every process developed in the garden works equally well in any other nature context.

* In Chapter 19 in this book, I give more ideas on retrofitting the processes to nature areas outside the garden.

Once you read nature's definition of "nature" and "form" you will know that we're talking about every aspect of life. There are many different gardens in life. The teacher's garden is the classroom. The scientist's garden is the laboratory. The therapist's garden is the client. The mother and father's garden is the family and home. If you are interested in establishing a co-creative partnership with nature in these kinds of areas, you will need the foundation of knowledge this book gives you plus the *Perelandra Garden Workbook II: Co-Creative Energy Processes for Gardening, Agriculture and Life.*** *Workbook II* presents the processes you will use with nature when working with and balancing these other gardens.

** Ordering information is in the back of this book.

Perelandra
February 1993

PERELANDRA
GARDEN WORKBOOK

A Complete Guide to Gardening
With Nature Intelligences

1

WHY BOTHER?
A MATTER OF
SPIRITUAL INTEGRITY,
A MATTER OF THE HEART

Why bother going through the effort it will take to incorporate an entirely different approach to your gardening? Especially in light of the fact that there are a number of approaches out there that are proven, established and successful enough.

I'm very aware that this is a valid issue. I've raised the question myself. I'm especially prone to raising it when crouched over in the garden working on the third day to do something that takes regular gardeners less than an hour to do. I've been known to stand my weary bones upright, look toward the sky, and give serious thought to the state of my sanity. But each year as I watch my garden flourish under adverse conditions and the other gardens around me struggle, even die under the same conditions, I find I raise the question less and less. I also realized over the years that my garden does not flourish because I'm a good gardener. I'm surrounded by good gardeners who have been at it a lot longer than I. And to be quite frank, in the world of gardening, there are many who are more technically advanced than I.

The Perelandra garden thrives because of the approach I have been taught, and the underlying consciousness and reality that motivates the approach. What I'm going to describe to you in this book does not fit comfortably in the recognized notions of tradition, logic or even sanity. In fact, it tends to thumb its nose at all three, especially sanity. Be that as it may, it works. And that's what drives traditional-gardening thinkers a little nuts. It's also what will drive you a little nuts. Everything you know which has gone into establishing your sense of order, stability and balance—in other words, logic—both in the garden and in your life, will be constantly challenged. For you see, this gardening is a metaphor for the whole of life. As you change how you approach the garden, you will, in turn, change the very fabric of how you approach your life.

It takes a lot of effort and struggle to change our way of thinking. It takes many times more effort to change our thinking, and then turn around and change how we actually *do* something. All the existing tools, information, expectations, manuals and charts are geared toward established ways. It takes effort to look at what is already available to us and change it to accommodate the new or invent what we need. I've been taught that everything on Earth is changing, and that includes how mankind responds to and works with nature. Well, this has to include gardening, too. Old traditions and proven practices must be updated in order for them to respond fully to our changing times. I've also been taught that because of the differences in environments between one spot on the planet and another—and here I refer to ecological impact as much as anything else—no one method can be used in two different gardens with the same exact results. So it would be useless to tell you step by step how to duplicate the Perelandra garden. In fact, *I* can't even duplicate it from one year to the next. Conditions change. There is constant ecological shifting which I have to make adjustments for each year. All I can do is share what I've been taught, how I get my information, and the processes I've developed as a result.

OVERLIGHTING DEVA OF PERELANDRA

I would like to address the issue of change as well—specifically, the change the planet Earth is experiencing at the present time. Understand that the change we speak of regarding the movement from one era to the next—in your terminology, "Piscean" to "Aquarian"*— is universal, and Earth is a part of this massive shift. Try to keep in mind that Earth is not experiencing some isolated process, but is actively and intimately linked with an overall process. I say this to you, and will most likely repeat it from time to time, in order to keep things in perspective for you. We on the devic level find that you on the human level have the habit of disconnecting yourselves from the larger picture. This is self-imposed isolation.

Now, regarding nature and this change. It only stands to reason that if the whole universe is experiencing a major shift, that shift would have to be fully demonstrated in form on Earth. Mankind has the idea that he is participating in a change, but he has not on the whole looked beyond himself and recognized that everything around him is also participating in the same change.

Those souls and intelligences who have been a part of Earth's evolution for the past two thousand years have diligently focused on establishing all functions of life in such a way that they fully demonstrated the energy dynamic of the Piscean era. All that existed on Earth, in whatever form, had to respond to the Piscean environment prevalent within the universe. To do otherwise would have been to place the planet in a position of disharmony within its own universe.

Earth is not of the Aquarian age yet. It is in a transition period that is moving toward the Aquarian age. This very same can be said about the universe as well. The laws of the universe dictate that there be transition between points of change. To go directly from point A to point B would place an unacceptable strain on all life forms, either on this planet or within the universe. There would be spasm. Instead, there is transition. During the transition all that existed during the Piscean age begins its movement toward the Aquarian age. Form, structure, action, intent, attitude—all of this begins to shift.

Earth is now fully participating in this transition. The chaos which you are experiencing and observing around you is in part a response to the transition. I say "in part" because, although a sense of chaos on some

* The Piscean era explored and worked with the dynamics of the parent/child, higher/lower and masculine-energy-dominant relationships; these dynamics were expressed in both action and structure throughout all levels of form reality.

The Aquarian era into which we are moving emphasizes the concepts of balance, teamwork and partnership. These dynamics will be emphasized in the pattern and rhythm of all life behavior.

level is inherent in change, the degree of chaos and how it is manifested in action is up to mankind and however much he wishes to fight the transition.

We turn our focus to gardening, for it is an excellent example of what we have been talking about. Those who were drawn to agriculture and gardening during these past two thousand years worked very hard to develop understanding, knowledge, tools and frameworks for action which successfully meshed with the nature with which they were working and in light of the Piscean environment. What they developed, by and large, responded to the Piscean dynamic. It had to if this aspect of reality on Earth was to be in harmony with the universe. Their struggles, growth and development were within this larger harmony. We on the devic level recognize their heart connection with the nature around them. Because of the present fragile state of the planet's natural environment, it is easy for mankind today to turn to these people and point a finger of blame. Accuse them of wrongful action. Even look to them as being stupid.

What they accomplished was not wrongful or stupid. It was Piscean, and for the most part worked well within that era. But then the planet began to make its movement in response to the transition. In Earth time, that would be approximately 1940. And those things that worked so well within the Piscean era began not to work quite so well. The demands of the planet began to change and the old forms could not respond in balance to the new demands. The clashing of the old forms with the new demands for change, along with mankind's reluctance to let go of the old, have created a mess.

What was developed in the area of agriculture and gardening during the Piscean era is not to be discarded, but rather used as the foundation upon which to build. Remember, you are in the transition, not the Aquarian era itself. Therefore, allow for growth and change, not destruction. For the sake of order and harmony, look to what was developed and what worked well, and allow that to be your starting point for the transition.

The reason the garden at Perelandra is so successful is because Machaelle has opened herself to us—what she refers to as "nature intelligences"—in a co-creative partnership, and allowed us to direct her through this period of change. Her description to you of standing up in the garden from time to time and questioning her sanity is her way of expressing the chaos around change which I have referred to. As you see, because she is willing to move with the currents of the times, her response to the inherent chaos is not one of destructive revolution, but rather gentle recognition.

The changes that have been instituted in the Perelandra garden work because they have the power of the existing dynamic of the universe behind them. If she were to hold onto those practices which worked so well in the Piscean era, she would then be acting contrary to the universal flow—and the Perelandra garden would reflect this. In short, to add our answer to the question "Why bother?," we feel that to do otherwise, to buck universal flow, would be akin to attempting to stop a tidal wave with your hand.

I would like to add one more insight. Just as humans are working to adjust to the changing times, so, too, is nature. In the areas where man comes into active partnership with nature—forestry, conservation, gardening, farming, landscaping, etc.—he has the opportunity to help facilitate nature's response to the transition. In these areas we not only need mankind's cooperation, we need his active partnership. Notice that the areas I have singled out would not exist if it were not for man's desire to interface with nature. Therefore it is essential to our evolution in these areas that mankind open the door to us and consciously join with us in a new level of partnership so that we may work together to bring into form the necessary changes.

Let me give you a brief background on how Perelandra and I got started in this partnership.

We moved from the city to the country in 1973. While city dwelling, I became interested in ecology and its corresponding responsible life styles. By the time Clarence and I moved to the country, the idea of putting in a vegetable garden on our new land was as practical and logical as putting a house on the land. I didn't give much thought to the matter. I just put it in. To do otherwise would have seemed odd to me. I had not had any gardening experience prior to this, so I spent the first couple of years educating myself as to the ins and outs of "good" gardening. I also listened to the advice of my neighbors, some of whom have fifty, sixty and seventy years of gardening under their belts. These are legitimate farmers who depend on the produce from their gardens for their main food supply. As a result, my

* In the first edition of the Workbook, *I called this process "co-creative **energy** gardening." Now, I feel "co-creative gardening" describes the process more accurately.*

* That meeting and my early education are described in Behaving As If the God In All Life Mattered.

** The pronunciation of "deva" is **"dey-vah,"** *not diva (the singer) or dee-vah.*

***The 1990 definitions, titled "Co-Creative Definitions Dealing with Nature, Life, Science, the Universe and All Else" are printed in their entirety in Appendix A.

first couple of years were quite successful. We had more food than we knew what to do with. However, the high amount of produce was directly related to the fact that I was using the insecticide Sevin. I began to think when I read on the back of the bag that I should not eat vegetables within twenty-four hours after spraying. Using Sevin pretty much assured me of successful production, but what was I doing to my body once I ate the food? And did spraying this stuff do anything to an already fragile environment? I didn't even raise the question of killing all those bugs—I still considered them pests who stood between me and a successful garden. But the questions I did raise led me to organic gardening.

Organic gardening certainly addressed my concerns over our health and the environment. Its focus on overall balance and building healthy soil as being keys to better quality food made all the sense in the world to me. It still does. I consider organic gardening to be the foundation upon which *co-creative gardening** (the term I use to describe the Perelandra gardening process) is built. But anyone who practices organic gardening knows that it is made up of a huge volume of hints, tips, ideas and practices—some of which, when tried, work and some don't, despite the fact that the organic gardener just down the road did exactly the same thing and got incredible results. Reading volumes on organic gardening in an effort to find the magical combination of practices that would give me the kind of garden one always sees photographed on the covers of books and magazines made me feel that not only would I not reach a respectable level of gardening until age eighty-five, but that I had no right to expect it before eighty-five. I had to put in my time like everyone else. I was just thirty-one years old, and the road to eighty-five seemed awfully long.

By this time, it was 1976 and that's when Clarence handed me the Findhorn garden books. They introduced me to the idea that there was an intelligence in nature and if one applied oneself just a bit, one could communicate with these intelligences and "be told" what to do, especially in the area of gardening. To say the least, I found the notion appealing and worth a try. This is when I met* and began working with devas** and nature spirits.

Let's define some terms. In 1990 I asked nature for some definitions.*** I had a feeling that nature's understanding of certain words was not the same as our understanding. Here's how nature defined itself.

NATURE: *In the larger universe and beyond, on its many levels and dimensions, there are a number of groups of consciousnesses which, although equal in importance, are quite different in expression and function. Do not misunderstand us by thinking that we are saying that all reality is human soul-oriented but that there are some aspects of this reality that function and express differently. We are not saying this. We are saying that there are different groups of consciousnesses that are equal in importance but express and function very differently. Together, they comprise the full expression of the larger, total life picture. No one piece, no one expression, can be missing or the larger life picture on all its levels and dimensions will cease to exist. One such consciousness has been universally termed "nature." Because of what we are saying about the larger picture not existing without all of its parts, you may assume that nature as both a reality and a consciousness exists on all dimensions and all levels. It cannot be excluded.*

Each group of consciousnesses has what can be termed an area of expertise. As we said, all groups are equal in importance but express and function differently from one another. These different expressions and functions are vital to the overall balance of reality. A truly symbiotic relationship exists among the groups and is based on balance—universal balance. You are absolutely correct to characterize the human soul-oriented dynamic as evolution in scope and function. And you are correct in identifying the nature dynamic as being involution in scope and function. Nature is a massive, intelligent consciousness group that expresses and functions within the many areas of involution, that is, moving soul-oriented consciousness into any dimension or level of form.

*Nature **is** the conscious reality that supplies order, organization and life vitality for this shift. Nature is the consciousness that is, for your working understanding, intimately linked with form. Nature is the consciousness that comprises all form on all levels and dimensions. It is form's order, organization and life vitality. Nature is first and foremost a consciousness of equal importance with all other consciousnesses in the largest scheme of reality. It expresses and functions uniquely in that it comprises all form on all levels and dimensions and is responsible for and creates all of form's order, organization and life vitality.*

꧁ⶌ꧂

*Nature intelligences (devas **and** nature spirits) have a joyful manner about them. They may make us smile, even laugh at times, but they do not engage in cruel jokes or dirty tricks. And they are scrupulously honest. It is not in their nature (pardon that pun) to be otherwise.*

"Deva" is a Sanskrit word meaning body of light. This has little connection to what I experience when I am open to the devic level, but I accept the word. I simply experience an energetic presense which I don't normally see, but can feel and inwardly hear. The devic level is the *architectural dynamic* within nature that creates the blueprints for all form. In other words, it is the force that formulates every individual aspect of form on Earth. It is the creative force which determines the size, color, shape, weight, texture, taste, life cycle, and requirements of all form, all of nature. Each form has inherent in it its own deva. There is, for example, the Deva of Soil, the Deva of the Shasta Daisy, the Oak Tree Deva, the Carrot Deva. Each deva holds, as in a computer bank, all the specific information relative to its form. It also holds the information pertaining to how its individual natural form fits into the grand scheme of things both on Earth and within the universe. If there are to be any physical changes made—for example, changing carrots from the color orange to pink—they must be made within the devic level in order to maintain natural balance. Change made through our pure will and desire of humans disregarding the devic dynamic is called "manipulation," and results in a weakening imbalance which becomes part of the ecological disaster we presently experience.

OVERLIGHTING DEVA OF PERELANDRA

Machaelle's understanding of what she calls the "devic dynamic" is quite accurate, as it should be since she has been directly working with this level for more than ten years now [since 1976]. *Over that period of time, her understanding has broadened and grown due to her continuous experience with us, as with a friendship which has gone on for years. We point this out so that you'll understand that your working relationship with us may be small in scope in the beginning when compared with what Machaelle has presented to you. Don't be discouraged with this. As you consciously open to our level, allow our friendship to touch you, and then slowly and organically grow. She does not consciously remember, but ten years ago Machaelle saw the devic level as little more than a giant phone bank in the sky. We considered her imagery creative and most workable. From this clear but limited scope of reality, our friendship has developed and along with this, so, too, has our understanding of one another.*

At this point, we might add one additional thought to Machaelle's description of our level. It is generally believed that form—that is nature or what you call "physical reality"— is indigenous to Earth only. This is only part of the picture, and we feel that in order for you to relate in a fuller, more balanced manner toward nature and the form around you, we must expand the understanding of the devic level.

All that exists on Earth exists in one dynamic or another in every dimension of reality beyond Earth. The form of the five senses is but one expression of what you see around you. That expression shifts and changes in countless ways that directly relate to the many realities which exist on all levels. There is not one thing on Earth that does not exist on all other levels of reality. The devic level, in its role as creator and architect, is the bonding dynamic between all that is physical on Earth and its corresponding levels of existence elsewhere. To relate and respond to, for example, the Carrot Deva is to relate and respond to all existing levels of reality on Earth and beyond, through the specific dynamic of the carrot. In basic language, it may be said that one simple carrot is the key to the universe.

We find in our attempts to reach out to mankind on Earth that the biggest stumbling block we presently face is his limiting and demeaning attitude toward form—nature. We find it impossible to work with mankind's allocating relative spiritual worth on a sliding scale—with physical form invariably being placed at the bottom of the scale. This is certainly the root of the massive ecological imbalance which man now faces.

In Co-Creative Definitions, nature elaborated on the word "form." This might help clarify the above session from the Deva of Perelandra.

FORM: *We consider reality to be in the form state when there is organization, order and life vitality combined with a state of consciousness. For the purpose of understanding form in a constructive and workable manner, let us say that we consider consciousness to be soul-initiated and, therefore, quite capable of function beyond what we would term "form." There are dimensions of reality in which the interaction of life reality is maintained on the level of consciousness only. There is no surrounding organization, order or life vitality as we know it. There is only consciousness.*

We do not consider form to be only that which is perceptible to the five senses. In fact, we see form from this perspective to be most limited, both in its life reality and in its ability to function. We see form from the perspective of the five senses to be useful only for the most basic and fundamental level of identification. From this perspective, there is very little relationship between this perspective and the full understanding and knowledge of how a unit or form system functions.

*All energy contains order, organization and life vitality; therefore, **all energy is form**. If one were to use the term "form" to identify that which can be perceived by the basic senses and the word "energy" to refer to that aspect of an animal, human, plant or object's reality that cannot be readily perceived by the basic senses, then one would be accurate in the use of these two words. However, if one were to use the word "form" to refer to that which can be perceived by the basic five senses and assume form to be a complete unit of reality unto itself, and use the word "energy" to refer to a level beyond form, one would then be using these two words inaccurately.*

On the planet Earth, the personality, character, emotional makeup, intellectual capacity, strong points and gifts of a human are all form. They are that which gives order, organization and life vitality to consciousness.

Order and organization are the physical structures that create a framework for form. In short, they define the walls. But we have included the dynamic of life vitality when we refer to form because one of the elements of form is action, and it is the life vitality that initiates and creates action.

Devas: *Creators of all form's blueprints; universal in dynamic* ***Nature Spirits:*** *Regional implementors of the blueprints*

Here is my understanding of nature spirits.

In *Behaving . . .* I referred to nature spirits as the blue collar workers within the realm of nature intelligence. I still hold to this imagery today but feel it is simplistic. My work with the nature spirits has convinced me that they are truly masters of understanding, bringing spirit into matter, energy into form. They tend to the shifting of an energy reality which has been formulated on the devic level, and assist the translation of that reality from a dynamic of energy to form that can be perceived by our five senses. In short, they constantly work with the principle of manifestation on Earth. They move the blueprints into form and action. They also function in a custodial capacity with all that is of form on the planet. That is, when not interfered with by humans, they tend to the care and needs of all physical reality, assuring perfection within form. The catch phrase in this is "when not interfered with by humans." One of my major learning areas at Perelandra has been to understand the relationship between nature spirits and form, to learn how to *cooperate* with it—even become an equal partner in it.

When I am in the design and layout period of planning the garden early in the season, I am primarily working hand in hand with the devic realm. Specifically, the Deva of the Perelandra Garden. It is from this deva that I receive what is to go into the garden, which seeds to buy and which vegetables are to go into which rows. This is all part of the creative process. Once I have the information, I shift my attention to the nature spirit level, for it is here that I receive insight and assistance on process. That is, the best way to bring this garden into form. My day-to-day work in the garden is a co-creative process with the nature spirits. My focus is on bringing that which is of spirit into form and facilitating the perfection of that process. This is the nature spirit role as I understand it, and it is to them that I turn for my insights and lessons concerning how I am to participate.

In terms of how I relate to nature spirits, let me assure you that I do not have a phalanx of little elves and gnomes wielding pitchforks and shovels in my garden. I experience nature spirits as individuated energy presences, but not in specific forms. In relating to humans, nature spirits have occasionally taken on specific form, but since my personal sensitivity is to energy, we connect on this level. I rarely see nature spirits. On a few special ocassions I have seen swirling, multicolor balls of energy. Mostly, I sense that I'm not alone or can feel a tingling on my skin that indicates I'm not alone. My communication with them can be through sudden insight, intuition, visualization, kinesiology* or a clear inner hearing. It all depends on what they're trying to get across to me and the most efficient and effective means for them to communicate what they wish to me. Their daily operations here at Perelandra are unseen by the naked eye. The results of their work, however, are very noticeable, and the energy that surrounds the quality of their work is easily felt.

There is another distinguishing feature about nature spirits that will help you understand them and the differences between them and devas. Nature

* Kinesiology: A simple form of muscle testing used in this instance to discern yes and no answers from nature intelligences. The method is discussed in Chapter 2.

If you're feeling overwhelmed about all this communication business with nature, and you are feeling uneasy about whether or not you'll know who to talk to and be able to "hear" all the answers to your questions, relax. This is just Chapter 1. By the end of the book, you'll know just what to do to get your answers. Why, you'll even know the questions!

spirits are regional. Although I do not have a phalanx of little people visible in the garden, I do have my group of nature spirits who are connected to this land and what is happening here. Your connection will be with your own group. They are an intelligent reality that is individuated enough to be connected with specific geographic areas on Earth. Devas, on the other hand, are universal in dynamic. When I contact the Carrot Deva, I connect with the very same intelligent reality someone in China would connect with when making the same contact. Your Oak Tree Deva is the same as mine. Consequently, you can get devic information about your oak tree even if at the time you are a thousand miles away from your land and looking at someone else's oak tree. You can also get information about your oak tree while connected to my Oak Tree Deva. They are the same deva. However, you cannot get information about watering your oak tree while connected to my nature spirits at Perelandra. They don't know about your oak tree. You'll have to ask the nature spirits on your land who are tending to that specific oak tree.

To my knowledge, there is only one exception to this regional dynamic within the nature spirit level. This is Pan. As you probably know, there is a huge volume of traditional literature around nature spirits and Pan. Usually nature spirits are portrayed as cute, and Pan is portrayed as powerful and demonic. I've experienced many individual character traits with nature spirits, but *never cute.* I experience enormous power when connected with Pan, but I have never felt anything that can even remotely be characterized as demonic—only his power, which is equally balanced by love and care for me, Perelandra, and all of Earth.

My working understanding of Pan is that he is "in charge" of the nature spirit level. He is devic in his presence. Pan is everywhere and available to us all. Whenever I wish to be connected to the nature spirit level in a general manner for whatever reason, I connect with Pan. If I have a question regarding an issue around spirit and form, and I don't know which specific nature spirit to contact for help, I go to Pan. If I have a question and I don't know if it's devic or nature spirit in nature (so to speak), I ask Pan to clear up my confusion. Then I connect with whomever he has recommended. It is my understanding that Pan oversees which nature spirits are where and doing what jobs. In essence, he is that level's organizing force. He's the nature spirit CEO.

In light of his special position within the nature spirit level, I'll open to Pan for further clarification.

PAN

Mankind's immediate relationship to Earth is through his contact and work with the nature spirit level. For, as Machaelle has pointed out, it is here that he learns the practical lessons concerning the fusing of soul power into form. This is why man has come into the Earth plane—to learn these lessons of relationship between the individual soul and physical reality. If one were to look at the dismal state of the natural environment on Earth, it would be easy to see that on the whole, man has barely begun to recognize the purpose of his existence on Earth, let alone explore ways to facilitate the fusion of soul energy into form for the perfect functioning of that energy through form. This same dynamic of purpose exists within all nature on Earth, and it is here man has the opportunity to learn these lessons and demonstrate them outside himself within the arena of nature. From this experience, he may draw what he needs in order to seat his own fully functioning soul dynamic into a fully functioning body reflection.

All within the nature spirit level not only understand precisely what I am communicating to you here but are especially adept, due to the nature of our work, at practically grounding universal and soul energy into form. So rather than relegating us to entertaining and charming you through your arts, I suggest that you seriously consider looking to us as your teachers. This is the contact with you that we eagerly desire. All you need do is open your heart and your intent to us, and you will be most surprised at how quickly we will work to communicate what we know and what you need.

Pan is actually a being without (or beyond) gender. I refer to him as "him" because his energy feels masculine to me during our communications. I don't feel comfortable calling this good friend "it." So I say "him" or "he."

The same holds true with the other nature intelligences I work with. The key here is that in the act of communication, when I am listening, I am in the feminine mode of receiving. When nature is talking, it is in the masculine mode of sending or projecting out. The opposite is true if I am talking, and nature is listening. However, since I mostly listen, my predominant experience of nature is a masculine one even though nature intelligences are without (or beyond) gender.

Also in Co-Creative Definitions, nature defined "devas" and "nature spirits." The following is what nature said.

DEVAS AND NATURE SPIRITS: *"Devas" and "nature spirits" are names used to identify two different expressions and functions within the nature consciousness. They are the two groups within the larger nature consciousness that interface with the human soul while in form. There are other groups, and they are differentiated from one another primarily by specific expression and function.*

*To expand our definition of form, it is the devic expression that fuses with consciousness to create order, organization and life vitality. The devic expression is the architect designing the complex order, organization and life vitality that will be needed by the soul consciousness while functioning within the scope or band of form. If the consciousness chooses to shift from one point of form to another point, thereby changing form function, it is the devic expression of nature that alters the organization, order and life vitality accordingly. The devic expression designs and **is** the creation of the order, organization and life vitality of form.*

The nature spirit expression infuses the devic order, organization and life vitality and adds to this the dynamic of function and working balance. To order, organization and life vitality it brings movement and the bond that maintains the alignment of the devic form unit to the universal principles of balance while the consciousness is in form.

*To say that nature is the expert in areas of form and form principles barely scratches the surface of the true nature (pardon the pun) of nature's role in form. It is the expert of form and it is form itself. A soul-oriented consciousness cannot exist on any level or dimension of form in any way without an **equal**, intimate, symbiotic relationship with the nature consciousness.*

It has been over sixteen years since I began gardening under the tutelage of these nature intelligences and the result has been a garden in which all inhabitants, be they animal, mineral or vegetable, are compatible with one another. Each member of the garden enhances the health and well-being of all the others. And this includes the bugs. This garden is inclusive, not exclusive. I do nothing—organic or otherwise—for the purpose of repelling insects or wild animals. The focus is to create a balanced, wholistic environment in which all within that environment are enhanced. The results are not only more food than I know what to do with, but also food that has contained within it a very high level of life energy—*light*. In other words, the garden demonstrates *balance,* and the food this garden produces embodies balance.

In Co-Creative Definitions, nature also defined "balance" as it pertains to humans and other form—such as gardens.

BALANCE: *Balance is relative and measured, shall we say, by an individual's ability to faithfully demonstrate the various elements comprising his larger reality through the specific frameworks of form in which one has chosen to develop. When what one is demonstrating is faithful in intent and clarity with these elements and the larger reality, one experiences balance. And those interacting with this individual will experience his balance. One experiences imbalance when there is distortion between what one demonstrates through the form framework and the intent and clarity of the elements comprising the larger reality as well as the larger reality itself.*

If you truly look at what we are saying here, you will see that balance as a phenomenon is not an elusive state that only an exulted few can achieve. Balance is, in fact, inherent in all reality, in all life systems. Balance is defined by the many elements within any individual's reality. And it is the dominant state of being within any reality and any form system. It is also the state of being that links individual life systems to one another and to the larger whole. When one says that he is a child of the universe, what one is acknowledging is the relationship and link of his higher state of balance to the universe's state of balance. Whether one feels linked to or distant from this relationship depends on the closeness or distance he creates within himself with respect to his larger personal state of balance—that dynamic which is part of his overall reality.

This brings me to why I bother. I was asked by several people what the Perelandra garden means to me. I can hardly believe the question is even asked, and I have barely been able to articulate even a sentence in response. I keep wanting to say, "Isn't it obvious!" Friends say I am naive to believe that it is. So I will try to answer.

The Perelandra garden is my life, my heart and my very breath. It is my friend, my healer, my nurturer and teacher—about myself, my planet and my universe. It is my key to the universe. It is my access to spiritual truth and universal natural law contained within the universal flow. It is the demonstration of these truths and laws played out before my very eyes. It is my proof that what is spiritual truth and universal law courses through all reality—and this includes a garden. It shows me that what I see and experience in that garden is beyond all structures, all forms, and well beyond the notion of worship.

It is my university of life. I draw from it my questions, answers, approach and direction. How I live springs from what I've learned and experienced in the garden.

It has been my spiritual teacher in the deepest sense. On a daily basis, within the mundane framework of the garden, I experience and consciously work with truth and natural law. This little garden links me to the greater whole and allows me to experience reality beyond space and time—the fact that it sits on land on this planet is purely coincidental. And it has taught me that we are a vibrant, active planet fully participating in a larger, loving whole.

It has taught me about power—my own and that which is contained in all life around me. About equality. About balance. About teamwork on a peer level. I have experienced an environment where the focus is maintained on the welfare of the individual parts as well as the health, balance and well-being of the whole. And I have experienced extraordinary results from that focus. It has taught me that life is truly beyond five-senses form and that form (five senses and expanded) is the essence of truth and life itself. Through it, I have dramatically changed my thoughts, my thought process, my knowing, actions and reality.

This garden is a way of life which touches the core of my soul and through which my soul sings. It reconnects my conscious reality to the truths held within both my heart and soul, and from this I am reconnected back into the universal life force itself.

This is what the Perelandra garden means to me, and this is why I bother.

When I was about to begin the *Perelandra Garden Workbook,* I felt that I was to draw one card from the Aquarian tarot and that this card would clarify the direction of the book. I drew "The Knower" which says in part:

> The Knower holds an egg to his heart and the egg sprouts a root
> with two leaves. The fruit of this plant is the winged and shafted
> Sun above his head. The Knower shall plant this egg in the earth
> and a new kingdom shall be grounded on Earth.*

* The New Tarot *by John Cooke and Rosalind Sharpe*

I took an egg into the center of the garden, planted it, and returned to my desk to begin writing this book.

2

CRACKING THE
COMMUNICATION CODE

The backbone of the Perelandra garden is communication. I depend on the devas and nature spirits to inform me of my direction and the step-by-step processes I need to take. Without that information, I would be guessing along with everyone else.

Communication also happens to be the biggest stumbling block people face when they consider gardening in conscious partnership with nature. Now, I think it's fair to say that some people use the communication issue as a convenient excuse. They can support, even admire this kind of gardening, but because they feel they aren't among the "gifted ones" and feel they can't get this kind of information, they don't have to practice it.

Well, I happen to be someone who feels deeply that this communication is possible for everyone. We are talking about a natural partnership between humans and nature, and it is not meant to be exclusive. It only stands to reason that there are simple ways for us and nature to communicate with one another. We're also talking about nature *intelligence*. The question is—can this intelligence be accessed? Can we create a common bridge that will allow an information exchange between us and nature?

From the beginning, I believed there had to be language frameworks that were just waiting to be developed.

I see the communication problem as being similar to the situation that arises when you are faced with someone from another country who speaks a language that is completely foreign to your ear. There isn't one sound they are making that strikes a familiar note. We can back off from the situation and say, "This is impossible." Or we can tackle it together with the other person, begin to learn each other's language, and build a bridge for communication.

The latter is what I've done with nature. I've worked to develop techniques which we can use for the purpose of sending and receiving information. And it's not difficult. In fact, it's embarrassingly simple. But that's as it should be.

TEANTROS

I have asked to share with you some of our views on the issue of communication. My name is Teantros. I am one of a large group of nature spirits who are working at Perelandra. My specialty, if I may say, is communication. This may seem strange to you. A nature spirit working in the area of communication. Traditionally, you see us as having our attention on the various forms within the nature kingdoms—the trees, the rocks, grasses, animals, clouds. But this is just one area of our focus and involves only some of us who are working within the realm of the nature spirits. We work with the universal principles of bringing spirit into form and shifting that form from one level to another. Wherever these principles apply, you will find us. Since Earth is the planet which deals primarily with these particular principles, you will discover that there is a large and active level of nature spirits connected in various capacities with the planet.

Communication is a dynamic which easily falls within both these principles. Energy* as thought is exchanged and translated into word form. The word "communication" is used to describe the exchange of intelligent energy from point A to point B for the purpose of transferring information. Up to now, communication as you know it has been primarily the transfer of intelligent energy between two points within the same level—for example, two people on Earth speaking directly to one another.

I don't wish to imply that there has been no communication between

* Energy: According to nature, all energy contains order, organization and life vitality. Therefore, all energy is form. However, we humans traditionally use the word "energy" to indicate that which can't be perceived by our 5 senses. In communication with us, nature will also use the word "energy" to distinguish between what can be seen and heard, and what can't be perceived by the 5 senses.

levels. That would be false. There has been within the soul of each human on Earth a constant link with levels beyond his physical* self. But the essence of this communication has been unconscious. Also, there have been some individuals throughout history who have developed the means for conscious communication between levels. But this has been viewed as an extraordinary development by the society surrounding the individual. The time has come for mankind in general to develop the ways and means to bridge the communication gap which has existed between levels.

This is not a job that is being left solely up to humans. We on the other levels are most eager to work in partnership with you for the purpose of developing the framework needed for easy communication access between levels. For one thing, you must realize that we on the nature spirit level, as is true with the various levels beyond us, need your assistance in understanding your language. I'll give you an example of the communication problems we face with you. We don't work with your set of physical measurements. There is no need for us to use them. For instance, we simply know where something is to be placed or how much of something is to be added for the health of a plant. We don't need to know inches or ounces. But you do. If we are to work with you in a co-creative partnership in the effort to return all that exists on the planet to a state of health and balance, we must then develop ways with you in which our knowing can be translated into inches and ounces. So you see, it is not just your issue; it is our issue as well.

Perelandra is a nature research center, and we nature spirits take full advantage of that fact. There are teams of us connected with Perelandra who work with research and development both within the wide area of nature itself and how nature as a whole can interface with man in new and better ways. Communication is one of the areas of research that fits into the latter category. We are excited about what has been developed and feel we now have a simple, workable framework for inter-level communication with humans. Don't forget that the frustration you have felt when you've been unable to hear and understand us, we have felt tenfold when we have been unable to reach or understand you.

* Physical: Nature will also use the word "physical," as well as the word "form" to indicate that someone or something can be perceived by the average person's 5 senses.

KINESIOLOGY

There are 2 issues to be faced in communicating with nature. One is how to ask a question. The other is how to hear the answer. I'm going to deal with how to hear the answer first. After all, that is the biggest psychological barrier we have.

There are several ways we can hear. There are some who can actually hear nature as in a normal conversation. Those people don't need this book. All they need to know is that they can get specific answers to specific technical questions from nature. Mostly these people need to be encouraged to ask nature simple questions, then shut up, listen and do what nature suggests they do.

The vast majority of people are not in this situation. However, there are several ways to hear without using our ears. For example, we can get gut feelings or intuitive hits about something. In both cases, these may very well be our efforts to translate nature intelligence input into gut feelings or intuition. But often we can't tell the difference between these feelings being initiated by desire or will on our part or by nature intelligence. This is a problem.

There is another way we can hear that eliminates most of the problems around distinguishing between just who is giving the answers. This is kinesiology*—muscle testing. With this, we let the body's electrical system act as a bridge and do the translation work. Everybody can do kinesiology because it links us to our electrical system and muscles. If you are alive, you have these 2 things. I know that sounds smart-mouthed of me, but I've learned that sometimes people refuse to believe anything can be so simple. So they create a mental block—only "sensitive types" can do this or (my personal favorite) "only women can do this." It's just not true. Kinesiology happens to be one of those simple things in life that's waiting around to be learned and used by everyone. It's a system that has been used among humans for some time now. Chiropractors and wholistic** physicians use it as a diagnostic tool.

Simply stated, the body has within and surrounding it an electrical network or grid. If a negative energy (that is, any physical object or energy vibration that does not maintain or enhance health and balance) is introduced into a person's overall energy field, his muscles, when having physical pressure applied, are unable to hold their strength. (The ability to hold

*"Kinesiology" is easy to pronounce. It only looks awful. Ken-**ease**-e-ol-ogy.*

**I spell "wholistic" this way deliberately. I prefer to use a word that connotes the whole of something rather than "holistic" which, in this day and age, implies religion or holy.*

muscle power is directly linked to the balance of the electrical system.) In other words, if pressure is applied to an individual's extended arm while his field is affected by a negative (energy), the arm will not be able to resist the pressure. It will weaken and fall to his side. If pressure is applied while affected by a positive (energy), the person will easily resist and the arm will hold its position. This is what happens if you have ever been to a chiropractor that uses kinesiology as a diagnostic tool. The doctor tells you to stick out your arm and resist his pressure. It feels like he's trying to push your arm down after he's told you not to let him do it. Everything is going fine, and then all of a sudden he presses, and your arm falls down like a floppy fish.

To expand further, when a negative is placed within a person's field, his electrical system will immediately respond by short-circuiting or overloading. This makes it difficult, if not downright impossible, for the muscles to maintain their strength and hold the position when pressure is added. When a positive is within the field, the electrical system holds, and the muscles maintain their strength when pressure is applied.

This electrical/muscular relationship is a natural part of the human system. It is not mystical or magical. Kinesiology is the established method for reading their balance at any given moment.

What does this kinesiology business have to do with "hearing" information from nature? Simple. If you ask a simple question using the yes/no format, nature can answer your question by projecting a yes (positive) or a no (negative) into your energy field. Then you read the answer by testing yourself using kinesiology. That's the bridge. *When you use kinesiology with nature intelligences, you are testing the results of **their answer** on your electrical system.* It's like surrogate testing. Nature uses your electrical system to send a yes or no to you. When you are properly set up and communicating with nature, you are *not* receiving answers from yourself. You are receiving them from nature.

← Important stuff!

Now, all you have to do is learn to muscle test yourself—easier than you think. And learn to ask questions in the yes/no format—trickier than you think.

For now, let's concentrate on learning kinesiology.

I don't mean to intimidate you, but small children can learn to do kinesiology in about 5 minutes. It's mainly because it never occurred to them that they couldn't do it. If I tell them they have an electrical system, they don't argue with me about it—they just get on with the business of learning how to do this simple test. Actually, I do mean to intimidate you. Your first big hurdle will be whether or not you believe you have a viable electrical system that is capable of being tested. Here's a good test. Place a hand mirror under your nose. If you see breath marks, you've got a strong electrical system. Now you can get on with learning how to test!

If you have ever experienced muscle testing, you most likely participated in a 2-person operation. You provided the extended arm and the other person provided the pressure. Although efficient, this method can be cumbersome while standing in the middle of a garden. Those arm pumpers have the nasty habit of disappearing right when you need them the most. So we'll be learning to self-test.

The Kinesiology Testing Position

1. THE CIRCUIT FINGERS: **If you are right-handed:** Place your left hand palm up. Connect the tip of your left thumb with the tip of the left little finger (*not your index finger*). **If you are left-handed:** Place your right hand palm up. Connect the tip of your right thumb with the tip of your right little finger. By connecting your thumb and little finger, you have just closed an electrical circuit in your hand, and it is this circuit you will use for testing.

Before going on, look at the position you have just formed with your hand. If your thumb is touching the tip of your index or first finger, laugh at yourself for not being able to follow directions, and change the position to touch the tip of the thumb with the tip of the little or fourth finger. Most likely this will not feel at all comfortable to you. If you are feeling awkward, you've got the first step of the test position! In time, the hand and fingers will adjust to being put in this position and it will feel fine.

Circuit fingers can touch tip to tip, finger pad to finger pad, or thumbnail resting on top of little finger's nail. Women with long nails need not impale themselves.

2. THE TEST FINGERS: To test the circuit (the means by which you will apply pressure on yourself), place the thumb and index finger of your other hand inside the circle you have created by connecting your thumb and little finger. The thumb/index finger should be right under the thumb/little finger,

touching them. Don't try to make a circle with your test fingers. They're just placed inside the circuit fingers which do form a circle. It will look as if the circuit fingers are resting on the test fingers.

3. POSITIVE RESPONSE: Keeping this position, ask yourself a yes/no question in which you already know the answer to be yes. ("Is my name _____?") Once you've asked the question, press your circuit fingers together, keeping the tip-to-tip position. *Using the same amount of pressure,* try to pull apart the circuit fingers with your test fingers. Press the lower thumb against the upper thumb, the lower index finger against the upper little finger.

The action of your test fingers will look like scissors separating as you try separating your circuit fingers. The motion of the test fingers is horizontal. Don't try to pull your test fingers vertically up through your circuit fingers. This action sometimes works but it's not as reliable as the horizontal action.

Another way to say all this is that the circuit position described in step 1 corresponds to the position you take when you stick your arm out for the physician. The testing position in step 2 is in place of the physician or other convenient arm pumper. After you ask the yes/no question and you press your circuit fingers tip-to-tip, that's equal to the doctor saying, "Resist my pressure." Your circuit fingers now correspond to your outstretched, stiffened arm. Trying to pull apart those fingers with your testing fingers is equal to the doctor pressing down on your arm.

If the answer to the question is positive (if your name is what you think it is!), you will not be able to easily pull apart the circuit fingers. The electrical circuit will hold, your muscles will maintain their strength, and your circuit fingers will not separate. You will feel the strength in that circuit. *Important: Be sure the amount of pressure holding the circuit fingers together is equal to the amount your testing fingers press against them. Also, don't use a pumping action in your testing fingers when trying to pry your circuit fingers apart. Use an equal, steady and continuous pressure.*

Play with this a bit. Ask a few more yes/no questions that have positive answers. Now, I know it's going to seem that if you already know the answer to be yes, you are probably "throwing" the test. That's reasonable, but for the time being, until you get a feeling for what the positive response feels like in your fingers, you're going to need to deliberately ask yourself questions with positive answers.

While asking questions, if you are having trouble sensing the strength of the circuit, apply a little more pressure. Or consider that you may be applying too much pressure, and pull back some. You don't have to break or strain your fingers for this; just use enough pressure to make them feel alive, connected and alert.

Hand artwork by Jim Brisson.

4. NEGATIVE RESPONSE: Once you have a clear sense of the positive response, ask yourself a question that has a negative answer. Again press your circuit fingers together and, *using equal pressure*, press against the circuit fingers with the test fingers. This time the electrical circuit will break, and the circuit fingers will weaken and separate. Because the electrical circuit is broken, the muscles in the circuit fingers don't have the power to hold the fingers together. In a positive state, the electrical circuit holds and the muscles have the power to keep the 2 fingers together.

How much your circuit fingers separate depends on your personal style. Some people's fingers separate a lot. Other's barely separate at all. Mine separate about 1/4 inch. Some people's fingers won't separate at all, but they'll definitely feel the fingers weaken when pressure is applied during a no answer. Let your personal style develop and change naturally.

Also, if you're having a little trouble feeling anything, do your testing with your forearms resting in your lap. This way you won't be using your muscles to hold up your arms while trying to test.

Play with negative questions a bit, and then return to positive questions. Get a good feeling for the strength between your circuit fingers when the electricity is in a positive state and the weakness when the electricity is in a negative state. You can even ask yourself (your own system) for a positive response and then, after testing, ask for a negative response. ("Give me a positive response." Test. "Give me a negative response." Test.) You will feel the positive strength and the negative weakness. Remember, in the beginning you may feel only a slight difference between the two. With practice, that difference will become more pronounced. For now, it's just a matter of trusting what you've learned—and practice.

Don't forget the overall concept behind kinesiology. What enhances our body, mind and soul makes us strong. Together, our body, mind and soul create a wholistic environment which, when balanced, is strong and solid.

If something enters that environment and negates or challenges the balance, the entire environment is weakened. That strength or weakness registers in the electrical system, and it can be discerned through the muscle testing technique—kinesiology.

Kinesiology Tips

If you are having trouble feeling the electrical circuit on the circuit fingers, try switching hands—the circuit fingers become the testing fingers and vice versa. Most people who are right-handed have this particular electrical circuitry in their left hand. Left-handers generally have the circuitry in their right hand. But sometimes a right-hander has the circuitry in the right hand and a left-hander has it in the left hand. You may be one of those people. If you are ambidextrous, choose the circuit hand that gives you the clearest responses. Before deciding which to use, give yourself a couple of weeks of testing using 1 hand as the circuit hand to get a good feel for its responses before trying the other hand.

If you have an injury such as a muscle sprain in either hand or arm, don't try to learn kinesiology until you have completely healed. Kinesiology is muscle testing, and a muscle injury will interfere with the testing—and the testing will interfere with the healing of the muscle injury.

Also, when first learning kinesiology, do yourself a favor and set aside some quiet time to go through the instructions and play with the testing. Trying to learn this while riding the New York subway during evening rush hour isn't going to give you the break you need. But once you have learned it, you'll be able to test all kinds of things, even while riding the subway.

Sometimes I meet people who are trying to learn kinesiology and aren't having much luck. They've gotten frustrated, decided this isn't for them, and have gone on to try to learn another means of testing. Well, I'll listen to them explain what they did, and before they know it, I've verbally tricked them with a couple of suggestions about their testing, which they try, and they begin feeling kinesiology for the first time—a strong "yes" and a clear "no." The problem wasn't kinesiology. Everyone, as I have said, has an electrical system. The problem was that they wanted to learn it so much that they became anxious, frustrated and tense—they blocked.

So, since you won't have me around to trick you, I suggest that if you suspect you're blocking, go on to something else. Then trick yourself.

If your testing has been going along just fine and you suddenly begin to get contradictory or "mushy" test results, consider:

1) This may not be a good day for you to do this particular work in the garden, and nature is trying to alert you to this with unclear test results.

2) You need to do something else in preparation for this process and, again, nature is trying to get your attention. Ask if something else is needed first.

3) You are not in the best shape for holding a session with nature. You're too tired or need to eat. Close everything down and come back the next day to begin the testing again

4) You may need to drink water. If you are dehydrated, your electrical system will feel weak during kinesiology testing.

5) Test yourself for flower essences. (Flower essences are explained in Chapter 16.) The essences balance and repair the electrical system, and this may be just what you need for clear kinesiology results.

When you care the least about whether or not you learn kinesiology, start playing with it again. Approach it as if it were a game. *Then* you'll feel the strength and weakness in the fingers.

Now, suppose the testing has been working fine, and then suddenly you can't get a clear result (what I call a "definite maybe") or you get no result at all. Check:

1. Sloppy testing. You try to press apart the fingers before applying pressure between the circuit fingers. Or you try to press apart your fingers *before* you finish asking the question. These things happen especially when we've been testing for awhile and become over-confident or do the testing very quickly. I think they happen to all of us from time to time and serve to remind us to keep our attention on the matter at hand. (Excuse the lousy pun.)

Especially in the beginning, start a kinesiology session by first feeling a few positive and negative responses. Ask yourself some of those obvious questions. Or simply say several times, "Let me feel a positive." (Test.) "Let me feel a negative." (Test.) This will serve as a kind of warm-up, and remind you what positive and negative feel like before you start.

2. External distractions. Trying to test in a noisy or active area can cause you to lose concentration. The testing will feel unsure or contradict itself if you double-check the results. Often, simply moving to a quiet, calm spot and concentrating on what you are doing will be just what's needed for successful testing. As your testing improves, you will be able to concentrate better despite noise.

3. Focus/concentration. Even in a quiet spot, one's mind may wander and the testing will feel fuzzy, weak or contradictory. It's important to concentrate throughout the process. Check how you are feeling. If you're tired, I suggest you not try to test until you've rested a bit. Or you may need to eat. And if you have to go to the bathroom, do it. That little situation is a sure concentration-destroyer.

4. The question isn't clear. A key to kinesiology is asking a *simple* yes/no question, not two questions in one, each having a possible yes/no answer. If your testing isn't working, first check your hand positions. Next, review your question, and make sure you are asking only one question.

And, while you're asking a question, don't think ahead to the next question! Your fingers won't know which to answer.

5. Match your intent with how you word your question. If you are prone to saying, "Oh, I didn't mean to say that!" when you talk to others, this might be an area you'll need to work on.

A woman at one of our workshops asked me about some strange answers she had gotten about what to feed her cat. She had asked, "What kinds of food would make my cat happy?" She got weird answers like chocolate, catnip, steak.... I pointed out that she probably asked the wrong question. She meant to ask what foods would make her cat *healthy*. She was a little surprised. She thought that this was the question she had originally asked. In short, her question and her intent didn't match. Nature will answer what you ask, not what you meant to ask.

6. You must want to accept the results of the test. If you enter a kinesiology test not wanting to "hear" the answer, for whatever reason, you can override the test with your emotions and your will. This is true for conventional situations as well. If we really don't want something to work for us, it won't work. Or, if we don't *want* to hear something, we won't. That's our personal power dictating the outcome.

Also, if you are trying to do testing during a situation that is especially emotional for you, that deeply stirs your emotions, or if you are trying to ask a question in which you have a strong, personal investment in the answer—such as, "Should I buy this beautiful $250,000 house?"—I suggest that you not test until you are calmer or get some emotional distance from the situation. During such times, you're walking a very fine line between a clear test and a test that your desires may override. Kinesiology as a tool isn't the issue here. It's the condition or intent of the tester. In fact, some questions just shouldn't be asked, but *which questions* should be asked is relative to who is doing the asking. So, think about this. We each need to develop discernment around which questions are *appropriate* for us to ask.

When I am involved with testing during emotionally stressful times, I stop for a moment, collect my thoughts and make a commitment to concentrate on the testing only. If I need to test an emotionally charged question or a question about something I have a personal investment in, I stop a moment, commit myself to the test and open myself to receiving *the* answer and not the answer I might desire.

A NOTE TO THOSE WHO ALREADY USE A PENDULUM: Using a pendulum is a form of kinesiology. If you are happy using a pendulum, feel free to continue using it with co-creative gardening. You will simply be using the pendulum to discern yes/no rather than your fingers.

QUESTIONS AND THE UNIVERSE

I've already stated that one of the keys to kinesiology is asking a simple question in a yes/no format. I can go even further with this and say that one of the keys to receiving *any* information or insight from intelligent sources beyond our conscious selves is the ability to ask a clear concise question regarding the information we'd like to receive. I can also say that the biggest stumbling block to the interlevel information flow, besides the fear that we can't "hear," has to do with asking questions.

Over the years, I've learned some pretty mighty lessons in this area. I've found out that there exists in the universe what I call a "cosmic code of conduct." Our worth as free-thinking individuals is recognized and deferred to by all other intelligences, all other life. The universe isn't going to just throw truckloads of information at us at will. We must indicate that we wish to know these things. And we must indicate precisely what areas of knowledge we are referring to. It is not enough for me to say I want to know everything there is to know. In order to respond to my desire to know, I must express what it is I wish to know. The universe looks to me to take on my own responsibility for the timing of my growth and expansion. Indicating what I'm ready to learn through the tool of asking a question is how I express my timing to sources beyond my conscious self.

In *Behaving . . . ,* I talk about what it meant for me to accept my position as creator of the garden. This required that I establish my rightful position as *co-creator* with the nature intelligences. It also required that I recognize my responsibility to do this. To be in any lesser position would place me on the level of an ignorant servant. This is unacceptable to the intelligences I work with, and as far as I am aware it is unacceptable to the universe at large. By accepting our responsibility to make known that which we wish to know for the purpose of expansion and growth is to accept our position as creator of our personal garden.

One consideration within the cosmic code of conduct has to do with timing: specifically, the universal acknowledgment of our personal timing. This is why we don't get truckloads of information coming at us from out of the blue. The following excerpt about timing is a lesson I received in 1984 from a consciousness known to me as Universal Light.

UNIVERSAL LIGHT

The process of evolution is continuous within each soul. And by association so is the concept of timing, since it is so intimately linked to evolution. Therefore if a man can point to only a handful of moments in which timing played a role, he has missed observing and very likely experiencing the many instances of timing in his life. If one were to see his life as a tapestry of design and color, the pattern of the weave comes significantly from timing. As man recognizes and responds to the phenomenon of timing, the weave in his tapestry becomes more dramatic and the color more brilliant. It is his choice. There are a number of phenomena available to him which he can choose to incorporate—at any level of intensity he desires—into his life.

Nothing in the universe, in all of reality, is held back from the individual living on Earth. Each person decides for himself the intensity with which he chooses to live his life. The limitations are his own. How much is available to him is not dictated by the universe. It is entirely dictated by the individual. Most souls who live on Earth, as they struggle through their lessons concerning the relationship of spirit flowing through form, feel that the universe and its truths are being held back from them in one degree or another because they are encased—or enslaved—in the body. This is not only untrue, it is an excuse. To think that something greater than yourself is dictating what you should or should not know, deprives you of the responsibility for self-growth, self-evolution. What is the use of working and seeking to improve, to open and expand yourself when you think you are dictated to by some intelligence, some consciousness greater than yourself, outside of yourself.

The evolutionary process in all souls involves the shifting and expanding of an individual's boundaries and limitations, or what has been termed the

*ring-pass-not: The boundary
or scope of limitations we each
have which separates our working and workable knowledge
and reality from the rest of all
knowledge and reality. As we
evolve, the ring-pass-not expands appropriately, so that we
have access to what we need
but are not overwhelmed by all
that there is.*

"ring-pass-not."* Do not think that when we use the word "limitation" we are being judgmental. All souls have some aspect of limitation. There is wise limitation and there is limitation that derives from fear. Wise limitation defines the individual who knows what level and part of reality he can enfold into his life and successfully integrate into his actions in form. Wise limitation admits that knowledge and reality which can be fully grounded by an individual. A wise man understands what he can take into his conscious knowing and what he can ground in action during his life. It is a sign of wisdom when he can say "enough," and give himself time to integrate that which he has come to understand, to successfully reflect it through his body, his actions, and into form. Once successfully grounded, he can shift his ring-pass-not and take in more.

When we garden in conscious partnership with nature, we are not only responding to our own sense of timing, we are also responding to nature's timing in the garden. In the same lesson, Universal Light addressed this issue.

UNIVERSAL LIGHT

Timing has been a major factor in the Perelandra garden, timing and the prevailing logic about what should and should not be done in a garden. Timing within gardens in general has been completely placed to one side and ignored, while the theory of logic has been the principal force. At Perelandra, this has been reversed. Natural timing has come to the fore. Year after year, through her observation of timing, Machaelle's concept of logic has changed. What was logical in the garden one year has become illogical the next.

Logic is meant to be active and ever-expanding. Often the individual reaches a particular level of logic and then the logic crystallizes into a static position. Anything that continues to move around him constantly butts up against his static logic. For example, a rock, seemingly on its own, changes position from point A to point B. In a static logic, the intellect dictates that what you just saw did not happen. One of Machaelle's lessons in the garden has been to loosen or de-crystallize her logic. That had to occur very early on for her to see the evolution of the garden. When the ring-pass-not expands, so must logic. In order for all that is new in the ring-pass-not to register consciously, logic must also expand to incorporate the new information in the ring-pass-not.

Machaelle has also seen that when one works out of timing with nature, a great deal more energy is used than if the job were done in the proper timing. She has retrained herself to observe and try to read the signals of nature's timing. When she saw another timing unfold in the garden, she became confident to look for different timing in herself. Usually the timing precedes her logical notion of what should be, so she has realized that if she waits for the timing the situation unfolds far more effortlessly. In timing there is grounding. In logic and intelligence there often is not.

I've had another major lesson around this issue of questions that has to do with the difference between asking a question of the intellect and a question which gives me information for integration. This is a fairly easy thing to distinguish between on paper but a bit tough to begin to discern personally.

You see, we live in an age where we are given deference and approval for the amount of information we know. Our school systems honor the student who can stuff a lot of information in his head and then repeat it at the correct moment. Not only do we admire individuals who can do this, we grow up to believe that to live well in society, one must remain intellectually alert. Ask questions. Take in information.

I don't mean to imply that there is something wrong with our being intellectually developed. But I do point out the pitfall: it has encouraged us to develop the habit of asking questions for the sake of asking questions. We do nothing more with the answer than file it. This is what I mean by an intellectual question. The more I have developed around this issue of asking questions, the more I have realized what a useless exercise it is for me to ask an intellectual question. What in the world can I do with all that information? It's useless baggage.

The integration question is one in which the answer is received in right timing, and we are able to integrate the information we receive into our life. It can change the way we think, how we perceive the reality around us, how we act, how we move through our daily schedule. When this type of question is asked, we are able to move the answer through a complete grounding process by however the information impacts our life.

I can't give you a formula for distinguishing an intellectual question from an integration question. Obviously, since we are all different, what is intellectual for one may be integrating for another. But I can give you some hints I've come up with in my own journey through the question issue.

One of the best ways to begin weeding out needless information gathering is to start making it a practice to act on every piece of information we take in. Just the thought of this will give us mental strain. Very quickly, as we attempt to actually respond, time itself will encourage us to be more discerning about the information we are gathering. There simply isn't enough time in the day to respond with some form of action to all the pieces of information we take in. We would die of exhaustion.

I experienced a gradual change around asking questions. At first I continued to ask all the questions that typically popped into my mind. As I began to understand the wisdom of taking in only the information I could integrate and use, I became sensitive to what was happening when I asked a question. I could feel some answers move as an energy right into my body system. Other answers I felt bounce off me like a rubber ball off a brick wall. I could hear what was being said to me, but the energy behind what was being said didn't come into me. After awhile, I could anticipate the effect an answer would have on me—I could feel whether the energy was going to be absorbed by me or bounce off—and know that I need not bother going through the exercise of physically hearing it. I'd just apologize for asking the question and indicate that I need not hear the answer. Further down the line, I realized I could think the question, feel the impact of the answer on me, and make a decision whether or not to even open my mouth.

Why am I going through all of this, you ask. Seems a bit overboard, doesn't it? Well, through kinesiology I've given you the means to "hear" the answers to all your questions. Kinesiology can open that door for you. And that's precisely what I want to happen for you. But I want to encourage you to use kinesiology wisely as a viable, living tool within your daily life, not as a tool for you to become cosmic scholars. I want you to use it to participate more fully in your life and your environment. I don't want to encourage armchair observers. You can easily bog yourself down with information overload and render yourself motionless.

Over the years, I've met quite a number of people who ignore what I'm saying here and, after learning kinesiology, start using it across the board

hey become kinesiology addicts and cos-
wake up feeling exhausted and thoroughly
laming kinesiology, swear off it entirely.
nother. In bringing this up, I'm trying to
rough this. Think. And use good old-
n and when not to use kinesiology.

gardening I do at Perelandra, one must
estions—all necessary. For your own
you weed out the unnecessary ques-
gy on the design, layout, preparation
er to ask why *this particular* design,
do it, and then I spend the summer
night have asked in the spring are
ations. The quality of the answers is
action, and observed the results of
n I'll ask questions on the basis of

to ask a certain question. This is because,
my present range of logic, I won't be able to understand their
answer. I must expand my logic first. I usually do this by continuing to
follow their day-to-day advice about the thing in question and simply observe over a period of months, even years. After this, I'll know to ask the
question again. It's then I can hear the answer. From this process, I've
learned something about patience.

OVERLIGHTING DEVA OF PERELANDRA

*In establishing our partnership with you, I feel it essential to add our
overview to this issue of the information which must flow between us. As
Machaelle has stated, we on the higher nature levels will not and cannot
decide for you what you are to know and when. You must orchestrate this
yourself. We take no responsibility for you in this area. If you ask us a
question or seek knowledge from us in a particular area, we will answer.
We will give you all the information you seek. What you do with the information is completely up to you.*

*However, the partnership we seek with humans is a partnership of action
and co-creative growth. Information is meant to be a dynamic energy, not a*

stagnant energy. Although we will give you all the information you seek, we do this in the spirit of action. We seek nothing less. The planet can tolerate nothing less. Too many shifts and changes face us for there to be time wasted on stagnant information gathering.

I point out one additional thing to you. If you humans are only interested in receiving stagnant information, you limit the scope with which we may communicate that information. We are reduced to interacting with you on the mental level. If you physically move with the information you receive, we can then expand our interaction through your physical movements. We can modify movement through intuition, and we can do it in the moment. Through the intuition we can pass along nuances in action that were impossible to pass along to you on the mental level, resulting in a much broader understanding of that which you desire to know. In short, our opportunity for communication with active information is far greater than with stagnant information.

NATURE SPIRITS AT PERELANDRA

We wish to join you at this moment because what is being said is of vital importance to us if we are to work directly with you. We **are** action. We **are** movement. And we dedicate our energy to health, growth and change. We cannot even begin to relate to the human issue of what has been referred to as "stagnant information gathering." We have no understanding of this exercise. Our intent is to interact with you in motion. Our very existence is one of continuous movement. Nature itself is in continuous motion. Where we find humans who are not moving, we back away. We know only to move away and tend to our purpose on the planet in separation from the human.

Regarding our participation in exchanging information with humans: We prefer to do this in a framework of action. As we have said, action is our natural mode of operation. We prefer to interface with you as you work in the garden, for instance. We prefer to communicate through action. If we wish to teach you something about energy and its relationship to form— something which you have indicated to us you wish to know—we will most likely **show** you the information: demonstrate it to you. This is one reason why those humans who consciously work in partnership with us in their gardens talk about the unusual things they see or experience there. Those *unusual happenings have our "fingerprints" all over them and represent times when we have been in communication with the human.*

THE NUTS AND BOLTS OF ASKING A QUESTION

Remember that to use kinesiology successfully, you have to rely on questions in a yes/no format. Short, simple, concise questions. This is easy—and it's not so easy! As thinking adults, we have learned to use compound and compound-complex question frameworks. After all, we don't want to sound like idiots. Simple questions are out of style, and consequently we are out of practice. However, with a little bit of thought, we can learn to rephrase any question we might have or anything we wish to know into a yes/no format.

I'll give you some common pitfalls to watch out for.

Let's say you want to know if you should remove an old apple tree from your backyard that looks to you to be diseased. You open yourself to the appropriate deva (deciding who is appropriate will be discussed later), and ask, "Should I remove this apple tree from the backyard?" Not, "Gee, this apple tree doesn't look too healthy and I was trying to decide if I should take it down, but the squirrels love it so and in the fall the apples are a nice source of food, but I don't want to risk the other trees and I certainly don't want to kill this one because it has been out there in the backyard for years and it's pretty in its own way...." The first response a nature intelligence would make to you is, "What *is* your question?"

I call asking a strung-out question like this "mash potato-ing." In essence, all you've presented the deva with is a glob of shapeless mash potatoes, thus giving no clear avenue for response. If you are faced with an issue that involves many considerations, simply present each consideration separately in a yes/no format. For example, if I were to break down the mash potato question, I would present it something like this:

Should the apple tree in the backyard be removed? (yes/no)

Is the apple tree healthy? (yes/no)

Does this tree's health risk the health of the surrounding trees in the yard? (yes/no)

Is this tree an important source of food for the squirrels? (yes/no)

Is this tree an important source of food for the wildlife in general in the backyard? (yes/no)

(If the tree is to be removed and it is also an important source of food) Should I provide another source of food for the wildlife after the tree is removed? (yes/no)

(If yes, then start listing possibilities one by one.)

Should I provide:

> apples? (yes/no)
>
> bird seed? (yes/no)
>
> suet? (yes/no)
>
> pepperoni pizza? (yes/no)

I've not only shown you how to break down a complicated situation into a series of simple yes/no questions, I've also shown how you can build your question process based on the answer to each question. This is how you receive complex information with lots of nuances—allow the answer to the previous question guide you to ask the next question and keep the process building.

Now, let's say you are looking at the aforementioned backyard and everything looks all right, but you have some vague feeling that something is wrong. Even this situation can be broken down into a yes/no format.

Connect with the overlighting deva of your backyard, and ask:

> Is there something wrong with the backyard? (yes)
>
> Does something need to be added? (no)
>
> Does something need to be removed? (yes)
>
> Is it my child's swing set? (no)
>
> Is it a bush? (no)
>
> Is it a tree? (yes)
>
> Is it the maple tree? (no)
>
> Is it the apple tree? (yes)
>
> (With surprise) Is that sucker sick? (yes)
>
> Should it be removed? (yes)
>
> Soon? (yes)
>
> Has the health of the other trees and bushes been compromised? (no)

(Breathe a sigh of relief and go find someone who will take that tree down for less than $18.85 an hour.)

In essence, what you are doing is playing *Twenty Questions* with a deva.

This may seem tedious to you, but this kind of simplicity is an excellent place to begin when learning something new. Don't let false pride and the fear of looking silly get in your way. If you take the time to build your foundation, eventually you will have a broader working relationship between yourself and the nature intelligences, and you'll develop refinements to your technique.

Part of my development has centered around the use of intuition. Once I began to feel comfortable with the *Twenty Questions* routine, I noticed that my intuition began to play into it. I paid attention to this and soon realized that the nature intelligence I was connected with was using my intuition to guide me more efficiently through the questions. I got to the point where, if I walked out into this mythical backyard and sensed something wrong, I would connect with the deva and ask:

> Is there something wrong? (yes)

Then my attention might be drawn to the apple tree or I'd get an intuitive hit that the problem was the apple tree, and I would ask, in light of the new input:

> Is it the apple tree? (yes)

As you see, I was able to get to the heart of the matter comparatively quickly. But intuition wasn't added until I felt comfortable with the more basic technique. Like any tool, the better we are with the basics, the more proficient we'll be with what develops later.

A Note on Clarity

If you're having difficulty wording a simple yes/no question, consider this an important issue to be faced and something worth spending time to rectify. You have not simply stumbled upon a glitch in your quest to use kinesiology. You've also stumbled upon a glitch in the communication between your higher self and your conscious self. If you can't even clearly phrase the question, you can't expect an answer. I've met people who cannot articulate a question. In a workshop they will attempt to ask me something and I can't figure out what they are asking—nor can anyone else in the workshop. Usually it turns out that they are frustrated because they can't get any clarity in their own life and are trying to ask me what to do about it.

For those of you who find yourselves in this boat, you have a terrific

CRACKING THE
COMMUNICATION CODE

*HINT: As you develop internal order, your intuition will become clearer and stronger. You'll see that when you ask a simple yes/no question, you will intuitively sense the answer before testing. This is a normal development. I recommend that you continue with the kinesiology testing as a **verification** that your intuitive answer is correct.*

It's helpful, especially in the beginning, to literally verbalize your questions out loud and not just think them. When we say something aloud, we tend to articulate it better than when we just think it. Also, I will ask something out loud if I'm a little tired and I need some extra sensory input (sound) to help me keep my focus.

opportunity to turn that around and develop internal order by learning how to articulate a simple yes/no question. If you do this, you not only develop the tool of kinesiology, you also develop clarity for communicating with yourself. I fully understand that it will take focus on your part, and in comparison to someone who finds articulating a simple question easy, to you it will seem herculean. But if you wish to function consciously on your many levels, you must have internal clarity and order.

I recommend that initially you devote your attention to learning to ask simple questions and not worry about receiving answers. When you need to ask another person a question, take time to consider what you really want to ask and how it can be most clearly and efficiently worded. It helps to write down the question. In this way, you can visually examine your words. If they don't convey what you mentally want to express, play with the wording. Keep doing this until you feel those words accurately and concisely communicate what you wish to ask. Then go to that person and ask the question. Notice the difference in quality of how the person answers you. Your clarity will inspire similar clarity in the response.

I urge you to continue this process for a fair period of time—even dedicating yourself to the process for a year or two. Quite often, that frustrating inner confusion exists because we've not had an acceptable framework for the development of mental ordering. Learning to ask questions gives the mind something tangible to work with and, in the process, you learn mind-word-and-mouth coordination. You'll find that as you develop the ability to clearly articulate a question, your inner fog will begin to lift, which in turn will automatically begin to lift your outer fog.

Either/Or Situations

I find myself faced with either/or situations quite frequently. (Should I do this or that for this plant?) This is simple to deal with. Let's say I must make a move, and I have 2 or more options as possibilities. I will open myself to the appropriate nature intelligence. Now, I learned early on that I can't assume that nature knows what is going on inside my head. So the first thing I do when I'm in an either/or situation is inform the intelligence what I perceive my options to be. I list them all. Example: I receive that the rose bushes need a dressing of phosphorus. I have options available to me as to what I can add to the soil for the phosphorus. I will tell whoever

I'm working with that it can either be bone meal, alfalfa meal, rock phosphate or liquid kelp. Then I will ask "Which would you prefer I use?," and go through the list again one by one thereby setting up the scenario in a yes/no format.

Would you prefer

bone meal? (no)

alfalfa meal? (no)

rock phosphate? (yes)

kelp? (no)

If I get a no on everything in my list, I will double-check myself by retesting. If I still get a consistent no, then I'll ask:

Is there something else you would prefer that I add? (yes)

I also have Nitro-10, greensand, cottonseed meal, dolomite lime and liquid seaweed. Is it one of these? (yes)

I then relist these fertilizers one by one in order to find the preferred fertilizer.

Another scenario: You get out of bed one morning with a driving desire to wear your yellow and green polka dot shirt. Then you saunter to the closet and as you look for your snappy yellow and green polka dot shirt, your eye catches the purple and orange striped one, and you're overcome with an equal desire to wear this one. Being a responsible person who desires to participate in the universal flow on a daily basis, you say to yourself, "Well, which one should I wear?" The "Well, which one is it?" question is a sure sign you are in an either/or situation. In such situations, I will ask "Does it matter which one of these 2 shirts I wear today?" (If I get a no, I can exercise free will and make a personal decision based on which shirt attracts me the most. If I get a yes, then I'll shift into a yes/no format and list each shirt separately to find out which one it's to be.)

You probably noted that I didn't connect with nature in the above scenario. Directing this question to yourself is akin to asking if it is healthy for you to include a couple cups of coffee in your life. Either your system can handle some caffeine or not. Caffeine will either weaken your system, thus giving you a negative when you test a cup of coffee or simply ask the question, or your system can maintain its strength, giving you a positive when tested. In the case of the shirts, it's a question of appropriate colors and types of fabrics if there's a difference between the 2 shirts. One day yellow and green may be a part of your system's balance, and another day the purple and orange may assist the balancing. Or both sets of colors are fine. (Or neither!) You get all this input by simply testing the state of your electrical system while literally holding the options or projecting the options through the format of a question. I call these "environmental impact" questions: physical things around you that impact your physical well-being.

Connecting with Your Higher Self

Sometimes the kinds of questions we're asking go beyond the simple environmental impact questions. Sometimes we might like to know something about certain life directions we are presently facing. For these we should have direct input from our higher selves—where information on a larger scale is "housed." Connecting with your higher self couldn't be more simple. (For all of you who are thinking about going to some fancy workshop just to learn how to do this, I'm going to save you the $500 cost of the workshop right now.)

1. Focus your attention on yourself and say aloud (softly):

    I wish to be connected to my higher self.

Keep your focus on what you are saying. The connection occurs within about 5 seconds. Sometimes you'll feel an energy shift in your body.

2. To get confirmation, test yourself using kinesiology. Ask:

    Am I now connected to my higher self? (Test.)

If you get a no, it just means you lost focus. Regroup and ask to be connected again. Then test for verification. You'll get a yes now.

3. Ask any questions in a simple yes/no format.

In my writings, where I have used the phrase "disconnect from your higher self," that's my short-hand way of saying "disconnect your special connection with your higher self." Again, it is impossible to disconnect or sever from your higher self.

IMPORTANT: Once you've finished, you will need to disconnect your connection with your higher self. Notice I said "disconnect your connection." I did not say disconnect from your higher self. It is impossible to disconnect from your higher self. It's with you always. Part of your standard equipment. You can't lose your higher self.

However, you have connected to your higher self in a special way and it requires physical energy on your part to maintain that connection. If you already had a conscious bridge to your higher self, you would not have needed to go through this exercise to begin with. But bridging the unconscious higher self to the conscious self costs you energy. This act is a physical phenomenon. This is exactly the same phenomenon that occurs when we connect with any other intelligence that requires special bridging. So, here's what you do to disconnect:

1. Say aloud (softly):

    I'd like to disconnect this special connection with my higher self.

This also occurs within 5 seconds. You may feel another energy shift in your body.

2. Verify the disconnection by asking:

    Have we disconnected the special connection? (Test.)

If you got a no, your higher self hasn't mutinied on you. It just means you lost your focus again. Refocus, and ask for the disconnection again. Then verify. You'll get a yes.

For those who insist on remaining consciously connected to their higher self beyond the question session: In about 12 to 24 hours you will feel fatigue, a drain. The cost of maintaining this connection is now beyond what you can easily endure. You're okay. No one has ever died of higher self overload. But you do need to disconnect or you'll just continue draining. Do the disconnection and eat some protein. You'll feel your energy begin to return in about 20 minutes. It may take up to a day or 2 to fully return, depending on how long you tried to hold the connection.

WARNING: I strongly advise you to limit your questions to only decisions you are presently faced with. Don't ask questions projected into the future. The answers you receive will be accurate in light of all the variables surrounding you now. It can only remain accurate if those variables remain exactly as they are now. Once the variables start to change, the accurate answer will change accordingly. Variables can change in an instant. In order to know the accurate answer to a question you asked your higher self a week ago or a month ago, you'll have to ask the question again, in light of the new variables. Personally, I won't ask a question that has to do with my future. I concentrate on what I'm facing in the present and have deep faith that if I address the present well, the future automatically takes care of itself.

I don't use kinesiology for the long sessions I have with nature. Also, I do not channel. The nature intelligences do not take over my physical being nor do they control my voice. I do what I call "translation." I am in full control of my consciousness. I connect with the specific devas and nature spirits in a 4-point coning (explained in Chapter 18). Information is given me in the form of energy. My job as translator is to assign to specific impulses of energy the word that most fully carries the intent of the energy I was given. I translate directly on a computer.

To understand this process more easily, just think of the job of the United Nations' interpreters. They don't go into a trance state. They develop the art of focused listening and the ability to translate intent, thought, expression and concept from one language pattern to another. If you take away the audible sound and have only the projection to the translator of the energy behind the sound, you have an idea of what I receive: communication in the form of energy. I just translate that communication into the form of words that are faithful to the intent and expression of the energy I "hear." And very like the U.N. interpreter, I am only as good at this as my innate ability combined with training, discipline, care and a lot of years of practice.

Kinesiology is like any tool. The more you practice, the better you become at using it. You need a sense of confidence about using this tool, especially when you get some very strange answers to what you thought were pretty straight questions. It helps you get over the initial "this-is-weird-and-the-damned-testing-isn't-working" stage if you have some confidence in your ability to feel clear positive and negative responses. The only way I know to get over this hump is to practice testing. You cannot mentally talk yourself over this hump. With practice, you will develop clarity in your testing and you'll learn your personal pitfalls.

In teaching kinesiology, I have found that something interesting happens to some people when they are learning it. Every block, doubt, question and personal challenge they have, when faced head-on with something perceived as unconventional, comes right to the surface. It's as if the physical tool of kinesiology itself brings to the surface all those hurdles. So they learn kinesiology right away and use it well. Then, all of a sudden it's not working for them. When they tell me about it, I realize that the thing they do differently now that they didn't do at first is double-checking their answers—and rechecking, and rechecking, and doing it again, and again. Each time the answers vary or the fingers get mushy and they get "definite maybes."

Well, again the issue isn't the kinesiology. The issue is really why they are suddenly doing all this rechecking. What has surfaced for them are questions around trust in their own ability, belief that such unconventional things really do work and are working for them. They are having a sudden lack of self-confidence.

Again, the only way I know to get over this hurdle is to defy it—keep testing. The other alternative is to succumb and stop developing with kinesiology. But, that doesn't really accomplish anything. So in cases like this, I suggest the person keep testing, *stop double-checking* and take the plunge to go with his first test result. Eventually, the action based on the first test result will verify the accuracy of the test. From this, your confidence builds. I firmly believe that only clear personal evidence can get us through these kinds of hurdles and blocks—and that means just continuing.

So, what can we practice test on? Everything. You could easily drive yourself nuts. What colors you should wear. What colors you should wear for a special event. What would be healthiest for you to eat for breakfast, lunch and dinner. You take 10 separate vitamin and mineral supplements as a matter of course on a daily basis. Try testing them individually ("Do I need vitamin E? B_6? Iron?") to see if you need all 10 every day. Or if there are some you don't need to take at all. You are sitting at a restaurant and they don't have Tofu Supreme on the menu. Is there anything at all on that menu that is healthy for you to eat? ("Should I eat fish?" [yes/no] "Should I eat beef?" [yes/no] "Chicken?" [yes/no] "Häagen-Dazs fudge ripple ice cream?!" [Yes!]) For all of these kinds of questions, you're just directly testing your electrical system. These are environmental impact questions. No higher self connection needed.

The point is to test everything you possibly can that doesn't place you in a life-threatening situation, follow through on your answers and then look at the results. As I have worked through the years to refine my ability to use kinesiology, I have, on many occasions, purposely followed through on answers that made no sense at all to me, just to see if the testing was accurate. Doing this and looking at the results with a critical eye is the only way I know to learn about ourselves as kinesiology testers, and to discover the nuances and uses of kinesiology itself.

One last piece of information: Give yourself about a year to develop confidence with kinesiology. Now, you'll be able to use it right away. This just takes sticking with your initial efforts until you get those first feelings of positive strength and negative weakness in the circuit fingers. But I have found from my own experience and from watching others that it takes about a year of experimentation to fully learn the art of asking accurate yes/no questions, and to overcome the hurdles. As one woman said, "You stick with this stuff a year, and boy, what a great thing you end up with!"

3

ESTABLISHING YOUR PARTNERSHIP

It's time to take the plunge. You've been kinesiology testing everything from here to Aunt Sally's kitchen. You have a fair sense of the positive strong and negative weak sensation in your fingers. Spring is barreling in on you. You are knee deep in the new season's gardening catalogs. And you want to get started in your new partnership.

To get started, I recommend a small, formal declaration on your part. I mentioned in *Behaving*... that this was how I got started, and I still feel that this is an excellent way to begin. My suggestions:

1. Go outside. Not only is this a symbolic gesture of your desire to physically link with nature, it might also facilitate matters as you direct your attention to nature for the declaration.

2. Direct your attention to nature—specifically, to the nature intelligences. If this is too vague for you, just pretend you are speaking into a telephone with nature listening in at the other end. Or sense that nature as an intelligent presence is sitting opposite you waiting for you to say something. The main thing is that you do whatever is needed to consciously link yourself with the nature intelligences. Be clear, precise and simple about it.

* About this energy stuff: Just as there is personal style about how people's fingers respond to kinesiology, there is also personal style when it comes to whether or not people feel energy. A person is not deficient if he or she doesn't feel energy washing over them, through them, around them—whatever. All the connections you will be making in this book are verified by kinesiology. You don't have to feel anything to successfully work with nature co-creatively. Just follow the steps, do exactly what they say to do and trust that nature will hold up its end. In time you may feel subtle energy changes, but this is just nice—not necessary. The physical changes you observe and the success of these processes will verify to you that nature is right there working with you.

3. Say aloud:

I would like to be formally linked with the devic realm.

Wait just a few seconds. You may feel sensations like a wave of energy gently wash over you.* It's fine if you feel nothing because you are going to verify your connection with this level using kinesiology. Ask:

Am I now connected? (Then test.)

Once you get over the shock of feeling a powerful and positive test result, go on to step 4.

4. Say aloud:

I would now like to be formally linked with the nature spirit level.

Again wait a few seconds, then ask:

Am I connected? (Test.)

You'll get another powerful positive result. I know I sound awfully confident about your test results, but remember I am aware of how much nature wants this connection with you and how eager it is to work with you in a consciously communicating partnership.

5. Spend a moment recognizing that you have just opened the phone lines to a new and expanded level. This is a significant time for you, and I doubt if you'll want to let it pass lightly. I suggest that you just sit quietly with the moment.

6. Now that you have their attention—and they probably have yours—it's time to declare the intent of your partnership. If gardening is your focus, simply say aloud:

I now request that we work in a co-creative partnership in the garden
and that I be connected to all the nature intelligences involved.

To verify that you have been heard, ask:

Is this declaration accepted? (Test. You'll get another yes.)

If you don't have a garden but you want to establish a partnership, go right ahead. If you have house plants, establish your working partnership around these. You can focus the partnership on a greenhouse or atrium. Or your backyard. Or the semi-precious geodes and crystals you have displayed around the apartment. All you need is one focal point around which you and nature can establish a working relationship. Having a focal point of some kind will allow you to keep the relationship active, and this will be essential for the dynamic exchange of information, lessons and ideas you seek.*

You are now consciously and actively linked with nature and ready to move on. While you are connected, you may take the opportunity to ask anything you'd like. Just make sure it's in a yes/no format.

If you feel that what you've accomplished is already enough, close out the session. You'll want to get in the habit of closing down a session because 1) it gives your sessions clarity—a beginning when you open a session and an end when you close, and 2) it takes energy on your part to maintain focus during a session, and if you are not clear about a session being complete, you might get into an energy-drain situation because of nature continuing to hold its lines open while it tries to figure out what you are doing. Nature will not automatically close a session you opened.

7. To close down a session, say aloud:

      I request that this session be closed.

This takes about 10 seconds. To verify, ask if the session is now closed. You should have a positive response. If you get a negative, focus yourself on the matter at hand (and not on what has happened during the session!) and make the request again. You'll get a positive result this time.

All of the connections you will be making will occur right away. All you have to do is request the connection and nature will immediately connect with you. It takes about 10 to 15 seconds for your body to adjust to and accommodate the nature presence. This is why you may feel energy shifting in your body. Nature will not refuse to make the connection. It does not get into an argument about these things. And it doesn't make some personality judgment and decide that on specific days it just isn't going to talk to you. Nature also doesn't get headaches. You ask, it connects. It's as simple as that.

As far as we humans are concerned, no special "spiritual elevation" is required of us. Any limitations we feel about this connection with nature are in our heads. All that is required of us is focus, concentration and clarity.

ESTABLISHING YOUR
PARTNERSHIP

* You can also establish a co-creative partnership with nature around focal points such as your home and your work. For this, you will also need the Perelandra Garden Workbook II. It explains the processes that can be applied in these kinds of areas.

A WORD ABOUT ETIQUETTE

The easiest way to describe the etiquette I use when working with devas and nature spirits is to say that I treat them as loving, intelligent teachers of the first order who also happen to be my best friends. I am friendly and fully open with them. I will joke and kid around at times. I also try to conduct myself in as considerate a manner as possible. For example, another reason I make it a point to close down my sessions is that in a discussion with a good friend, I would not simply get up and walk out of the room leaving them to figure out if the discussion has ended or not. (I wouldn't do this with a stranger either!) I have discovered over the years that *I* am treated as a good friend and with the most loving consideration by nature. I try to respond in kind. I say "thank you" and "excuse me" and "I'm sorry." I take a moment to acknowledge when something special has occurred between us. I don't just let those moments slip by and even after 16 years, I don't take these moments for granted.

I think if in your growing relationship with nature you should get stuck and not know how to respond to a situation, you'll be on safe ground if you consider what you would do if the situation were between you and a good friend—someone you care enough about to make an effort not to offend.

I don't wish to imply that nature is temperamental and needs to be tip-toed around. But some people don't understand that courtesy is a universal dynamic that is demonstrated on all levels beyond us. And there are other people who, when beginning their partnership, become overwhelmed by the power and majesty they experience from nature and place it on a pedestal. That's the last place nature wishes to be placed. Good friends aren't placed on pedestals. Still other people can be taken by the sudden friendly informality they experience with nature and throw all good sense to the wind and act in most inconsiderate and thoughtless ways. I am bringing up the issue of etiquette in an effort to encourage you to develop a sound middle road of care.

PAN

I would like to add to this issue from our point of view. We intelligences within nature do not discern between good etiquette and bad etiquette.

*Etiquette, as such, is not an issue with us. We exist within the dynamic spirit of love and naturally respond within that spirit. This is extended to humans whenever we have been able to make any contact. We do not **try** to respond as such, or seek to respond in love. We **are** love—love in action. Therefore that spirit is the underlying intent in all we do. To act otherwise is alien to us and for the most part causes confusion because we are not familiar with action or intent outside the spirit of love. The human's free will allows him to choose action either within or outside the spirit of love. Nature does not have this choice.*

From our point of view, Machaelle's use of the concept of etiquette is her way of bringing human attention to this issue of action within the spirit of love and our confusion around action outside that spirit. We would say that good etiquette is love in action.

THE ELEMENTAL ANNEX

One of the very first things I was told to do when establishing my partnership with nature was to open what I call the "Elemental Annex"— the nature spirit sanctuary. I set aside an area in the woods near the garden, roped it off and announced that this piece of land was for the exclusive use of the nature spirits. Immediately after this pronouncement, I felt a tremendous rush of energy enter the area and sensed myself surrounded by readiness, action and organization. I also sensed that my gesture of setting aside this piece of land had been accepted as a bridge between the nature spirits and me. From that point in time, our working relationship has been clear and vital—tangible.

I have since moved the site of the garden, and a year after that move, I was told to rope off an area near the new garden for the nature spirits. Their shift occurred during the spring equinox in 1984 and was as dramatic the second time as the first.

I strongly recommend that you establish a nature spirit sanctuary. It can be any size* and should be in an area where people don't need to enter. It is to be for the sole "habitation" of the nature spirits, traditionally regarded as an area where humans are not to enter. The rope is to remind humans to stay out, not keep nature spirits in. This means that the nature spirit sanctuary is not to double as a sitting area for you or a play area for your

* It can be a 1-foot square of land, a rock or, if your partner is the original mad mower and refuses to allow any area to be untouched by a blade, you can choose several nice tree limbs to be the sanctuary.

children. The intent is that this is an unencumbered gift from us to the nature spirits. Aside from being a tangible gesture of recognition on your part, it also becomes the base of nature spirit operations on your land and can have quite a vibration of activity emanating from it.

How to Open a Nature Spirit Sanctuary

1. Choose a suitable area. If you are gardening, it would be good to have it near the garden.

2. Rope off the sanctuary. Or mark the boundary any way you wish, making sure it is easily discernable.

3. Standing just outside the area, ask that the nature spirits accept this sanctuary and join you in full partnership as you develop your new relationship with nature.

4. If you would like to verify that all of this has happened, open to the nature spirit level (you can now direct your attention to that level by looking directly into the sanctuary) and ask if your roped area has been accepted by them. Then test.

PAN

The nature spirit sanctuary that Machaelle has described to you is more important than ever before. There are areas around the planet that can best be described as sanctuaries which have been established by the nature spirits themselves. Some of these areas have been discovered by humans and called "fairy rings." If a human stumbles upon such a place, he describes it as enchanted and indeed heightened with a strong and vital energy. This is the energy of the nature spirits he has felt.

Long ago, when man and nature co-existed on more friendly terms, the nature spirits felt free to establish their area of concentration nearby. These were special points of intense power strategically spaced around the planet through which Earth could be spiritually infused not only by nature itself but by the universe as a whole. But as man's age of development caused him to infringe on the very existence of nature, these points of concentration were either de-activated or moved to safer ground, shall we say. They took on an energy of protection—protection from humans. One must remember that so much of man's modern development has been contrary to the well-being of all that is natural on the planet. This may be extended to include the nature spirits, for their role on the planet is intimately tied into the well-being of all that is natural. The shifting of the points of concentration away from man's proximity has been a retreat by the nature spirits resulting in a significant diminishing of the scope and intensity of the natural power grid around the planet. Consequently, today there exists an isolation between man and the nature spirits, and a planetary environment of de-spiritualization—form devoid of vital life energy.

The initiation for the reunion between humans and nature must come from humans. The time has long passed where it is appropriate for such an action to be initiated by nature without the conscious participation of the humans who will benefit. The age we are all moving into is one of conscious teamwork, not blind benevolent trust that all will be well.

The benefits of such a reunion are indeed great. The actual operating principles around the notion of spirit and matter perfectly united, which will move man and the planet forward, exist within the dynamic partnership between man and the nature spirits. It is these two who work most directly with spirit and matter united, and the problems that arise from this union.

As each sanctuary is made available by man and activated by the nature spirits, it will send out the word that once more man and nature are ready to work together—only now they are ready to work in an equal, co-creative partnership. And as each sanctuary is activated around the world, you will feel, even see, the nature spirits moving out of their protective isolation to re-enter the world at large for the purpose of respiritualizing the planet.

Dismantling a Nature Spirit Sanctuary

Sometimes it becomes necessary to dismantle the sanctuary. For example, you are moving and the new owners of your property are not into co-creative gardening. Or, you are renting and now you must move. The owner and/or the new renters are not likely to be into co-creative gardening. Or, your spouse was into co-creative gardening and you know that a sanctuary was set up. Now your spouse has left or passed on and you are moving forward into a new life—and you feel it's right that the sanctuary be dealt with appropriately. In these kinds of cases, it is important to dismantle the sanctuary. This is easy.

1. Connect with the nature spirits of the sanctuary. Say:
   I'd like to be connected to the sanctuary nature spirits. (Verify the connection by testing. A positive answer means you're connected.)

2. Explain what is happening that brings the sanctuary's existence into question.

3. Ask, in light of this, if it is appropriate to dismantle the sanctuary. (Test.)

4. If you tested yes, request that the sanctuary now be dismantled.

This should take no more than 30 seconds. If you feel nothing happening, just wait the 30 seconds. Then thank the nature spirits for their assistance and remove all the markers that were placed around the sanctuary area. The land is now free to be used in any way someone wishes.

Before leaving, disconnect from the nature spirits you linked with for this process. Say:

   I'd like to disconnect from the nature spirits of the sanctuary. (Test.)

If you tested no to step 3, ask if the nature spirits wish for this sanctuary to remain open. (Perhaps the new people really are into a co-creative partnership and you don't know it. Nature would know this, however.) Assume nature knows what it's doing, and that your responsibility is now complete. Leave the site marked, disconnect from the nature spirits of the sanctuary and that's it.

It is also possible that a no means that nature would like to shift this sanctuary to a site at your new place. If this is the case, don't close the sanctuary down, but remove all the markers. Once you've found a suitable spot at your new place, work with the nature spirits as you would when opening a new sanctuary. Only this time, nature will simply shift the old sanctuary to the new spot. Mark the new site. Now you have the sanctuary up and running at the new place.

If you intended to open a sanctuary at your new site yet when you asked nature about closing down the old sanctuary they said to close it, go ahead and close it. It is up to nature whether or not a sanctuary should be closed, shifted or a new one opened at another site. Let nature lead the way in this.

4

BREAKING GROUND

From this point on, much of what I will be doing will be giving you the questions you'll need to ask nature. For example, you are standing in the middle of your 1000-square-foot backyard or looking out over your 40 acres, shovel in hand, ready to start this new garden. You have a clear idea of the garden size you wish based on your needs, desires and the reasonable amount of time you can give to the garden. This is very important for you to have these things clear in your mind in order to ask the first question. To answer, the deva will want to take into consideration your garden intent and needs, and must have that information supplied by you. It is your job to supply this information.*

    1. Ask to be connected with the deva of your garden. Test to make sure you are connected.

    2. The first question:
        Where should this garden be placed?
(Now I know this is not a yes/no question, but this is the first question. I'll show you how to translate it into a yes/no format shortly.)

    Even if you already have an established garden, you have a related question to ask:

        Is this present garden placed in the appropriate spot?

*It really is important that the gardener define the garden. You can't just say to nature that you want a garden. It will ask what kind of garden you want. Remember, nature's idea of a garden is Yosemite National Park. So you better give them some specifics. You define the garden by telling nature about its purpose, its various uses, the size family it will serve.... Nature needs this input before it can locate the garden and create the design and layout.

53

If you get a negative, then you need to consider:

1) Are you willing to move the garden?

2) Where should it be moved?

If moving the garden is an unwieldy or unacceptable option, you have the right to say "no" to the suggestion. You always have that right. But if you wish to establish a partnership with nature, you won't be able to stop with just your "no." You need to make a commitment to do what nature will suggest to you in order to make the present area more workable. To move a garden is an exhausting proposition, I readily admit. But remember, nature would not suggest a move if it did not have good reason. It's just that *we* don't understand the reason. I personally would give serious thought to moving the garden even if I had no idea why nature was suggesting this to me. I'd do it just to find out what nature knows that I'm not seeing. It's at times like this we really learn from nature.*

If you are faced with starting a new garden or moving the site of the old one, you still must deal with the issue of where to put it. There are do's and don't's already established in good gardening practice regarding where one should locate their garden. A southern and eastern exposure. A northern and western protection. On a knoll or rise for good drainage, etc., etc. Although you may know these points very well, they are not the issue now. The issue is where *nature* wishes you to place the garden.

I do not suggest you throw out all your learned knowledge. In fact, it will be most useful to you to observe different thought, different approaches, and overall changes to new concepts. You'll have a springboard for comparison. When learning, this can be handy. And nature itself will use what you already know as the foundation upon which you will build together.

However, it's important in co-creative gardening to put what you already know to one side and ask the deva of your garden where the garden should be placed. Having asked this question, you need only establish a framework for translating the answer, which you do by breaking down your land area into sections. You can do this visually as you stand there on your land or make a line drawing of the area and indicate each of the sections or grids. Then focus on each section and ask:

Do I put the garden here? (Test.)

Keep doing this for all the sections. Once you identify the section and it in

* I have had some pretty interesting experiences when I found out I'm to do something that I swore I'd never do—like move a garden. If I am just sitting around thinking about the possibility of this kind of task, every fiber of my being would be shouting, "No way!" However, when I actually find out I'm to do it, my state of mind and the circumstances surrounding me have all "magically" changed to support doing this previously unthinkable task. I now have desire, good will and energy for the task.

*My suggestion is that you not sit around and list all the things you would refuse to do if nature asks you. And don't sit around what if-ing nature. (What if nature asks me to move my house.) Nature isn't goofy. You're just projecting your own fears. I suggest concentrating on what nature is suggesting to you **now**. If something big is to happen in the future, nature will help supply the ways and the means.*

itself is a fairly large area, break that section into subsections and identify the exact location through the same elimination process.

If at the end you have only 1 positive response, then you now know where to place the garden. If you have 2 or more positives, you are being told there is more than 1 spot and you are being given options. In this situation, I always ask if there is 1 option better than all the rest. If I get a yes, I'll identify which one by asking the question, "Which one is the best?," looking at each of my options and asking "Is it this one?," and eliminating. If I get a no, I get to give my free will free rein and make a personal choice between the options. Sometimes several adjacent sections will test positive. This means that once the garden is properly oriented, its borders will pass through a portion of each of these sections.

THE OBSTACLE ISSUE

If you haven't already guessed, your partnership with nature can be a constant test of commitment on your part. Issues will come up again and again which will challenge your heart in very fundamental ways. The obstacle issue is but one example. You have gone through the elimination process and have found that the garden is to be right where the 10-year-old oak tree is standing or where you already have a rose bed. You have an immediate heart conflict.

There are some things to think about before you yell "no" and ask for a secondary placement.

1. You asked where the garden should go and this is the answer. You did not give any conditions to nature prior to the question. I don't give conditions because I really want to know the answer (no matter what) and then I'll deal with any complications that might arise.

2. Nature does not have an emotional attachment to form. It has a godly relationship with form in that it has a divine love for life. It designs and organizes with the intent of divine love inherent in all those decisions. We humans do not have to teach nature how to properly love and respect the world of form. In light of this inherent divine love, it still told you that the best position for the garden is right where that oak tree is standing.

3. The direction nature has given you regarding the garden takes into

consideration input, facts, reality, balance and energy from all sorts of levels. The deva has the health and balance of the whole as its primary consideration, not just the oak tree. If I were looking at that oak tree, I'd have to consider that there is a bigger picture involved here.

Still before yelling "no" to taking out the tree or any other obstacle, I'd ask some more questions:

Is it to be moved?

Can this thing be easily moved?

If so, where?

(Follow the same positioning process you did with the garden. This time you'll receive the answer in light of the future garden being placed in its position. That potential placement for the garden is now new input when the deva considers your land area.)

If it is not to be moved, is it to be removed altogether?

If yes, then you can pursue the issue by asking if this decision has to do with overall energy balance (if the tree is healthy) or if the tree is actually weakened in energy by its being in this position.

A 10-year-old tree is not easily moved. But if you get a positive answer when you ask if the tree is to remain part of the whole picture of your yard or land, you might ask if you are to plant a younger tree of the same kind in the new desired location. If you get a yes, what nature is most likely planning for is an energy shift from one form to another. That is, the life energy of the first oak tree will be shifted, prior to your taking it down, to the form of the young tree. This is done on the nature spirit level and is part of that cooperation between man and nature that is available to us. In actuality, you won't be removing a large tree. You will be setting up the vehicle for a complete energy shift by planting the second tree. The spirit and life force of the first tree will remain intact but in a different form.

Participating in an Energy Shift

1. Supply the new form to which the energy will be shifted. Sometimes nature will use a form that is already in the area. For example, you may have another oak tree in the yard and nature will indicate to you that no other form needs to be added and it will use the other oak tree as the receiver of the life energy from the tree to be taken out. (Energy is completely flexible when it comes to size and shape. The life energy from

1 tree can be received fully in another form without causing overcrowding.)

2. Once the second form has either been added or identified, connect with the nature spirit level. Say:

I'd like to be connected to the nature spirits working with this tree.

Make sure you are connected:

Am I connected with the nature spirit level? (Test.)

3. **Initiate the shift** by asking the nature spirits to now shift the energy from the old form to the new.

4. Although this process is immediate and takes a matter of a minute, do not disturb the old form for about 2 weeks to make sure the shift fully stabilizes. Before removing the old form, test to make sure all is ready for removal.*

There is another wonderful and amazing verification that the energy has shifted which you can see for yourself. Before removing the old form, take a good look at it. Really look at it carefully. Then remove it completely from the spot. As soon as it is away from the area, look where the form used to stand and try to visualize its being there. If the energy was shifted, you won't be able to visualize the form even though you just looked at it less than 5 minutes before. This is because not only the form but the energy within the form are no longer present, and there is nothing before you on any level of reality from which you can draw for a visualization.

Don't panic if you can still see the form. Once again, connect with the nature spirits and ask that they shift the energy even though you have already removed the form. They will do this. Don't assume a mistake has been made on anyone's part. The nature spirits use opportunities such as this all the time for teaching. Show us something different. Give us a new nuance. Change process slightly to meet individual need. Understand that something is happening, and remain alert and open for input either through what you observe or what you sense intuitively. Also, you may not have the complete lesson until you go through the process a second time with another form to be removed, and they show or communicate to you in this scenario again. So don't hesitate to keep moving forward even if you sense you may have made an error and you no longer have any idea what you

You can also use this process with nature to shift energy from a stand of trees that is slated to be cut down or bulldozed. In this case, the energy from all the different trees in the endangered area will shift en masse to their corresponding forms in a nearby safe area.

Also, you can repair an area that has been suddenly leveled by working with nature to shift the remaining energy to nearby appropriate form.

*However, it is not appropriate to do this kind of work on someones else's property without their **conscious** permission. It's a matter of ethics. So, you may only be able to do this for land you own or rent. Or on land owned by the general public. In this situation, you own a piece of the rock.*

* If you understand the Soil Balancing and Stabilizing Process from both Chapter 18 of this book or the Perelandra Garden Workbook II *(henceforth known as* Workbook II*), this can be done right after the shift is complete. The 2-week waiting period won't be necessary then.*

* Nature is a wonderful teacher. It takes into consideration our individual strengths and weaknesses. It gives us lessons that enhance those strengths and helps us understand and modify those weaknesses. With this, our partnership with nature deepens.

are doing. If you get information from nature to participate in another energy shift, do it.*

For the sake of clarity, let me add that nature does not need our participation in order to do an energy shift. Nature spirits do this all the time—moving energy from one level to another and then into form, or from one form to another. It's an energy dynamic that is as much a part of the nature spirit level as breathing is to us. But I remind you that we are moving into an era of conscious teamwork. In those areas where man and nature interact, such as gardening, landscaping, land management, etc., there is constant opportunity for co-creative partnership, and nature will not assume sole responsibility for quality interaction with us. It looks to us to participate in kind.

If, in light of all this, you do not wish to move or shift the obstacle, ask the deva for a secondary position for your garden and commit yourself to doing what must be done to stabilize or enhance it. As you become sensitive to working with nature, you'll notice that you won't be feeling a judgmental energy coming from it to you. If you ask for a secondary or alternative decision, you won't feel nature calling you a jerk. It's okay to make that decision, but what nature looks to us for is an understanding that our decisions have implications. An alternative is an alternative for a reason and requires a different approach or different action. If we keep that in mind and remain open to further input from nature, we'll maintain a good, flexible relationship.

DEVA OF THE PERELANDRA GARDEN

Machaelle has touched on an area upon which we would like to expand, and that is garden placement in the context of the whole picture. The purpose of the approach to gardening being presented here is to establish a highly planned and cooperative space where man and nature can work in partnership for the purpose of the enhancement of man's health through the heightened quality of his food, and the enhancement of the surrounding land area itself through the radiation of heightened nature energy from the garden. The direction of vibrant, life-giving energy not only moves into the plants and their vegetables. It also radiates from the garden into the surrounding land and impacts all form within that area. Perhaps it would be easier to visualize what we are saying if one saw the garden as an energy generator. As man and nature work more closely together, the garden ener-gy shifts, clarifies and strengthens, which in turn makes the garden a finely tuned generator. And the life energy contained within all surrounding form is enhanced that much more.

As you can see, a garden where the power of man and of nature have come together in a truly creative endeavor can be in itself a very powerful thing. It has been fairly easy for humans to grasp how this power can impact them personally through the higher quality food they eat from that garden. But humans have tended to miss the powerful impact that the gar-den can have outside itself.

It is for this reason we must be very careful about the placement of such a potential power area within the context of the whole. When you open to us seeking the information for where to place the garden, we will position it where not only the internal garden process is most positively enhanced, but where the external relationship of the garden to the whole is most ad-vantageous.

Consider several things: If you are seeking this information from us, by the mere fact of your opening to us you are saying that this garden will be consciously linked in partnership with nature. That tells us that the power potential in this specific garden is great. It is a potential that may not be fully attained for years, since man and nature will need time to work together in a building process, but it is a potential that must be taken into consideration by us on the devic level. There are areas within the whole of your land which are more appropriate than other areas for holding such a power point.

So when we look to place such a garden, we take three questions into consideration: 1) Where on the land is the physical activity of garden growth best supported? 2) Where will the internal movement of energy and the development of a powerful energy environment best be supported? 3) Where will the external movement of power energy into the surrounding environment best be enhanced and supported? We will place a garden in the most positive position in light of these three considerations. And quite frankly, because the energy and the power questions are so important, we may place a garden in an area which looks to you to be not the best grow-ing area technically (and you may be right), but will better address the power and energy issues. From our point of view, it will be better to im-prove the form sources available in a specific area for the garden growth process because this can be easily accomplished within the spirit of team-work between us, the nature spirits and man. Preparing an area with power and energy in mind deals with deeper, more fundamental issues that must be addressed within the intelligent levels of nature.

I bring one additional issue to your attention. If a person considers the quality of food both in energy and form to be of importance, then we can assume that he is grasping the relationship between the quality of food and the health of the individual. There is a direct correlation between the two—the health and well-being of the human physical vehicle and the quality of the food fuel introduced into that vehicle. I point this out to emphasize what we in nature see as the internal movement of healing energy within the garden: The healing relationship between the food the garden produces and the physical form into which the food goes. It's a healing dynamic. The external movement from the garden, that is that power/energy which radiates into the whole, is also healing—a radiating power/energy which has inherent in its makeup the dynamic of healing. As food can transform the physical health of one's body, the radiating energy from the garden transforms the physical health of the environmental form it impacts. So you have an internal healing dynamic and an external healing dynamic. You have learned from the nature spirits that the re-introduction of nature spirit sanctuaries into the planetary whole will serve to respiritualize Earth. On the same order, we say to you here that as these co-creative gardens are established around the planet you will have the establishment of power points which will radiate healing energy into its environment. As these points establish, they will link with one another forming a healing grid around the planet, thus enveloping Earth with its own vibrant, healing energy.

This is one of the potential results we refer to when we say that although nature is powerful beyond your imagination and humans are powerful beyond your imagination, man and nature come together hold the promise of many times their individual power. A potential of this union is the creation of the Earth's own healing energy grid through its gardening system around the planet. And the healing power which will radiate from the gardens and ultimately from the grid formed by the link-up of the gardens will be equally available and usable to both humans and nature because it was created by humans and nature united.

This is an issue which really should have been settled prior to your locating the garden site, but if you didn't, now is definitely the time. If ever there was a call for sensibility and moderation, this is it. In my travels I've gotten to see plenty of gardens that tend to be either the appropriate size for feeding all of Philadelphia with 1 burnt-out gardener working it, or the size of a Raggedy Ann baby pool with 6 eager gardeners pressing the soil to produce enough to feed the aforementioned Philadelphia.

Obviously individual need is a major factor to be considered. But with the approach we are presenting here—co-creative gardening—your ability and willingness to maintain responsibility for your end of the partnership throughout the gardening season also becomes a factor. Anyone who has gardened knows that in the spring we have all sorts of energy and excitement to draw on. It's fun to be outside again. Then July and the heat hit, and the gardening work starts to get tedious. I've always heard from the farmers around me that July is the acid test for finding the *real* gardeners. If you've got a garden that still looks nice in July, you're a *real* gardener. If you've got one that looks like it went to hell in a hand basket and ought to be mowed down, according to the old timers around here, you're a fake.

So when thinking about size, I suggest you consider not just your food needs, but also try to make a fair evaluation of how much energy you really have to give to this project throughout the entire season.

One more thought on this issue: There are books written about all sorts of different gardening methods with different time and space requirements. If I were just starting out, I would do a little research in this area to identify the type of gardening practices that appeal to me in light of my own time and space requirements. Then I would connect with the deva of my garden and ask if any one of these practices could be used as the base method for the garden. Let nature make the final decision. This, after all, will form the foundation of how you will work in the garden. For example, after all this warning about being reasonable about the size of your garden, I have to admit to you that mine is 100 feet in diameter and produces enough food to feed Philadelphia. But my garden is primarily a laboratory where we do the kind of research I'm sharing with you in this book. My garden's location, size, shape and layout are what is required, as far as nature is concerned, for the support and operation of a nature research garden. If its intent was to be a family kitchen garden, its location, size and shape would no doubt be different. Up to this year, I was the primary human worker. (I now have an assistant.) What enabled me to garden this space was that nature suggested that I use as my base method Ruth Stout's mulch gardening method. I keep 6 to 8 inches of mulch on the entire garden at all times. It's an ecologically sound and labor-saving process that eliminates watering, weeding and tilling except to work up the rows in the spring for planting. It is a method that accommodates the size nature and I need for the research work and the fact that up till this year there has been one human doing the work.

The issue here is not to push any one method of gardening onto you. The fact is, there is no one right or wrong method. Each has its points, pro and con. What's important is to find the method that accommodates you, your needs, the needs of your nature partners and the land. Whatever method or combination of methods you choose, you can be sure nature is going to modify it as you go along so that it can better respond to change and what is really happening in your garden. In essence, the method chosen is just a starting point.

GARDEN SHAPE

Gone are the good old days when we went out to that special plot of land, paced off a 30-by-50-foot rectangle, plowed it, tilled it and then staked about 15 straight rows for planting. Well, maybe those days aren't completely gone but the *assumption* that this is what one does is definitely gone.

At Perelandra, I started out with that rectangle. This was when the garden was a kitchen garden. As the energy of the garden increased, my abilities to work within the partnership improved and I made the committment to shift the garden to research, I got the word that the garden was not only to change location but size and shape as well. I went from the usual rectangle to 18 concentric circles, the outermost measuring 100 feet in diameter. I also have 3 paths which spiral to the center. It took 4 years of fine-tuning to finally get the combination of shapes well defined into the garden.

Why bother with this craziness? (Especially when all the existing gardening tools and machinery work best in a straight row garden!) Nature has taught me and I have certainly experienced that shape and energy are related; that a circle contains more power than a straight line. One simple way to explain this is to point out the obvious. A circle is a straight line with its 2 open ends connected, thus forming the circle. A simple straight line has 2 open ends. The energy contained within the line that is connected and held in the circle is released out the 2 open ends of the straight line.

For some gardens, it's fine to have straight rows. For others, it's important to have circular rows. I do not mean to sell you the concept of gardening in circles. Remember, I started out with a rectangular garden with straight rows. That was the appropriate layout for my kitchen garden—and it was designed by nature. And what I do at Perelandra may be completely inappropriate for your garden. What I am trying to impress on you is that there are options, and these options should be discussed with nature. Ask nature for the shape that is best suited for your garden *now*. Please don't get into a competition with what I'm doing at Perelandra. If you get that the rectangle shape is best for you now, trust that nature knows what it is doing and put in a rectangle. You may or may not get word to change that shape at some point down the road. Simply understand that there is an appropriate shape or combination of shapes that you need to establish for the overall vibrancy and health of the garden, and your source for finding that out is nature.

On a practical level, I suggest drawing on paper all the various shapes you can think of, then connecting again with the deva of the garden (remember that issues like the shape and size of the garden are all formulated on the devic level) and testing each shape separately. The one that tests positive is the one for you now. If more than one tests positive you may be getting an either/or choice or you might be getting a recommendation to combine the 2 shapes into one more complex shape. To discern what's going on, simply break this down into 2 questions:

Is this an either/or situation? (Test.)

Are both shapes to be used? (Test.)

The positive result will tell you which way to go.

I really suggest that regarding the shape issue you test all your ideas with nature and let nature have the final say. I've seen some gardens where the gardener has become entranced with this idea of shape and energy and

Warning: You are totally missing the point of co-creative gardening if you do anything in your garden because this is what I do at Perelandra. In order to accommodate locale and the ecology unique to that locale, nature will design each garden differently. In co-creative gardening, plans, designs and layout are not interchangeable.

has laid out the most complicated labyrinth possible. I can tell just by looking at it that this is the work of a human mind. It may be doing all sorts of things on an energy level but those things may not be very helpful to what is trying to happen in the garden. I find nature tends to lean more toward simplicity.

NATURE SPIRITS AT PERELANDRA

We wish to add insight to the issue of shape from our vantage point. We work with the concept of shape and energy constantly. It is an example of spirit and form, energy and matter. There is an intimate and vital relationship between the two. You see and feel this with the relationship between your soul energy and your body. Your soul energy could not function comfortably within the form of a tree and vice versa. There is what can be called "universal appropriateness" when teaming energy to form. Now, don't get us wrong. We are not dealing with judgment here. We are not saying that the form of a tree is too low for the soul of man. But we are saying that there is such a thing as universal appropriateness between energy and the shape it needs in order to function fully within form.

This notion which we bring to your attention is why shape is so important. If we were given the assignment to establish an area such as your garden and we were left on our own to do it, we would immediately know what shape this specific garden was to have for it to function within form. The question is not only essential but basic when considering energy on Earth. Up to now, we have primarily been faced with the individual arbitrarily choosing the form for his garden. He doesn't take into consideration the garden as an energy reality seeking to come into form, nor does he understand the relationship of that garden to the whole. So he simply chooses a shape that suits his purposes. Our job, if we may state it this way, is to assist the dynamic process that goes on between energy and its form. If a garden is laid out in an overall inappropriate shape, we are left with, at best, an uphill battle in our work. You are left with a battle in the garden. In order to keep that garden alive (and we mean "alive" not "healthy"), you must address a constant demonstration of weakness. In the past, this issue has become so intolerable, so impossible from our position, that we have simply had to leave altogether and release the area completely to the human to do with as he wishes.

Regarding the issue of changing the shape from time to time: Remember that a garden is dynamic, a constant energy flow which shifts and changes on a continuous basis. We read these changes and shifts. We know the nuances. All these nuances are multi-levelled and varied because all that is of form within a garden is multi-levelled and varied. Everything is in a state of evolution—that is, a state of progressive change. Form must adjust appropriately to evolution. To force form to be static while expecting it to house energy that is dynamic is foolish, to put it simply. It doesn't work and will result in the deterioration of both form and its energy. An unhealthy relationship is created between the two.

We do not wish to scare you and make you believe that you will receive promptings every year to completely change the shape of your garden—or else! We said that evolution is progressive change and form changes respond accordingly—progressively. Once you have established the initial appropriate form, you will receive from us in time information for a series of progressive changes that will not tax your energy or your patience at all.

The Perelandra garden had a major change in 1979 because it was then that Machaelle made certain personal commitments to the level of research she was willing to explore. This necessitated that the intent of the garden (and its shape) be adjusted accordingly. A major evolutionary step concerning the garden which dramatically shifts the future and its direction requires a corresponding major change in that garden's form.

We point this out so that you won't feel that all the work and effort you will put into establishing a garden in its proper shape is temporary. In fact, it is the primary design upon which you will fine-tune as its progression dictates. There will be some gardens whose initial intent will be consciously changed by their gardeners, as what happened at Perelandra. In these cases, there may be major changes in location, size and shape to accommodate the new intent. But remember, although you as the creator of the garden dictate the intent, you will not be alone in working out that new intent. You will have the new information, energy, cooperation and power from our level as well as the devic level behind you. And you will find that the work involved in such a massive change will feel effortless.

5

SETTING UP TO RECEIVE THE DEVIC INFORMATION

The success of the garden rests on information. What goes into the garden? Where do I put it? How many of each should I put in? Do I put rocks in or do I take rocks out? Will there be interplanting? Does that mean flowers or herbs, or what? Basically, you are faced with a piece of land laid out in an unusual shape and now you need to know what to do with it.

All of the information you need is held within the devic level: specifically that of the deva of your garden. Your job now is to receive the bits and pieces of that information and translate it into useful and usable form. In the past, this has been the big stumbling block for many who have wanted to move into co-creative gardening. But by developing some planning tools for yourself and using kinesiology, this process of getting the specific information from the devic level has become quite simple.

I'll give you as much as I can from my 16 years of figuring out how to get all I need from the Deva of the Perelandra Garden, and the charts and tools I've developed for translating that information into visual form on a small scale—namely, the garden chart.

I start the planning process in early February, and I work to have all the necessary charts and information completed by the end of the month. This gives me enough time to order the seeds (*which seeds* is part of the devic information) and start the early seeds for transplants (again, part of the devic information), so that all I have to do in the spring is translate my planning information into the garden.

During your first year, you're going to feel like you're stuck in a slow motion movie while you work with nature and get your information. In the beginning, it is normal for kinesiology to go slowly for you. It's a new tool. Patience is the key here. As you go through all the testing this first year, you'll notice that your kinesiology technique will speed up. By the time you get into your second and third years, it will get much faster and feel very efficient. Just expect that especially during the first year you'll need to have patience and allow more time for getting all your information.

Remember you are learning a whole new process, and things will go slowly as you go through your learning curve. After the first year, you'll see that you will move more quickly through the process.

CHARTS AND LISTS

The usual comments I receive from first-time co-creative gardeners has to do with the incredible boatload of information they have to deal with from nature. It can be overwhelming. It is especially overwhelming to people who are a little short on organization. To keep from feeling swamped or downright sinking from the sheer volume of information, you'll need to get heavy into information management—specifically, charts and lists.

Now, usually when I talk about this, people's eyes begin to glaze over. They expect co-creative gardening to be freeing and fanciful and a little floaty—or something like this. They did not expect it to be technical and require organization. And they certainly didn't expect to be discussing charts and lists.

In co-creative gardening, you ask nature to supply all the technical information about the garden and the techniques for working that garden. There is *a lot* of information coming from nature. You can't keep it all in your head—unless you have a photographic memory. You'll need to write it down. Now, you can write it down in a spiral notebook as you receive it—that's what most people choose—but this causes problems. You're not just recording information and then putting it away as you move on to something new. You are also required to refer back to that information in order to shift it from paper into the garden. If you need to find something specific in a notebook filled with 40 pages of information, it's going to take time to hunt through all those pages. This can be frustrating. A lot of time is wasted. Having the ability to separate and file the information in related chunks is helpful. This is the advantage of a loose-leaf notebook with dividers over the spiral notebook.

Also, charts and lists help organize this massive body of information. Besides being timesavers, good charts and lists function as common "playing boards" between you and nature. They organize both of you. They're like focal points. Believe it or not, your kinesiology will work more easily because you are working in a more organized environment. You'll just function better, and this saves time, too.

Use a chart when the information you are working with flows better in the context of graphs or tables. Charts need grids and lines in order for them to work well. I've given you a couple of charts to start with in the back of this book. Just cut them out and make photocopies before you use them.

A simple list is a single column of information that gets tested over and over. For example, the kinds of minerals or crystals you might have in your garden can be a list. (See page 87 for an example.) If you don't work from a list, you will have to remember all this information about stones year after year. This is a waste of time and brainpower. Keeping a list that you can refer back to whenever you need to test about crystals and minerals greatly facilitates your testing process.

You will need to design most of your own charts and lists as you go along. You know you need a chart or list when you are writing the same words over and over again. For example, you want to find out something about fertilizers. As you go through the testing, you find that you are writing the names of your fertilizers over and over. Broccoli needs *bone meal*. Sage needs *bone meal*. Squash needs *bone meal*. It gets real tedious writing "bone meal" so many times. So you make a chart like the one in the back of this book where all you have to do is list the fertilizers you are to work with across the top and supply spaces for listing the vegetables along the side. This way, you never write "bone meal" again. All you do is write the amount (1/2 cup) of bone meal needed in the appropriate box. Also, this kind of chart is easy to work with when tranferring all that fertilizer information into the garden. You don't have to read a bunch of notes spread throughout all those spiral-bound pages. Instead you're working with one very efficient chart. You'd be surprised how much a good chart like this can facilitate your garden work.

Another good situation for a chart is if you have a bunch of small flower beds around your house and lawn. Draw a simple layout of where the house/lawn are and locate the beds. Then give each bed a name or number. Now nature knows which bed you are talking about when you ask questions about bed #6 or bed #8.

So, although I counsel patience when it comes to kinesiology speed, I counsel a kind of impatience with information mismanagement. You've got to feel that writing the same words over and over or tripping all over yourself trying to describe the location of a bunch of flower gardens are unacceptable before you'll say, "Ahhh, this is a chart," or "This is a list, if I ever saw one." Then you'll take the time to create a chart and make a list.

For my research work, I've designed approximately 25 different charts and lists. My information gathering and management feel effortless as a result.

A key to good charts or lists is modification. I've seen people create charts and then, after starting to use them, find they missed something in the design and have to keep adding extra words or columns to accommodate other information. I design a chart and then work it a couple of times. Anything I've missed will surface. Then I go back and change the design of the master chart. And I look at my charts (and lists) at the beginning of each year. If they need to be updated, do it. It may seem like I'm spending a lot of time on charts and lists, but the time these things save me is manifold when compared to the time I spend keeping them current.

THE GARDEN CHART

This is an essential tool that will benefit you and the process enormously if you take time to do it well. First, you'll need to draw a scale layout of the garden: its shape, the placement of the rows and any focal points. Make it a simple line drawing, and I suggest you do the final copy in black ink. Once you make this layout, you can save yourself all kinds of time next year and the years after by having the original blank photocopied. (Black ink will give you a good, clean copy.) Don't let an 8-1/2-by-11-inch sheet of paper limit you as to the size of your scale drawing. You're going to want enough space to comfortably add all the writing and symbols for the layout of the vegetables. So if 1 sheet is going to give you permanent eye strain, scotch tape several sheets together (or get larger paper) in order to create your reasonably sized, easily used garden chart. There are photocopy centers that will make large copies of this original for you. The Perelandra chart is on a 14-by-18-inch sheet. Also, consider that you are going to be referring to this chart a lot throughout the season. You may even want to put it up on a wall. It will be very irritating, if you have trouble reading it.

Questions You'll Need to Ask

1. *Is there a focal point in the garden?*

2. *If so, where?*

A focal point is a point in the garden where something special may be going, such as a crystal, a special plant, special herbs, a seating area.... It can be any number of things and is usually considered a position of power within the garden as a whole. At Perelandra, the focal point is the very center of the garden where we now have crystals sitting inside a genesa crystal (explained in Appendix B), all on slate and surrounded by a ring of herbs. This focal point has changed in content but not position over the years. It began as just a natural white quartz rock sitting right in the middle of the garden and has changed as the garden energy changed. (Nature told me what to add or take out and when.)

Regarding your focal point, if you have one, don't assume it is in the middle of the garden. Ask the deva of the garden if there is one and if so, where is it to be placed. Then use kinesiology and the elimination process you used to locate the garden (squares and grids) to locate the focal point. (Don't discount it if you find that your intuition is working with you as you direct these questions to the deva of your garden. Ask the deva if what you are sensing or "seeing" is correct. Nature will use your intuition as one of the communication tools as you work together. But to be sure you are perceiving accurately, double-check your intuition with kinesiology.)

Another note on focal points: There is no value judgment placed on whether or not a garden has a focal point. They are there for specific reasons that have nothing to do with one garden being better than another. The important issue here is if a garden is to have one. If so, put it in and position it correctly. And if a garden is not to have one, don't arbitrarily manufacture one.

3. *Which direction are the rows to run?*

> North/south?
>
> East/west?
>
> Circular?
>
> Serpentine?

For those of you who know traditional gardening practices, don't assume east/west.

4. *How many rows?*

With this question, we add a new twist to your kinesiology technique. This is not a yes/no format. It requires a different approach. It's called sequential testing. Are you still connected to the deva of your garden? (Test.) Ask:

Sequential testing using kinesiology. ⟶

> How many rows are to go into the garden?
>
> > 1 row? (Test. You'll get a positive.)
> >
> > 2 rows? (Test. Another positive.)
> >
> > 3 rows? (Test.)

Keep progressing in numbers until you test negative. Let's say you test positive all the way up to 15. On 16, you test negative. This means that the number of rows which are to be in the garden is 15. Sixteen is too many and that's why you got a negative.

5. *What is the distance between rows?*

> Should the distance between the rows be equidistant? (You'll most likely get a positive on this, but it won't hurt to check.)
>
> How far apart should they be? (Use the same sequential testing setup as in #4.)
>
> > 1 foot? (Test.) If positive, ask:
> >
> > 2 feet? (Test.)

And keep going until you get a negative. Let's say "4 feet?" tested negative. That means 3 feet is your distance. Four feet is too far apart. You can get even more precise by asking if the rows are to be wider than 3 feet. If you get a positive, this means nature would like the rows between 3 and 4 feet apart. Start the sequential testing at 3 feet and add in increments, testing after each increment.

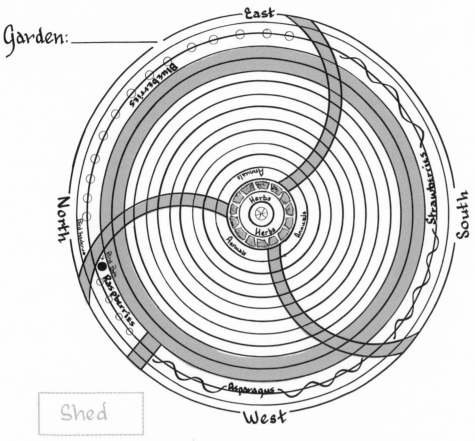

Garden: _____

Blank Perelandra Garden Chart

3 feet? (positive)

3 feet 1 inch? (positive)

3 feet 2 inches? (positive)

3 feet 3 inches? (negative) This means that the rows are to be
   placed precisely 3 feet 2 inches apart.

What has impressed me with this part of the process is that I didn't have
to work the row placement out mathematically in order to get all of them
to fit. This devic information fit perfectly. But if after placing the rows on
your chart you have space left over, check:

   a) The accuracy of your chart's scale.

   b) Double-check the number of rows you are to have.

c) Double-check the distance between the rows.

d) If the space is still there, ask if you are to have this space left-over. Something may be planned for that space that you aren't aware of yet. If you get a positive and this remains one of life's little mysteries, just keep moving on. Somewhere down the line you will receive clearly what is to happen here. I don't waste a lot of time demanding to know what is going on. I've made it a practice to move on the basis of the information I receive and trust that at some point all of the mysteries will clear up. And they have. Quite frankly, working with the mysteries and then watching them disappear is such fun and so much a validation of the partnership, that I wouldn't want to change this.

If you have more rows than space, double-check your information, including the measurement of the borders of the garden itself. This should clear up any problems.

THE PLANNING CORK BOARD

I do not use the blank garden chart during the actual devic receiving process. I use that chart for the final transfer of all the information once I've received it. In essence, the chart is my final layout.

For the actual process of taking down all the information I get from nature, I find my garden chart to be unwieldy. I was constantly spinning it around in order to read it. So I purchased a cork board. Then I simplified the layout (straightened the rows!) and marked this more simple layout on the cork board. You'll notice that the Perelandra garden chart has 3 sections created by the shaded spiral paths. I named each section according to what perennial is planted in the outermost band. There are 7 rows in each section that are used for the annual garden planting. The other rows make up the large circular path (the shaded band), the focal center encircled by slate, the annual flower band, and the outermost band which is 3 rows wide and contains all the perennial vegetables, fruit and bushes. The planting changes which I deal with each year and in which the devic information is referring to occur within the interior 7 rows. Each spiralled section contains 1/3 of each band or row.

So here's how I laid out the simplified chart using spiralled sections to organize rows:

A. Blueberry	B. Raspberry/Asparagus	C. Strawberry
1.	1.	1.
2.	2.	2.
3.	3.	3.
4.	4.	4.
5.	5.	5.
6.	6.	6.
7.	7.	7.

Herb Band:

Annual Band:

Outer Band:

(Row 1 is the row closest to the center of the garden and row 7 is closest to the perennial band.)

As I have said, this simplifies the garden layout in order to better accommodate the devic information process. If you need to simplify your garden layout, I strongly suggest you do it. If you have straight rows, you won't need to do anything but transfer your main garden chart design to the cork board.

THE TAGS

You fill in the empty rows on the cork board by pinning small tags into the rows. Each tag has written on it the name of a vegetable, flower or herb you will be planting in that row. (You will get the information of what you will be planting in Chapter 6.)

Also include a handful of blank tags for any duplicate plantings you might have. Nature may want sage planted in more than 1 row, for example. You'll need more than 1 sage tag.

So, cut about 100 rectangles—1/2 inch by 2 inches—out of regular paper or card stock. (Since you'll be using the tags for many years to come, card stock will hold up better.)

As what goes into each row is identified (Chapter 6), simply pin the

Don't forget to purchase a bunch of push pins when you get your cork board.

appropriate tag in the corresponding position on the board. This allows you to watch the garden develop and you can more easily see the relationship between the sections and between the rows. The tags also give the flexibility you'll need to correct any errors you might make with the kinesiology, or as you work with the devic level if you are given several options in specific areas. You'll just be moving tags around.

THE COLOR SQUARES

This is purely an option. Once thinking it over, you may decide this suggestion isn't for you. But, when you're trying to figure out how to interplant 9 gold marigold plants and 11 onions with 20 broccoli plants, these squares come in real handy. Quite often, however, the devic information concerns only the ratio of your interplanting and leaves its pattern in the rows up to you and your taste, and the squares allow you to play around and visually see the different patterns.

Get some colored paper (colored construction paper will do nicely) and choose 6 colors. One color each for above-ground vegetables, root vegetables, flowers, herbs, fruits, and one color for rocks, crystals or stones. Mine are about 1/2-inch square.

COLOR SYNCHRONIZATION

The colors I chose for my squares are the same colors I use throughout the entire planning and charting process. My colors are:

> red — annual flowers
> orange — herbs
> green — above-ground vegetables
> purple — root vegetables
> burgundy — perennial fruits
> white — minerals
> lavender — roses

When I set up a chart where color coding is helpful, I keep the above coding. I have a supply of felt-tip pens in these colors for maintaining the synchronization when I label the tags. For example, I write "broccoli" in green, "onions" in purple and "dill" in orange. I do this for several reasons. By keeping the colors consistent, my eye and brain get trained to them, and I can quickly and efficiently translate this coding from chart to chart—ultimately into the garden. So even though this may seem like a bit much detail now, it is actually another one of those information management tricks and a real timesaver.

And there's another very good reason for not only using color this way, but also for working with the tags and cork board, as well. The cork board becomes the microcosm of working in the garden. What goes on in terms of energy in the garden is created in energy on the board. With the colors, you can see the patterns develop between all the interplantings in the rows. As you work with the board, you'll find yourself becoming more sensitive to what is happening on it, and maintaining consistency helps this development. That sensitive interplay between you and the board will help you feel the balance and power of the garden as it's building, as well as sense areas where more devic information is needed or you've made an error. You'll feel that weakness or instability right from the energy in the chart. Something will feel wonky. Or you'll get an intuitive hit about some area. You can save a lot of work and heartbreak by catching errors and working them out at the dart-board stage rather than planting the error and dealing with the problem throughout the growing season.

SETTING UP
TO RECEIVE THE
DEVIC INFORMATION

My assistant also uses this same color coding. This way we don't have to work with two different color codings when we're reading one another's charts and notes. Keeps the headaches down.

6

WHAT GOES WHERE

By the time you finish this chapter, you will know what is going into your garden, how many of each, where you're going to be putting it and in what pattern, and what color everything is to be. Pretty impressive, isn't it?

I've broken this information down to a series of progressive steps for each situation. You will notice as you go along that you are following the same basic 4 steps* over and over. They are:

1. Get comfortable. Relax. Get pen and paper.
2. Connect with the appropriate deva (or nature spirit).
3. Ask your questions and test.
4. Disconnect with the deva (or nature spirit).

If you need to set up a nature session that isn't specifically broken down for you in this book, these 4 steps are all you need.

*This is the **basic 4-step procedure** for working with nature intelligences. Remember where it is. I refer back to it later on in the book. This is a test.*

DEVA OF THE GARDEN CONNECTION

You'll be receiving the content and layout specifics from the deva of your garden. You've worked with this deva already in order to find out where the garden is to be placed and what shape it is to take. Remember that the devas hold the architectural information in nature—the blueprints,

HINT: Keep breathing. Relax. You'll do just fine in this chapter!

79

shall we say. What you'll be getting is the step-by-step readout of the blueprints for your garden.

The direction and goal of the deva of the garden is to create as perfectly a balanced environment as can be achieved taking into consideration the land upon which the garden sits, the weather and ecological factors. Each individual aspect of the garden is chosen and placed with these in mind and aims toward the ultimate creation of a wholistically balanced garden environment. It is that balance which will provide the health and vitality of your garden.

NOTE: What follows is the overall planning and layout process, and as you go through it you may wonder why you would even want to consider putting some of the flowers, herbs and minerals identified for you in your garden. For now, simply concentrate on identifying what is to go into the garden and trust that you'll understand purpose and reason later.

Letting Go of Control

One of the hallmarks of co-creative gardening is the need for the co-creative gardener to let go of control of all aspects of the garden. Once we give nature the purpose and direction of the garden, we have to let go and let nature have its head, so to speak. Based on our stated purpose and direction, nature then designs a garden that is both a healthful and a healing addition to the property and our lives.

Now usually when I mention the issue of control, people immediately begin thinking about big guys in bulldozers knocking down 100 acres of prime woods to make room for yet another shopping center. I definitely agree that this is a situation in which humans have taken complete control of nature.

But there are more subtle kinds of control in which we all participate without even knowing it. Let me list a few examples. (In each case, the person in the example is a co-creative gardener and has every heart intention of working with nature.)

1. You went grocery shopping one lovely spring morning and saw a display of beautiful red and white petunias for sale at the store. You love petunias. Especially red ones. Overcome by the beauty of the spring morning and those red petunias, you bought 10 packs—that's 60 petunias. You

Our fears can cause us to keep a tight control on things. With co-creative gardening, some people fear doing this kind of work, yet at the same time they are drawn to it. Other people fear what their friends and neighbors will think—of the gardener and the garden. For these situations, I suggest quiet. You don't have to talk to others about what you're learning and doing. You don't have to place yourself on a firing line deliberately. Just quietly learn and work. In no time at all, your experiences with nature will lessen your personal fears—this happens automatically. And your garden will go through its changes and speak for itself to your friends and neighbors.

return home and take your flowers out to the backyard, connect with the deva of your yard and ask,

"Well, where do you want these petunias?"

In this case, it never occurred to you that the first question should have been asked at the grocery store. (You can connect with nature anywhere. If you need seclusion, sit in the car and consult with nature. You'll eventually learn to do kinesiology in a subtle way so as not to alarm the people around you or get yourself arrested.) The first question that should have been asked is,

> Can I put petunias in the yard and still maintain the healthful balance
> we are attempting to achieve?

If you get a yes, then ask if they can be red. You may need to ask if you should get some white ones, too, for balance. Or they may need to be pink or yellow instead. In this case, look around elsewhere for the recommended color.

2. You just spent $569,742.87 on a new home. It is the home you have been dreaming about for 10 years. In your mind, you have landscaped the front yard a thousand times. It's going to have a combination of maple trees and dogwoods—your favorite. You move into the house, get all set up with the deva of that yard and find out nature recommends oak trees for the yard. In fact, after checking the trees to be put in the backyard as well, you find out nature isn't talking about putting maples and dogwoods anywhere. Well, dammit, you just paid $569,742.87 for these yards! You own them. You can bloody well do what you want. You paid for the right!*

Now, this may sound like a ludicrous argument. But this kind of thinking surfaces far more often than you might imagine. In this example, you are disappointed; rather than working with nature to find out if there are maples and dogwoods in the devic plan for the future or if there's something simple you can do to your property so that it can accommodate maples and dogwoods, you get mad at nature and pull rank. Many people in this situation assume control and plant the trees they want. Then, once they've shown nature who is boss, they'll shift back to a co-creative partnership, connect with the deva again and ask what else is to be done in the yards. Unfortunately, now nature has a great deal more imbalance to contend with and this could result in additional labor on your part as well as nature's just to get this area of the property into some kind of balance.

** Does the phrase "**custodianship** of land" come to mind here?*

One other point in this example: Nature had a reason for steering clear of maples and dogwoods in the first place. Nature landscapes from the perspective of balance, not personal aesthetics. Often the planted maples and dogwoods would not do well, even die. In short, nature knows what it's doing.

3. You have strong opinions about aesthetics. What if nature asks you to do something ugly.

Please, people. You are talking about the creators of the Grand Canyon, Mt. Everest, sunsets, wildflowers, prairie grass and the rainforests. Nature doesn't create ugly. *We* do when we interface badly with nature.

My experience from working with nature is that the finished design may not be at all what I had envisioned, but it's beautiful all the same. It's *different* than what I originally had in mind. Often it's a lot better than what I could have created on my own. In working with nature in this manner, I have learned new things and my personal sense of aesthetics has broadened. That's been one of the benefits of co-creative gardening.

4. How we choose to word our questions is an easy way of exerting control. You are looking at your lawn that has a fair amount of weeds growing in it. You connect with the deva of the lawn and ask,

> What do I do to remove those weeds? After all, this is a lawn and not a hayfield.

You controlled the situation by the question you asked. You did not leave open the option that your lawn, in order to be healthy, needs those weeds. Their deeper roots might be aerating a pretty compact soil situation, and you don't realize this. The insect population around the house might be nicely balanced (and therefore not troublesome to you and your family) because of the environment those weeds give the insects. Remove the weeds, and you might be overrun with all kinds of pesky bugs that used to be kept in check.

Control is an issue you will be working with *a lot*. Your heart and mind can be behind co-creative gardening 100 percent, but this commitment will not eliminate the need to be ever-vigilant about those times when we exert control over nature. It's a constant learning process. Part of becoming a mature adult is to learn to assume control. Society judges us favorably when we are in control of things. There is a place for this in life, but a

It is also helpful if we maintain a good sense of humor about all this as we bump and grind our way through the learning process. We're not dealing with sin and damnation here. We are modifying how we think and act so that we can better accommodate partnership. A mirthful appreciation of our fantastic creative ability to control in the most subtle ways is really helpful. Nature won't be yelling at you, calling you an idiot or a jerk. It will join you in your laughter. And it will assist you by setting up situations where you maintain control even before you realize it! You're really celebrating a learning process and nature will want to join you in this celebration.

partnership, any partnership, won't work if one person controls the interaction between the parties. In co-creative gardening, our partner is nature. For this partnership to work, we have to accept that nature is the expert on nature and then allow nature to have input in its areas of expertise. In this case, we relinquish control and replace it with wisdom. We are wise when we recognize true expertise, learn from that expertise and act as a result of what we've learned.

IDENTIFICATION AND SELECTION PROCESS

Calling in the Devic Plan

1. Get comfortable. Quiet yourself. Have pencil and paper handy.*

2. Ask to be connected to the Deva of the Garden. Test to verify that you are connected.

3. Call in the garden plan. Say something simple like:
    I would now like to receive the devic garden plan. Are we connected for this?

Then test to verify all is set and ready to go.

Selecting Your Vegetables

1. Get a good seed catalog. This way you won't have to rack your brain trying to remember all the vegetables, herbs and flowers. (Don't forget the paper and pencil.)

2. Connect with the Deva of the Garden. Test to make sure you're connected. Ask that the garden vegetables be identified now.

3. Using the catalog, go through the list of vegetables one by one, asking the Deva of the Garden:
    Are _____ (artichokes, green beans, lima beans, etc.) to go into the garden? (Test.)
Keep a list of every vegetable that tests positive.

4. Look at your completed list. You have now identified what vegetables nature suggests for your garden. But, let's say your favorite vegetable in the entire world is the artichoke, and it's not on the devic list. You can

* Always plan to keep notes during your sessions with nature. If you try to remember what you have asked and what answers you get, your mind will bog down and become cluttered. It's hard to function in the sessions under such stress. Keeping a clear mind greatly facilitates the process. Besides, notes give you something to refer back to.

If you have a funny feeling that the neighbors are spying on you, and it's making you self-conscious about kinesiology testing in the garden, do the testing indoors. You don't need to be in the garden to get your information from nature.

* Here's a refinement I've added that has been quite helpful. After I identify the vegetables, I let the information sit a full 24 hours. Then I open another session with the deva and ask if there are any changes in that information before going on to the next section of testing. If I get a yes, it doesn't necessarily indicate that I have made a mistake in testing. Nature said that if we give 24 hours, it (nature) will do a final check of the balance contained in this area of testing, and adjust or strengthen it accordingly before we move on to another area of testing.

So, I test for what vegetables are to go in the garden. Make my list. Then I wait 24 hours, open a new session and retest the devic list. If there are any changes, I make them. Then I'll wait another 24 hours and test the revised list. I do this until the list has no changes after a 24-hour period. Once it tests clear, I go on to the next section of testing—identifying those flowers! I keep this process going till I have all the information for my garden layout and can fill out my main garden layout chart. (Nature says this process is needed for chapters 6 and 7 only.)

It takes about a month to get all of my information this way. But this gives nature a chance to iron out any weak spots while the garden is still on paper! It makes for a very strong garden.

request that artichokes be included. I suggest you ask first: "Can artichokes be included in this garden this year?" If you get a negative, consider backing off your request this season, trusting that the deva knows something you don't.

If you get a positive, add artichokes to your list. But, adding artichokes has ramifications. It was not originally included for a reason. In order to maintain the garden's balance, you'll need to ask the deva if anything else needs to be added to the list now that you've gotten the okay to add artichokes. If so, go back over the main catalog list and test to see what vegetables are to be included.

One more question to ask the deva: Since you added artichokes, is there any vegetable on your devic list (the list of the vegetables that tested positive) that now needs to be *removed*? If so, read through this list, 1 vegetable at a time, and ask if it is to be removed. Then remove anything that tests positive.

During this step it's important that you check out your personal wishes because they must be taken into consideration for you to receive the proper layout of the garden. Inserting the artichoke information at this point and having the full garden layout reflect that addition is much easier on you and the deva than asking to insert a personal wish after you get the full layout. A lot of erasing will go on at that point. Every vegetable has its unique power and vibration which require adjustments when included as part of the whole.

5. You now have a complete list of the vegetables which are to go in your garden. You may double-check this list by asking:

Is the garden to include _____?

Then, read the list and test each item one by one. Every vegetable should test positive. If one doesn't, test that vegetable again. If still negative, assume you made a little testing error when you went through the catalog and remove it from the list.

6. If this is enough testing for the day, close the session by disconnecting from the deva. (Closing a session would also include any gesture of thank you you would like to offer the deva, if you're so inclined.) Say,

I'd like to close this session and disconnect from the Deva of the Garden. (Test.) *

1. If you continued right on to this section after identifying the vegetables, you are still connected to the Deva of the Garden. Test just to be sure.

If this is a new session, ask to be connected with the Deva of the Garden. (Test to verify.)

2. Ask if you are to include herbs in this garden. (Test.)

3. For a positive response: Turn to the herb section in the seed catalog, or use any other source available to you, and go through the list one by one, asking if each herb is to be included. Keep a list of your positive responses.

4. Double-check the list as you did the vegetable list.

Is the garden to include _____? (Read your devic list.)

HINTS: The deva didn't include your favorite herb. Again, ask if it can be included as a favor to you. If you get a negative response, I again urge you to pull back from this request. If you get a positive response, add it to the list. Again, you'll have to check to see if any other herbs are now needed in light of this new addition. And then check to see if anything is to be removed from the devic list. Then, I'm afraid you'll need to go through the same process with the devic vegetable list. I know this is a pain in the butt, but control has its costs—and ramifications. Remember you're still aiming for a nature-balanced garden. If you don't let nature adjust for any changes, you might as well forget co-creative gardening and go back to a human-designed garden.

Also, you love herbs. You cook like crazy—especially Italian stuff. And when you asked if herbs were to be included in the garden, you got a negative response. It doesn't mean you can't have herbs. It is only saying that they are not to go into the main garden. Herbs may not be appropriate as part of the main garden package. Ask if you are to have an herb garden separate from the main garden. If so, do the same elimination process you did for locating the main garden and treat the herb garden as a unit within itself, designing and planning it with the deva of the herb garden.

HINT: About those vegetables on your devic list that you don't want and have no intention of eating: First of all, nature considers them crucial to your garden's balance or they wouldn't be on the list.

But there's another consideration. They may be on the list because nature knows something you don't yet know. I received a letter from a woman who said nature told her to plant mustard greens, a vegetable she would not normally have planted, and that, on top of this, a sizable portion of her garden was to be planted in mustard greens! A little like adding insult to injury. Well, the woman dutifully planted the seeds with only minor grumbling. That summer her daughter became quite ill. The doctor suggested, among other things, that she eat as many greens as possible—especially (you guessed it) mustard greens. The large patch supplied her daughter with greens all summer long.

5. If you don't wish to continue with the next section of testing, close down this session and disconnect from the deva.

Identifying the Flowers

1. If this is a new session, connect with the Deva of the Garden. (Test.) If you are continuing right on after identifying the herbs, make sure you are still connected to the Deva of the Garden.* Ask now to receive the identity of the flowers that are to go into the garden. (Requests such as asking to receive the flower list are important in that they direct the deva as to what information you want. The requests coordinate the 2 of you.)

* Test only as long as your fingers and focus hold out. Both will strengthen with testing experience. It's important that you not extend a session beyond your finger/focus limits. The testing could be compromised.

2. If your seed catalogs are anything like mine, there are about 200 pages of every flower known to mankind, and the idea of going through the pages one by one is exhausting you. I wouldn't tell you to go through all those pages. I wouldn't do it myself. I have my limits! Now is the time to call on your intuition. You can approach this list in a couple of ways. One is to simply leaf through the catalog looking at the pictures and casually taking in the names. Notice which pictures you are attracted to and which names stick in your mind. Make a list of all of these. Or, you can spend a little time thinking about flowers. Make a list of all the different kinds of flowers that pop into your mind.

3. The list that you have made is not what is going into the garden. It is the elimination process of all those flowers presented to you in the catalog. To be sure your list includes everything you need, ask:

Does this list include everything I'm going to need? (Test.)

If you get a negative, ask that the missing flowers be identified and either allow them to pop into your mind, or leaf through the catalog again. Trust that the deva will get this information through to you. Add what you get to the list, and once again ask if the list has everything. Keep doing this until the list tests positive. This is the flower list to be tested. I suggest you keep it for future reference so that you won't have to go through the elimination process again next year.

4. The list tests positive. Now, go through one flower at a time, asking if that individual flower is to be included in this year's garden. Make a list of your positive responses. These are the flowers that are to go into the garden.

Identifying Special Minerals and Crystals

1. Are you still connected to the Deva of the Garden? If this is a new session—you got it!—connect with the Deva of the Garden. (Test.) Request that the mineral and crystal information be given to you now.

2. Ask:

> Are there specific minerals or crystals that are to be included in the garden? (Test.)

3. If positive, go through the same process you've been doing for the vegetables, herbs and flowers. Your seed catalog isn't going to have a working list for you, so I'll give you a fair list right now.

Brazil Agate	Enstatite/Diopside
Carnelian Agate	Flourite
Fire Agate	Garnet
Moss Agate	Golden Beryl
Alexanderite	Hiddenite
Amber	Ivory
Aquamarine	Bloodstone (Jasper)
Azurite	Brown Jasper
Benitoite	Green Jasper
Cacoxonite	Picture Jasper
Coral	Poppy Jasper
Diamond	Red Jasper
Emerald	Yellow Jasper

Jade	Rutilated Quartz
Kunzite	Rhodochrosite
Labradorite/Spectrolite	Rhodonite
Chalcedony	Ruby
Sard	Rutile
Lapis Lazuli	Sapphire
Malachite	Smithsonite
Malachite/Azurite	Sodalite
Moonstone	Tigereye
Obsidian	Topaz
Opal	Tourmaline Tourmalinated Quartz
Star Opal	Blue & Red Tourmaline
Pearl	Catseye Tourmaline
Peridot	Green Tourmaline
Amethyst Quartz	Green & Colorless Tourmaline
Blue Quartz	Indicolite Tourmaline
Citrine Quartz	Opalized Tourmaline
Clear Quartz Crystal	Rubellite Tourmaline
Dendritic Quartz	Watermelon Tourmaline
Green Quartz	Turquoise
Rose Quartz	Variscite

Before you panic and think you're going to have to get a second mortgage on the house, go ahead and test this list just to see what minerals and crystals the deva is talking about here. You might be pleasantly surprised at the modest results you get. As I've said, I started out with a natural quartz rock in the middle of the garden. Through the years, as the garden energy refined, nature told me to add such minerals as amber, coral, emerald, lapis lazuli, malachite/azurite, clear quartz, amethyst quartz, topaz, tigereye, and rhodochrosite. The size has not been an issue, but quality and clarity have been. So I've bought small but clear stones, and the cost has been most reasonable.

I would suggest you first find out the devic information on the minerals and crystals, then look around your area for a dealer or jeweler who can steer you in the right direction for obtaining the stones on your list. If something is unobtainable either through a jewelry maker, gem dealer or from your personal jewelry, connect with the deva again with a list of minerals that are available to you, and ask for alternative choices. Go through your list, test each item and record the positive results.

If you would like to understand some of the properties—esoteric and otherwise—of the minerals you are going to put in your garden, I recommend a little book called *Healing Stoned** by Julia Lorusso and Joel Glick. (See Supplies and Resources at the end of this book for publishing information.)

* That is the correct title of this book and not a typo!

APPROACHING THE CORK BOARD

It's time to work with the cork board* and the tags. You have the full list of what is to go into the garden. Now is the time to find out where to put everything.

To simplify the transfer of information from the devic level to you, make sure your board has the garden rows numbered and that the numbers correspond to the layout of the garden. This numbering is a way of identifying each row both to yourself and to the deva. So when you request the vegetables that are to go into row 1, you have a clear picture in your mind where #1 is positioned in the garden, all of the charts you work with correspond to this positioning, and the deva knows precisely which row you are referring to.

At Perelandra, row 1 is actually a circle which is divided into 3 sections. For clarity, I have identified each row/circle according to its section. Row 1 is either strawberry 1, blueberry 1, or raspberry/asparagus 1. Each corresponds to the section which has these specific perennials. If the layout of your garden is in sections, I suggest you break down your rows accordingly.

The keynote here is clarity. The clearer you are, the easier time you will have in this process of transferring devic information to your board.

* Since writing the first edition of the Workbook, *I have refined my process by using a cork board instead of a simplified chart on paper. If you use (or wish to use) the chart on paper for this part of the process and you feel comfortable with it, please feel free to continue. However, if it felt a little clunky, I recommend the cork board.*

Positioning the Vegetables

1. Connect to the Deva of the Garden. Test for verification.

2. Request the information for positioning the vegetables. You can verify that this request was received and all is ready by asking:

   Are we ready to receive this information? (Test.)

3. Say:

I'd like to know the vegetables that are to go into row 1.

Again, saying these things is how you order and clarify your own intent, and how the deva knows precisely what you are asking for. Saying something aloud requires us to order our thinking that much more. So whenever possible, I suggest you ask the questions and read through the lists aloud.

4. Either read through your vegetable list one by one, testing each vegetable, or go through your stack of tags one by one. Ask for each vegetable:

Does _____ go into row 1? (Test.)*

5. Pin the corresponding tag(s) of the vegetable(s) which tested positive onto the row 1 position of your board.

6. Repeat this same process for each row.

Also, if you have a focal point in the garden that is outside the row pattern, extend your testing as you go along to find out what is to be included in this space. Treat the focal point as a row and test it exactly as you have been doing for the other rows.

7. After you have completed the process, I suggest you double-check your testing. You can do this quickly by reading aloud row by row the tags that are sitting there. Then ask:

Is row 1 correct? (Test.)

Any additions or subtractions? (Test.)

This is your double-check. A positive response means the row stands as is. If you got a negative to the first question, ask the second question differently.

Is there some vegetable to add? (Test.)

Is there 1 of the vegetables to take away? (Test.)

The positive answer gives you an indication of the direction to take to correct row 1. If you are to add a vegetable, just test your list again. The positive is the vegetable you missed the first time.

If you tested positive to the second question, test each tag sitting on row 1 by asking:

Should _____ be in row 1?

The negative response tells you what tag to remove. If you got a positive response for both questions, you need to add 1 and take 1 away.

HINT: When reading through a list of items, asking the same question for each, you don't have to repeat the whole question over and over. Ask the full question for the first or several items/plants on the list. Then, for the rest of the list, simply read the name of the item being tested. The question is now implied and doesn't need to be repeated. Example: Does broccoli go into row 1? (Test.) Does cauliflower? (Test.) Spinach? (Test.) Cucumbers? (Test.) This saves time and isn't nearly as tedious as repeating the whole question each time.

HINTS: If broccoli tested positive for rows 2 and 7, then make an extra broccoli tag and indicate broccoli in both rows. Remember, the garden layout is based on energy dynamics, not logic.

If you have some vegetables that had tested positive for the garden but were not placed, read those vegetables aloud and ask the deva if they are to be placed in *this* year's garden. If negative, assume they are to go in another year's garden. If positive, ask if you have missed them in the testing so far. If positive again, go through each extra vegetable asking:

Does _____ belong in row 1? (Test.)
> Row 2? (Test.)
> Row 3? (Test.)

And so on, until you test positive. Then read all the vegetables in that row and ask if it is now complete. Test.

If the extra vegetables test negative for this year's garden, just put the tags aside to be used next year.

Positioning the Flowers

1. Connect with the Deva of the Garden. Test for verification.

2. Go through the same process you used for positioning the vegetables. You'll probably need several tags for each variety of flower. Quite often a specific variety will be placed in more than 1 position.

3. Double-check your information by reading through the rows one by one as you did with the vegetables. Read and test the vegetables *and* flowers together for each row. (If needed, refer back to "Positioning the Vegetables," #7 for the double-checking procedure.)

Positioning the Herbs

1. Connect with the Deva of the Garden. Test for verification.

2. You guessed it. Go through the same process you used for vegetables and flowers.

3. Double-check your information.

HINT: Onions, leeks, shallots, etc. are considered herbs and vegetables, and I have onion tags made for both. When I am positioning the vegetables, I treat onions as a vegetable and have tags written in purple to indicate this. When I'm positioning the herbs, I treat them as an interplanting herb. This tag reads "onion herb" and is written in orange so that I can differentiate it from the vegetable. This will make a difference a little later when we're laying out the pattern the row is to be planted in.

Positioning the Minerals and Crystals

1. Make sure you are connected with the Deva of the Garden.

2. Go through the same process you used for vegetables, flowers and herbs.

3. Double-check your information.

Interplanting with Color

Considering the color of the flowers used in interplanting is another refinement of gardening with energy dynamics. Just as each plant variety in itself has its own energy, so, too, does color. If you have red cabbage interplanted with petunias, you can't assume that means red petunias. It could mean pink or white, or whatever color it takes to achieve the desired energy strength and stability needed in the row with the red cabbage. So now turn your focus to color.

1. Don't forget to connect with the Deva of the Garden.

2. Address each row individually, as you have been doing all along. If there are flowers in row 1, you can either go through a mental list of the colors you know this flower comes in, or use your seed catalog as a source for its colors, or make an all-purpose list* of the different colors flowers tend to be and use that as the guide for testing each flower.

* Flower colors: Here's another master list for you to create and keep.

3. To set up your process clearly, say:
    What color is the _____ (flower) in row 1 to be?
Then test the colors one by one. The positive response is the color. I suggest you write the color on the tag in pencil. This way, if the color for this flower is different next year, you need only erase and change the tag.

HINTS: If you get a positive response for 2 or more colors (this is rare), double-check to make sure your positive responses hold. If they do, it just means you are to have more than a single color in the row. (Determining the ratio of each color is explained in the next section.)

If you have 2 vegetables positioned in a row and there have been 2 flowers identified for the same row, you'll need to know which flower is to be interplanted with which vegetable. This is simple. Pin either one of the flower tags with one of the vegetables—pin them in such a way that you are indicating them to be a pair. Then ask:

> Do these 2 belong together?

If you get a positive, you now know how the vegetables and flowers pair up. If you get a negative, reverse the pairing. (Test to verify.) If you have herbs and minerals also indicated for that row, just keep pairing the tags until you get what is to be interplanted with which vegetable.

HINT: Sometimes nature interplants a row rather than just 1 vegetable. In this case, the flower, mineral or herb will not pair up with a vegetable. It is to be planted in its own position in the row. If this is the case, just pin the tag in its row and treat it like a vegetable when identifying its position.

4. Double-check your work.

Ratio

You know what is to go into the garden, in which rows, what is to be interplanted with what, and their colors. You are progressively building the energy base of your garden by addressing all of these issues. It's a process of refinement. The next step is to find out how many of each vegetable, flower, herb and mineral are to go into each row.

The concept of energy building is really a precision art. Not only are the rows being laid out with an energy balance in mind, but each row's relationship with all the other rows also has an energy balance. It matters to the other rows how many of a particular vegetable you place in any 1 row. Changing the ratio within a row shifts the energy balance of the garden and the other rows must be adjusted accordingly.

To find the ratio:

1. Yep. Make sure you're connected to the Deva of the Garden.

2. Starting with row 1, address the vegetables first. Set up for sequential testing. Ask:

> How many _____ (vegetable) are to be in row 1? Then test, asking:
> > 1? (positive)

2? (positive)

3? (positive)

And so on sequentially until you test negative. Go back a number to the one which last tested positive, and that's the number to go into that row.

If you have an herb, flower or mineral in that row, do the same process for them.

How many _____ (flower) go into row 1?

How many _____ (herb) go into row 1?

How many _____ (mineral/crystal) go into row 1?

HINTS: Again, since I use the same tags every year, and each year the ratios are different, I write the ratio information on the tags in pencil.

A little timesaver (and finger saver) in this process is to not always go through your count sequentially. For example, you have a 30-foot row that calls for broccoli. There's a good chance you're going to have more than 2 plants. I approach the numbering in blocks.

Are there more than 5? (positive)

More than 10? (positive)

More than 15? (negative)

This tells me the number is between 10 and 15, and I start the sequential count at 11.

Is it 11? (positive)

12? (positive)

13? (positive)

14? (negative)

I go back to my last positive and I know the row is to take 13 broccoli plants.

For vegetables such as beets, carrots, loose leaf lettuce, spinach, green beans, lima beans (vegetables which have a closer planting) you don't have to deal with precise numbers of plants. That definitely would be tedious. If a row calls for beets, you can approach your ratio in 2 ways.

a) How many feet in this row are to be planted in beets?

5 feet? (Test.)

10 feet? (Test.)

And so on until you get a negative on your increment question and can begin your sequential count. You can get something as precise as 27 feet of beets.

b) Approach the row not in feet but in segments by asking:

Is 1/4 of the row to be planted in beets? (positive)

1/3 of the row? (positive)

1/2 the row? (positive)

2/3 row? (negative)

The answer is 1/2 that row is to be planted in beets.

Another situation: You got that you are to plant a specific row completely with green beans. You also got that the interplant for the beans is radishes. (For the past 11 years, I've been given this information at Perelandra.) I don't deal with precise numbers in a row such as this. I approach it as follows:

Is this to be a full row of green beans? (positive)

Is this to be a 1-foot-wide row? (negative)

Is this to be the width of 6 inches? (positive) (Any time you might be considering wide row planting, get this cleared with the deva. It will affect your ratio information.)

How many pounds of seed are to be planted in this row?

1/2 lb.? (positive)

3/4 lb.? (positive)

1 lb.? (positive)

1-1/4 lb.? (negative)

It's 1 pound of seed to be spaced into this row. Now I address the radish interplanting.

Are the radish seeds to be mixed with the bean seeds when planted? (positive)

How much per 1 pound of bean seeds? (You'll notice in most seed catalogs that you can buy radish seeds by the fraction of an ounce and the ounce.)

1/2 oz.? (positive)

3/4 oz.? (positive)

1 oz.? (positive)

1-1/4 oz.? (negative)

The ratio of interplanting is 1 ounce radish seeds mixed with 1 pound bean seeds. If you have more than 1 row of beans, don't assume this ratio is the same. Test the second row separately. And don't assume the ratio will be the same if you get next year that you're to interplant radishes with green beans.

3. Once you've completed the ratio count for row 1, move on to row 2 and the rest of the rows.

4. Double-check your work by reading the ratio of each item, row by row. For example, the Perelandra garden row 1 (strawberry section) has chives, leeks and gold marigolds. The ratio is: 2 chive plants, 10 leeks, 2 gold marigold plants. I would double-check this row by asking:

> In strawberry row 1 are there to be 2 chive plants? (positive)
>
> 10 leeks? (positive)
>
> 2 gold marigolds? (positive)

This way, if I've made a mistake, I immediately know where the problem is. If I had read the row in its entirety with just 1 test for the whole row and had gotten a negative, I'd have to go back and break down the row plant by plant to find the problem.

Hills

Some vegetables traditionally have been planted in hills—a mound of soil with 2 or more plants. Watermelon, squash, melons and cucumbers are the usual ones. In co-creative gardening, I ask the deva if anything is to be planted in hills. Then I test my list to find out which ones. Ask,

> Is _____ to be in hills? (Test.)

For the ones that test positive, I'll ask how many hills and do the kinesiology sequential testing. Then I'll ask how many plants per hill.

Changing the Ratio

You have just made the horrifying discovery that, according to your chart, row 6 calls for 8 hills of zucchini, 3 plants in each hill. That's 24 plants of zucchini! Now, if you can't imagine the impact 24 zucchini plants will have on your kitchen—and sanity—around July, you have never gardened before. Trust me, this is a dilemma. You have several ways to approach the situation. No matter what approach you use, keep in mind that the ratio of all the plants in your garden is not arbitrary. It responds to an energy balance and is part of the building toward that balance.

1. Trust in the process and accept the 24 zucchini plants. This happens to be the option I would choose. I would be curious to see what 24 zucchini plants do for a garden balance. So, my reason would be educational, but then this is the major thrust of my relationship with the Perelandra garden, and often leads me to accept the unusual and seemingly impractical. Besides, it's only for one growing season. Next year you'll get to put in 30 okra plants! Yum.

There would still be this little issue of what to do with the produce from all those zucchini plants. You could line up a bunch of unsuspecting city-dwelling friends and let them figure out what to do with their 200-pound allotment of zucchini. Or, you could do something I heard on the radio. Someone discovered zucchini floats. They suggested we haul all the extra garden zucchini in the country to the Great Lakes, stake a sail on them and float them all to Canada.

2. You could also consider returning the extra produce back to the garden in the form of compost. A fair feeding exchange.

3. You could simply refuse to deal with the problem and request that the zucchini ratio be reduced to a manageable 4 plants. This can be done. *But in order to maintain the garden balance, you'll need to go through all the rows again for changes in position, ratio, color, even interplanting.* In essence, making a ratio change has an impact on the entire garden. If you don't accommodate the resulting changes, you'll be breaking down the very energy dynamic you're trying to build.

Energy Devices and Generators

By energy devices and generators I mean things like genesa crystals, pyramid/tensor energy posters and devices, copper rods, ionic generators—anything that is put into the garden for the purpose of shifting, changing or cleansing energy. There are a number of such devices that have been developed which you may be interested in trying. Usually they're placed at focal points.

At Perelandra, the center of the garden includes (beside the quartz crystal) a tensor energy poster and a genesa crystal. The poster generates what is called "tensor energy," but is familiarly known as "pyramid energy." And the genesa crystal is an antenna device made up of 4 copper circles, 2 feet in diameter, which when placed together at specific angles creates a ball. This serves as an antenna which attracts to it the life-force energy from all form within its range, cleanses the energy, and spins it back out into the environment. (See Appendix B for more information on the genesa crystal.)

The introduction of these 2 devices at Perelandra was gradual and part of the long-range building process of the garden—and *always* as a result of information given to me by the Deva of the Garden. If you have an interest in something like this, I suggest you check with the Deva of the Garden to make sure the device is appropriate and is in keeping with the balance of your garden environment. Also, if you have already done the devic planning for the year and you are requesting a device be put in although it was not part of the devic plan, it would be important to make sure the addition of such a device does not change the other devic plans and information. You'll have to double-check everything for any changes. These devices can be extremely powerful. When used as a harmonious and timely addition to the garden, they strengthen and enhance the balance that is already there. When they are out of place, they can throw a garden environment into a state of chaotic disaster. This is not to say that the device itself is a disaster, but when used improperly it can wreak havoc.

A sudden interest or attraction to one of these devices should not be ignored. This could very well be the interplay between the nature intelligences and your intuition to call attention to something that is to be added to the garden. So check your hits and insights with the Deva of the Garden by asking:

> Is my sudden interest in _____ important to the garden? (Test.)

If positive, pursue what you are to do and *when*.*

* NOTE: Just because you get a hit about something and it tests positive, don't assume you are to act on that hit immediately. Always check timing. Sometimes nature will only be able to tell you that yes, your hit is accurate but you are not to act on it now. In this case, nature can't say precisely when you are to act. There's a tricky timing involved. What this means is that nature wants you to be prepared to act when it (nature) says, "Now." Usually, in these cases, something a little time consuming is to be made (like a genesa crystal) or bought (like a mineral) and held till the right moment. When that time comes, you'll get another hit. I've had to wait up to 6 months between the time I got the first hit and the time to act.

Don't panic about whether or not you'll feel/sense the intuitive hit to act. You got the original hit just fine. You'll get the second one also.

Planting Position and Pattern for Each Row

Now's the time to use the 1/2-inch color squares you cut out. You have the ratio of each vegetable, herb and flower in the rows but you don't have the pattern of interplanting. This is the final piece of information you'll need for the overall design of the garden.

1. Again, be sure you're connected to the Deva of the Garden.

2. Address each row separately. While focusing on row 1, the very first question to ask is,

> Does the interplanting pattern matter?

Quite often, I'm given the freedom to design the row as I'd like, as long as I keep the proper ratio. If I get a negative response to the first question, that means I can play with my color squares until I come up with a pattern I like. I have a different color for vegetables, herbs, flowers and crystals. To help clarify, I'll give you an example of a row pattern.

In 1985, row 4 of the strawberry section had 5 brussels sprouts (BS) interplanted with 8 white petunias (P), plus 11 celery (C) with 5 white petunias (P). My pattern was as follows:

2P . BS . P . BS . P . BS . P . BS . P . BS . 2P / 11 C . 5 P

In this one row, I show even interspacing (brussels sprouts and petunias) and cluster spacing (celery and petunias). Since I had full freedom in the patterning, I chose this layout for both practicality and personal aesthetics.

If I have 2 vegetables interplanted in 1 row, as with the example I just used, I will determine direction in the row—for example, north half/south half, or right end/left end—and ask which vegetable is to be planted in which half of the row. To clarify: In the above example, I had both brussels sprouts and celery plus their interplantings positioned in row 4. I determined right side/left side of the row, a direction decision I keep consistent throughout my garden, and asked:

> Does it matter which vegetable is planted on the right half of the row? (positive)

> Are the brussels sprouts to be planted on the right? (negative)

Now I know brussels sprouts are on the left, celery is on the right.

3. Once I have the pattern laid out with the squares, I transfer that information over to paper using the initial of the plant, and reproduce the patterning. I find that when it comes time to move that pattern into the garden, it's easier to work from a piece of paper than to haul around a cork board. Below is an example of how the final positioning and ratio might look on paper.

1. Chives (2) Leeks (10) Marigold: gold (2)
C . M . L (10) . M . C

2. Red Okra (4) Petunia (3)
2RO . 3P . 2RO

3. Yellow Snap Beans (16 feet) Red Basil (6)
3RB . 16 ft. YSB . 3RB

4. Br. Sprouts (5) Wh. Petunia (8) / Celery (11) Wh. Petunia (5)
2P . BS . P . BS . P . BS . P . BS . P . BS . 2P / 11C . 5P

5. Carrots (27 feet) / Green Peppers (3) Red Basil (3)
27 ft. C / GP . RB . GP . RB . GP . RB

6. Snap Peas (17-feet-by-2-feet) / Corn (36 feet)
17-by-2-ft. SP / 36 ft. C

7. Sweet Banana Peppers (3) Anaheim Peppers (3) / Corn (36 feet)
3SBP . 3AP / 36 ft. C

HINT: I color-code the pattern on paper. Above-ground vegetable initials in green. Root crops in purple. Annual flower initials in red. Herb initials in orange. Again—visually, this facilitates matters quite a bit when it comes time to transfer all the information into the garden.

FURTHER HINTS: Sometimes I am told to interspace equally the flower or herb with the vegetable, and in so doing I find I have extra color squares left over in my hand. For example: I have 4 zucchini interplanted with 12 nasturtiums to be equally spaced with nasturtiums at the beginning and end of the row. I can easily lay out:

Z . 3N . Z . 3N . Z . 3N . Z

I have 3 nasturtium squares left in my hand to be divided and placed at each end of the row. My first question to the Deva of the Garden is:

Does it matter which end gets 2 nasturtiums? (positive)

Is it the left end? (positive)

So now the row pattern reads:

2N . Z . 3N . Z . 3N . Z . 3N . Z . 1N

Important! Attention!
The infamous poker chip hint.
Do not miss this!

This may be the most important hint I have given you yet! Transferring the patterning information into the garden can be a bit time-consuming and frustrating. The problem of properly spacing the pattern in the row is greatly facilitated if you use poker chips! If you saw the Perelandra garden in early spring, it would look like a bizarre poker game gone awry. What's nifty about the chips is that they're convenient, easy to move, easy to see, waterproof, cheap, and come in 3 colors. In a pattern, 1 color can indicate the position of a vegetable, another an herb, and the third a flower. When you plant, just look at the positions of the poker chips and go to it. The chips already have the patterns spaced out for you.

THE GARDEN CHART

You have all the information you need to fill in the large garden chart. As much information as you like can be transferred over. At this point, I transfer position, interplanting and ratio, and I color code the vegetables, flowers and herbs. I used to transfer the row patterning onto the chart by using symbols, but found that made the information too intricate to read easily. So I keep the patterning on separate paper.

I have included the complete Perelandra garden chart for 1985 so that you can see what all the information, once pulled together, can look like. (See page 102.) In the past, I've been reluctant to flash this thing in public—invariably someone will reach for pen and paper and begin madly copying it to use for their garden. I feel confident that in the context of this book, you realize that it would be useless and counterproductive to ignore all that is being suggested here and reproduce this chart for your garden. ***But in case you have any doubts, let me assure you that it would be a colossal waste of time and effort and that it would not give you the desired results of a balanced garden environment.*** It did, however, give *me* a beautiful, balanced, abundant garden in 1985, and the base upon which the subsequent gardens were built.

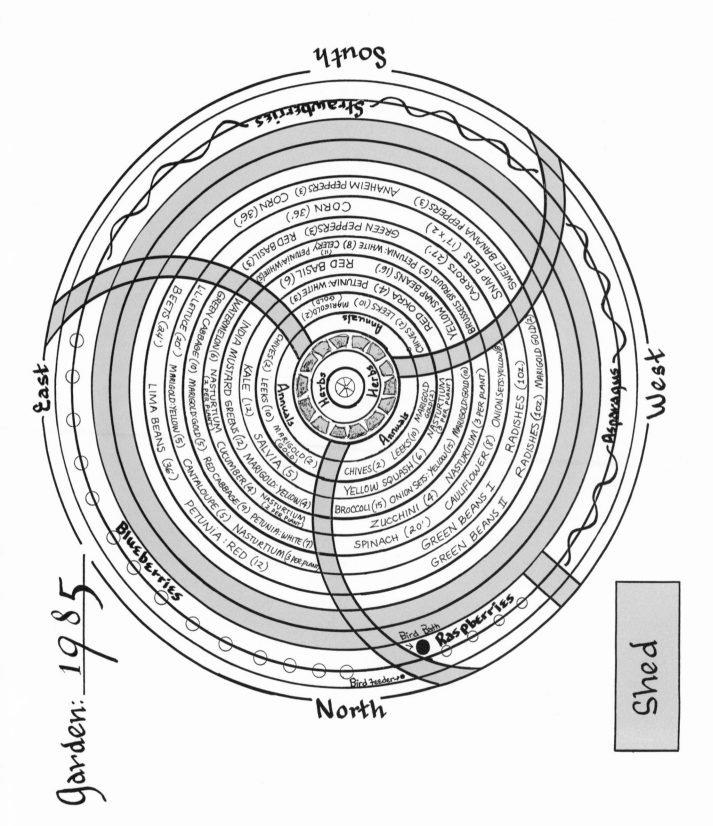

Garden: 1985

South

West

East

North

Shed

Strawberries

Blueberries

Raspberries

Asparagus

Bird Bath

Bird Feeder

1. There are billions of nature spirits and devas. Be sure you identify who you need to work with and ask for the appropriate connection.

If you would like information about a plant, for example, and you don't know the name of the plant, therefore you don't know who to connect with, here's what to do. Walk over, touch the plant and say,

> I'd like to be connected to the deva of *this* plant.

Or look directly at the plant and hold your focus on it while you ask the question.

When you test to verify the connection, you will see that, indeed, you are connected to the deva and that the connection occurred instantly. There was no confusion as to who you wanted. You don't have to know the name of anything to connect with either the deva or nature spirits working with it. You only need to indicate *clearly* the thing you want to ask questions about and then ask for the connection.

2. Nature answers only what you ask. If you don't ask the question about something, nature isn't going to talk about it to you on its own. So be clear about what you want to know and ask good, simple, clear questions.

Also, don't get goofy about asking questions. Don't ask nature to give you the answer to all existence as seen from the perspective of broccoli. Nature knows the answer to this and will tell you, if asked. The question is: can you hear the answer? If so, it's bound to be a lengthy one. Do you have time to hear it? And what are you going to do with this information?

3. Many practical questions, when answered by nature, beg for a follow-up question from us. For example, after a rainy spell early one spring, a fellow asked the Deva of Sweet Bell Peppers if it was too wet to plant. He got a no. He planted the pepper plants that day and they died within a week.

After asking if it was too wet to plant and getting the no, he should have followed up with these questions:

> Should I plant the pepper transplants today?
>
> (If no) When should they be planted?
>
> (If yes) Once planted, should they be protected in some way?

There's no limit to the number of questions you can ask. Knowing just what to ask is a bit of an art form and will develop naturally with practice. But be careful about coming into a session with all your questions already hammered out. Know what your first question is and what direction you'd like to get information about. Ask the first question and really listen to the answer nature gives you. Then ask the second question based on that answer. The questions build on top of one another and the final direction you take with the questions depends on the answers nature gives you.

4. Listen to/think about what you are asking. Do you really mean to ask *this* question? Don't forget the woman who wanted to ask what cat food was healthy for her cat but instead asked what food her cat would like. Two very different questions. Nature will answer only what you ask!

Also, think about whether or not what you want to ask will take more than one question. If so, think about how you'd like to break it down.

5. Remember you are creating a partnership with nature and not a religion. Think about your word usage. Think in terms of *working in partnership*, having *meetings* and *sessions* with nature according to an *agenda*, *batting around ideas* and receiving *input* and *advice*. It is very difficult to create a partnership with nature when you say you are *channeling* and getting *guidance*. This language closes down the dynamics of a partnership and places you in a childlike relationship with nature.

6. When working together, consider nature to be like a computer that needs good data input. Nature is working with *you*. Consequently, it needs to know what you know, what you are understanding and what you are doing. So tell nature everything you can that's relevant when discussing something. The quality of nature's final output to you directly corresponds to *your* input.

7. Nature automatically functions in a balance that is in step with universal laws. We do not need to teach nature these things. (I've actually met some people who get on a high horse, and want to teach nature a thing or two.) When we see ecological disaster, what we see is nature's plan after it has been impacted by ecological variables that have been created by us. We really don't need to teach nature about how to be nature—and this includes nature's role in the big picture, too.

8. Nature works with us personally. Our individuality, talents *and* limitations are taken into consideration. Nature will not ask a 100-pound woman to move a 600-pound boulder out of her garden—unless she's a dynamite weightlifter or has a husband with a bulldozer. In the beginning, lots of people get nervous about the possibility that nature will ask them to do something they can't do. Trust me, it's a non-issue. Nature just doesn't do this kind of thing.

Also, let nature know right up front what you are not willing to do. For example, after a few weeks of planting in the moonlight (per nature's direction), I decided I did not want to plant in the garden at 3 A.M. All I did was tell nature I didn't want to do this anymore. This was fine with them.

9. Get flexible around making mistakes. Some people get all tight and tense about the possibility that they might make a mistake. I think they feel nature will run them out of the partnership if they make a dumb mistake. Well, I'm the queen of mistakes—and they haven't run me out yet. Some of my best lessons have been the result of a mistake.

Another point: Nature prefers teaching through action and experience. It will deliberately set up a situation that, to us, looks like a terrible mistake. But it's actually a learning experience set up by nature. Don't panic. Just look at the mess, turn to nature and ask,

> Now what do I do?

Nature will lead you right out of the mistake.

D E V A   O F   T H E   P E R E L A N D R A   G A R D E N

It might simplify one's understanding of the planning stage if one saw his garden as a fine, delicate, gourmet soup in which the eventual success of the soup depends on the lightest and most careful of touches. A pinch of salt would add to the perfection, but a pinch and a half would break the delicate balance the gourmet chef attempts to create, and reduce his soup to an ordinary, perhaps even unpalatable experience.

When we work with humans to consciously create a garden environment, we approach the task with the lightest of touches so as not to tilt the balance at any given moment. A specific crystal placed in one position may be the perfect pinch of salt, in another position it is the pinch and a half. This applies equally to everything placed into the garden, be it mineral, vegetable or animal.

We might also add that we do not view any particular season as an isolated moment in time. We have an overview of the garden and a sense of direction that can be translated into a span of many years. We see one season as a unit within itself, but we also see how that particular unit connects with the whole, plus what lies ahead in terms of its growth and development toward environmental balance. All of these issues are part and parcel of what we consider when called on by man to help him create the co-creative garden.

Each season is a step in the healing process of the garden and its over-all environment.* Although you may balk at the notion of the twenty-four zucchini plants, as Machaelle has used in one illustration, we urge you to seriously consider bearing with us as we move your garden through its healing processes. At this point in time, we of the devic level understand the healing steps in which nature must travel. In the garden environment where man and nature join in partnership, we look to him to help us by implementing those steps. Man will not experience much understanding or logic toward what we are suggesting he implement, for these moves will be beyond present human logic. In time, as we grow together in our partnership experience, man will learn through observation and a new logic and reason will enfold him. For now, as Machaelle suggests, we ask that you trust our input. And see the garden, in the individual season, as a delicate gourmet soup, but also as a progressing unit of energy moving through a long-range healing process. Both of these dynamics are fully present in the planning information we give you.

We recognize your right at any time to say "no" to any suggestion we give you. We fully recognize your position as intelligent souls of the universe with the unencumbered right to dictate the direction of your life and environment. We will accept your "no" without hesitation and will adjust our information to you accordingly. But we wish to point out two things to you.

One. Although we can accommodate an arbitrary change in the planning and progression of the garden, it may only serve to unnecessarily slow the healing process your garden must go through.

Two. We of nature are also intelligent life within the universe. For the sake of the evolutionary growth on the planet, we not only ask but demand that humans fully recognize our position.

* This is important. I've heard from co-creative gardeners who have followed some pretty bizarre instructions from nature for a couple of years. Although they had no idea what was going on while it was happening, it was clear, in hindsight, that nature was moving their garden through an intense healing process. It's as if the garden had to move through a basic, general healing process before the specifics of a garden could be addressed. The gardeners may have felt frustrated, slightly insane, even disappointed for doing what they were being told to do—in some cases they had little produce to show for their efforts during this period—but now they had a beautifully producing garden that truly felt balanced.

7

SEED

The issue of selecting seeds can be quite an emotional experience for us gardeners. Quite frankly, I completely skirt the issue by allowing the intelligences connected with my garden to pick their own seeds. I don't make the assumption that seeds obtained from organically grown plants are better for my garden than the seeds from the large seed companies. I also don't make the assumption that organically grown seeds aren't better. As I said, I skirt the issue.

Right about here, I'd like to add an insight I've had about the large seed companies. Nature looks to us to form co-creative partnerships, not manipulative ones. From my interaction with other gardeners—especially organic gardeners, because they have developed a fine sensitivity around the quality of all that they put into their gardens—there is a general opinion that the horticultural research and development supported by the large companies is *all* manipulative and geared toward economical convenience only. Case in point is the development of the square tomato so that it can be packed more efficiently and shipped more easily. The result is that we're stuck with a fairly tasteless, but conveniently shipped square tomato.

I point this out to illustrate that I am not insensitive to the opinion held by these gardeners. But my insight is simple. It dawned on me that not all traditional scientists working in the area of plant development are manipulators. And if *I* wanted to dedicate my energy and efforts in this area, I would certainly consider working with a large company for very practical reasons. They have the money to back the research and give me a decent salary. So it seemed reasonable to me that tucked away in these large research centers are scientists with caring hearts who think and work in partnership with devic intelligence—although it is most likely an unconscious partnership.

One thing I've learned over the years is that because of the ecological and environmental changes on the planet, we cannot assume that the same plant that flourished 100 years ago would flourish today. The conditions have changed. The plant most likely needs to be "updated." And this is where sensitive scientific development comes in.

So here we are, back to the original question of what seeds are best for my garden. I have found that the deva of each vegetable knows the quality of all the types of seeds available that will produce that vegetable. I also have learned that each vegetable doesn't have just one "correct" seed. Determining the proper seed has to take into account not only the quality of scientific plant development, but also the conditions of your garden and the environment around that garden. So although I plant the De Cicco broccoli in the Perelandra garden and the choice was based on devic information, it doesn't mean that the De Cicco broccoli seed is the one for your garden. Plus, it doesn't mean I'll plant De Cicco broccoli in my garden next year or the year after.

Again, I sidestep the issue. I let the deva of each vegetable do the deciding. Up to this point you've primarily worked with the Deva of the Garden. Now you're going to branch out and begin working with the individual devas of the specific plants you have identified for your garden. This is easy, too.

1. Collect your seed catalogs and have a seat in a nice, warm (because you should be getting ready to order your seeds in late February or early March) comfortable chair. Bring your fingers along. You'll be using them. Also paper, pencil and the list you made of the plants to go into the garden—or your garden chart.

A digression: If you do not have a seed catalog, I suggest you write to W. Atlee Burpee Company and Park Seed. They will gladly oblige you.

I'm suggesting both companies because you should work with at least 2 lists of seed selections. Their addresses:

W. Atlee Burpee & Company   Park Seed Company
300 Park Ave.   1 Parkton Ave.
Warminster, PA 18974   Greenwood, SC 29647-0001
Tele: 800-888-1447   Tele: 800-845-3369

I have another address to give you for a very different kind of seed catalog. It is published by the Seed Savers Exchange and is called *The Garden Seed Inventory*. In its fourth edition, it is a 630-page inventory of 244 U.S. and Canadian seed catalogs. It lists nearly 6,500 non-hybrid vegetable varieties that are still being offered commercially and includes the variety name, range of days to maturity, a list of all the companies still carrying that variety, and the plant's description. The book is in paperback, and you will need to contact Seed Savers Exchange for the current price. Their address:

Seed Savers Exchange
Kent Whealy, Director
3076 N. Winn Rd.
Decorah, IA 52101

Back to the seed selection. You are armed with your catalogs and comfortably seated.

2. Let's say the first thing on your list is green beans. Connect with that deva by saying:

I wish to be connected to the Deva of Green Beans. (Test.)

(You may feel a sense of energy washing over you, very much like the sensation you may have felt with the Deva of the Garden. This is just your feeling the actual connection occurring. But again, don't be bothered if you feel nothing. The connection is verified using kinesiology.)

If the test result is negative, check your situation to make sure you are in a quiet place, feeling calm, and don't need to eat or go to the bathroom. Check also to see if you need to eliminate any other distractions. Focus your attention fully, and again request to be connected with the Deva of Green Beans. Test. (You'll get a positive this time!)

As you open to the individual devas, you will be "meeting" them for the first time, and may wish to spend a moment getting acquainted before getting down to business. There are a number of ways you can do this. One is to quietly be with the deva. Feel its energy around you and sense its presence. Another is to literally talk to the deva. It doesn't hear—devas don't have ears. But it easily and readily translates the intent of the energy behind your words. You could spend time talking about your feelings about the plant to which the deva is connected. If you wish to enter into a dialogue, simply say what you'd like, and then spend a moment being quiet. Quite often, the deva will use your intuition or your sense of visualization to communicate with you. Or you can ask yes/no questions, and have a dialogue with the deva through the use of kinesiology. When you have finished and feel comfortable, you can get down to business.

3. For green beans, you'll need to know if you are to plant bush beans or pole beans. Use the same yes/no format you've been using.

Are the green beans to be bush beans? (negative)

Are they to be pole beans? (positive)

By testing the second time, you double-checked your answer to the first question. You can bypass this by assuming a negative on the first question automatically means a positive on the second one. But I would recommend that until you feel very confident about your testing, it might be a good idea to double-check your answers.

4. I'll assume you are using the Burpee and the Park catalogs. Open one to the pole bean listing. Read the list to yourself or aloud. What you are doing here is making known to the Deva of the Green Beans the choice of variety from this particular catalog. The Deva may know the quality of the seed in question but it does not keep a listing of which company carries which seed. Once the list is read, ask:

Is the correct seed available in this list? (Test.)

If positive, go back through the list and test each variety until you find the one that tests positive. The implied question in this testing is:

Is _____ the correct variety?

If you get more than 1 positive, ask if 1 variety would be better than the other. If positive, eliminate your choices by asking which is the best, and test again. The positive is your best choice.

If you got a negative result, they are considered equal choices and you get to pick.

5. If, after reading the list from 1 catalog, you received a negative result to that list, go to your second catalog and repeat the above process, starting with reading the list aloud. There will be some different varieties listed, and most likely the deva's choice will be there. If not, go to a third catalog. I have 4 different catalogs on hand for this. I always start with the same catalog, using it as my base list. This gives me about 90 percent of the seeds we use. Rarely do I have to use all 4 catalogs.

6. Repeat this process for each vegetable, flower and herb that are to go into your garden.

HINTS: If you have gardened for years, you probably are aware of the specific variety of each vegetable favored by nearly everyone in your area. Word gets around. When I began getting my seed information devically, I was quite surprised at how different my list was in comparison to the favored varieties used by everyone around me. So don't be surprised if you get different information from the deva.

Second, I get the devic information on the seeds each year. I don't assume last year's list to be correct for this year. Changing conditions can have that much of an impact. And so can the evolving healing process that goes on in the garden year after year.

DEVA OF BROCCOLI

I would like to give you insight into how we of the devic realm view seeds. Humans tend to see them as that which contains a miracle. From a small acorn eventually comes a large oak tree. We of the devic realm can truly appreciate this notion, but we view seeds differently.

When we create on the devic level that which you help bring into form on the physical level, we collect, if we may say it this way, a variety of independent and individual energies which when combined, form one unit of complex but harmonious energy. In my specific case, you have named this unit "broccoli." Every trait and dynamic, seen or unseen by the human eye, has in back of it a specific energy that we on the devic level have drawn into the unit.

Each time a seed is produced by the plant, that full unit of energy, in its most powerful and condensed state, is passed on in the seed. When the plant is assisted and allowed to flourish in the state of the perfect harmony

SEED   *which is inherent in the devically created unit, that perfection also is passed on through the seed.*

However, if the plant itself does not develop in form to its full potential, that original devic unit is altered. What is then passed on is not the original unit, but an alteration of that unit. I point this out to show you that there is a relationship between what we of the devic realm create and the quality with which that energy of creation expresses in form.

Now, if left alone without the interaction of humans, the broccoli unit of energy would manifest through the levels of reality and eventually come into form on the planet. There, with the assistance of the nature spirits, the devically created energy would be released from the seed and allowed to develop to its full potential. The combination of the creation, the release, and the development would combine into a more expanded energy dynamic, and that would be transferred in total within the seeds from the plant to then be dropped onto the soil, and in right timing, once again would be released into form.

For a long time, humans allowed nature to take its own course and for the most part, even when humans became directly involved in their food production, nature was still allowed to take its own course. In recent times, however, technology has given man the ways and means to interfere with the process of the devic unit grounding into form through the conduit of the seed. He can either change the timing and development of the plant to such a degree that what is passed on in the seed is an alteration caused by not allowing the form to fully express its own perfect energy. Or, he can intrude by way of his own desires and wishes into the very core of the unit energy, breaking into the devic code as it were, and alter the unit so that the form that develops from this fully expressed energy is also altered. In both cases, what you call "hybridization" occurs, and in most cases you are left with a plant in a weakened state that requires, as do most things in weakened conditions, special care.

It is too late in our evolutionary development on planet Earth for man to simply recognize his interference and back out of the picture completely to allow nature to repair itself and once again take its own course. The interdependence between man and nature is too vast and the development of technology too sophisticated to allow such a move.

As has been already mentioned, the coming together in a co-creative partnership is presently the appropriate and sought after move. One does not have to be a scientist to join us in this particular partnership. One need only know how to listen, and then act. I have stated that there are two ways to alter the devic unit. One is to enter the unit itself using specific technologies already present in order to change the combination of energies we created on the devic level. This route is not where our overall partnership can be created. This is where we seek to unite with the scientific community in order to co-creatively repair that which already exists and develop that which must be for the future.

It is the second way a devic unit is altered where the person outside the scientific community can work with us. If physical form can be manipulated so drastically by humans that the devic energy becomes misaligned with its form, it is also possible to work co-creatively with the form to realign it to the devic energy.

In very practical terms, when I am asked to identify the specific broccoli variety that is best suited for your garden, I choose the seed that maintains the strongest connections to that inner devic unit. As Machaelle has stated, there is more than one broccoli variety whose seed maintains a strong connection. Even when left on our own, there would be more than one variety of each plant to accommodate the various conditions in which the plant is likely to grow.

Once the seed is selected, I will work to give you the information upon which you may act in order to assist the development of the form in ways that will strengthen and even alter that complex inner core of energy. In a very real way, we of the devic realm will function in the position of the overseeing scientist, and you will function as our assistant with the aid of the nature spirit level. Through a series of gradual and healing changes, the form and the devic unit will be reunited. And once again, the relationship between the devic creation, the encapsulation of that energy in the seed, and the releasing of the original creation into its full form potential will be manifest on the planet.

8

TRANSPLANTS VS. DIRECT SEED PLANTING

Here we go with another emotional issue. In light of the subtle energy fields and stabilizing energy lines which develop around plants as they sprout and grow, is it right to disturb this by moving plants around in the transplanting process? Some feel adamant that all plants should be started from seed in the garden so that none of nature's energy will be disturbed. Others who live in the northern climates have to transplant if they want to harvest their gardens before the first snow fall.

I completely sidestep this issue also. I go through the list of vegetables, herbs and flowers one by one, using this quick process:

1. Open to the Deva of _____ (the deva of each plant). Then test to verify your connection.

2. Ask:

Is _____ to be transplanted into the garden?

I make a list of all the positive responses. The negative responses are the plants that are to be started from seed in the garden.

3. Disconnect from each deva by:

a. saying "thank you" to indicate you are finished, and

b. requesting that the deva now disconnect.

(It is a good idea that you get into the habit of releasing or disconnecting in a clear manner anytime you have completed working with a deva or nature spirit. This helps each deva understand what you are doing and that you are finished working with it for now, and keeps the lines of communication clear between you. It is especially helpful when you are calling in individual nature intelligences, one right after the other, such as when getting information about a list of different vegetables.)

I have found through the years that the transplant vs. direct seed distinction has more to do with the overall garden timing than anything else. There is a planting rhythm in the spring which reflects the energy-building process, and relates to weather and insect patterns throughout the entire growing season. (I explain how to get the planting rhythm in Chapter 10.) Because it is based on variables, I get this information annually and do not assume that since broccoli was transplanted last year, it will be again this year.

One of the fun parts of co-creative gardening is to adhere to what look to be totally illogical and somewhat arbitrary spring rhythms, and watch how they play out to the garden's benefit throughout the season.

One more thing: By skirting the transplant/seed issue, I do not answer the question about disturbing all those subtle energy fields which form around plants. I know these energy fields exist, and that the health and balance of plants are greatly enhanced when these fields are undisturbed. By letting nature make its own choice in the matter, I also make the assumption that whatever is to be transplanted will have its energy fields taken into consideration and established accordingly.

PAN

I will address the energy fields surrounding plant life. The establishment of these fields falls within the domain of the nature spirits. The pattern of the appropriate energy fields to surround all physical life is established on the devic level and is part of the energy unit handed to us in the seed. (I use the word "seed" to describe any primary means of propagation within the nature kingdoms.) Once we receive the energy unit through the seed, we of the nature spirit level "read" the specifics contained within the full devic blueprint and begin the process of assisting it into form expression. As I have said, part of the unit information we receive is the pattern, timing and intensity of the energy fields which are to surround the form.

From the instant the seed moves toward germination, which is initiated on an energy level within the seed, the appropriate surrounding energy environment begins to develop. Those humans who have witnessed this phenomenon either through their own sensitivity or the technology known as "Kirlian photography" have developed an understanding of the complex and unseen reality that surrounds form. There is also evidence compiled by humans that when form is physically moved from one location to another, this energy reality is at best damaged. Often, it is destroyed. Both insights are technically correct.

When form, especially plant form, is relocated by humans in an abrupt manner without the assistance of the nature spirit level, the nature spirits will still attempt to reestablish the surrounding energy reality. But the timing of the form and the corresponding development of the energy reality have been thrown off. Consequentially, the reestablishment of the energy reality never has the chance to reach the level of development it would have reached had the plant not been relocated. Sometimes the weakness created by the form and its energy reality being out of sync with one another will prove too intense, and result in the death of the plant. More often, however, the plant does not die but continues an abbreviated growth process in a weakened state, surrounded by an undeveloped energy reality. The word "runt" accurately describes such a plant on all its levels.

What I have described is what occurs when humans shift and move form, especially plant form, in response to their own desires and needs without regarding the well-being of the natural plant process. I fully recognize that in order to plant a garden entirely from seed, one must limit his vegetables to only those that are indigenous to his specific area. At one time in Earth's history, this was precisely what occurred. And unconsciously, humans allowed the nature spirits to go about the business of establishing a full, dynamic energy reality around each plant.

As we have all noted and pointed out several times so far, times have changed. Technology has developed which allows humans, with a change in approach and different care, to plant just about anything they wish. A garden, be it vegetable, flower or herb, which is totally indigenous to the area is a thing of the past. We in nature recognize this fact.

It is important to remember that the problem I have been addressing arises from human need and desire, not nature's. Left on our own, the problem does not occur. We know better. Also, we have the power to override human ignorance and arrogance and establish perfection within the nature kingdoms. But to do so, we would first have to isolate humans from the natural processes which exist on the planet thus leaving the human population surrounded with the illusion of form—that is, form which is spiritually devoid, and for all intents and purposes, useless. We have the power to do this as well. But we choose not to.

*Instead, we choose to bring the issue to your attention and suggest alternatives, which when worked on by humans and nature spirits together, will solve the problem **and** establish a new co-creative process which will better address the needs of current times.*

When transplanting information is devically received, that devically created energy unit is appropriately adjusted so that what we on the nature spirit level receive to work with is a blueprint that has included the transplanting timing and development. When the plant is relocated, we have all the tools necessary to completely reestablish its energy reality. The result will be no break in the plant's development (which is the case when careless transplanting takes place), the plant itself will have as part of its devic unit all the protective dynamics needed during the transplanting process, and the form and energy reality will be synchronized.

Deva: *Creator/designer of*
the blueprints
Nature Spirit: *Implementor of*
the blueprints

It is important that the information of what is to be transplanted be given to you devically. Nature spirits can only work with what is received from the devic level. We do not alter or create blueprints of life energy. So although the process which Machaelle suggested earlier in this chapter is what can be called a devic process, you can see why I, representing the nature spirit level, would urge you to use it.

9

SOIL

I find soil building and soil work to be one of the more exciting areas of co-creative gardening. But then, I spring from the organic gardening tradition, and soil emphasis is one of organic gardening's best legacies.

If ever I had to start a garden again from scratch, I would love to use the first year to lay out the shape and build the soil. I would grow nothing. Ask nothing from this piece of land. Every time I say this, when I'm asked my advice or opinion about such things, I'm looked at as if I were just released from a rubber room. "Why in the world," say these people, "would anyone go to the trouble of establishing a garden, and grow absolutely nothing during its first year? That doesn't make a lick of sense, lady." Well, I suspect we would reap the benefits many times over when we did begin growing vegetables the second year and thereafter.

This is just an idea to bat around if you have yet to begin the garden. Perhaps after reading this chapter you might seriously consider doing what I have suspected for some time would be a marvelous experience for both garden and gardener.

Most of us interested in this kind of book already have a garden. I had the Perelandra garden in and working several years prior to my developing the strong, direct and precise relationship I now have with the soil.

SOIL   There are three issues around soil: 1) how to approach the soil in a new garden, 2) how to build and improve soil, and 3) how to work it.

APPROACHING THE SOIL IN A NEW GARDEN

The Perelandra garden is positioned in a field which had been farmed and grazed for many years—since before the Civil War. In the fall of 1979, when I had been told to move the garden to this new area and was given its exact location, we had the land plowed and turned for the winter. Then in the spring, the soil was disked, tilled, chemically tested for nutrient deficiencies, given hundreds of pounds of the different appropriate organic fertilizers (such as greensand, dolomite lime, nitrogen, etc.), and re-tilled.

If I had that to do over again, I would not have plowed and turned the soil. I would have broadcast the appropriate fertilizers, put a foot of hay and straw mulch right on top of the land, and let it "simmer" for that first year. I did something similar to this when I opened the tomato patch near the large garden a couple of years later. The result was a finely-textured, easy-working soil. By plowing, I kicked up a layer of clay subsoil that would make any bricklayer proud and then I dealt with the results for several years.

Now, let me confuse you a bit by updating what I've just said. If I had to do it over again, knowing what I know now, I'd be sitting down with the Deva of Soil and asking what I should do with the soil to properly open this garden. I wouldn't just assume it is best not to plant for a year and then act on that assumption. I'd do whatever I was told by the deva. Since everyone's garden has so many variables, I'm sure all our devic answers would be different, yet all the answers would work.

To set up this initial session, consider the questions involved and present them in a yes/no format to the Deva of Soil using the following process.

1. Get quiet. Ask to be connected with the Deva of Soil. Then test to verify your connection. (Since this is a new deva to you, you might wish to spend a little time with it before moving on to the matter at hand.)

2. Clarify the purpose of your session by stating that you wish to know what procedures to follow for preparing the soil as you open the new garden.

3. Begin to ask questions. I'll give you an idea of some questions. Keep a record of the ones that receive a positive response. When you finish the session, the combination of these questions and answers will give you the precise procedure you are to follow.

> Should the land be plowed? (Just because I feel I made a mistake in the beginning does not at all mean that no garden land should be plowed. I'd leave the issue completely up to the Deva of Soil and if I got a positive, I'd trust in the wisdom of that decision and do it.)
>
> Should the land be disked?
>
> Should it be tilled?
>
> Should the land not be turned in any way?
>
> Should it be aerated (as one would aerate a lawn)?
>
> Should it be hand dug?
>
> Double dug?
>
> Should the soil be tested for fertilizer?
>
> (If fertilizer is needed) Should it be:
>
>> a. added on top of the soil?
>>
>> b. worked into the soil?

(You can receive the precise soil needs from the Deva of Soil and I will give you that procedure in the "Building and Improving Soil" section in this chapter. For now, simply establish if fertilizer is needed and if it is to be broadcast on top of the soil or worked into the soil.)

> If it is to be worked into the soil, ask how many inches deep.
>
>> 1 inch?
>>
>> 2 inches?
>>
>> 3 inches?

And so on sequentially until you get a negative response and go back 1 number to the last positive response.

> Should the soil process begin in:
>
>> Spring?
>>
>> Summer?
>>
>> Fall?
>>
>> Winter?
>
> Should the soil sit/rest undisturbed before planting?
>
> Are we talking about days?
>
>> Weeks?

Months?

Whatever gets a positive response, find out how many days, weeks or months by testing sequentially.

(If it is to sit) Should the fertilizer be added before the resting period?

After the resting period?

Is mulch to be added?

Is it to sit on top of the soil?

How thick?

What kind of mulch?

Hay?

Straw?

Grass?

Leaves?

Sawdust?

Black plastic?

Newspaper? (not the slick color magazine sections)

(If you got several positive responses, you are being advised to have a combination for your mulch.)

Is it to be turned into the soil?

Plowed in?

Tilled in?

This list could continue for pages. But what is here gives you an idea of the kinds of questions to ask. Don't let the size of the list scare you. Just start at the top, ask 1 question at a time, record your positive responses and any issue that will apply to your garden, and at the end you will have all you'll need to know. Also, free your intuition. As you go along, the Deva of Soil will give you insight and direction. So if you are using the above list as your guide, be aware of questions that might pop up intuitively and go with them. If you have an intuitive insight, you can check its accuracy by wording the insight in a yes/no question.

HINT: As you ask your questions, think about what is available to you. If you live in the city and are planning to put in a 10-by-15-foot garden in the 20-by-20-foot backyard, you most likely will not have access to or need for a John Deere tractor plus driver to come plow your space. You may not even have access to or any idea of where to rent, borrow or steal a rototiller. That leaves hand digging, aerating, and/or mulching and not turning your soil at all as reasonable options for you. Your responsibility is to know what options are available to you, and present them to the deva. It will choose the best from your list.

4. Look at the list of advice you've just received and coordinate one cohesive procedure from it. This process will bring questions you should have asked to the surface, point out what look to be contradictions in the advice, and call your attention to possible errors. I'll give you some examples. Your procedure as is may say to hand dig the area in the fall, then cover with 10 inches of hay for 6 months before planting. You'll need to know if after 6 months you are to turn the mulch into the soil, leave what is there, or add more to it. In essence, as you pull your procedure together, you'll discover any gaping holes. Just ask the Deva of Soil the pertinent questions, and fill in the holes.

About contradictions: You had hand digging and tilling as options for turning the soil. You were told to hand dig your garden and not till. Then in the spring, after letting it sit over the winter, you are told to till. Something like this can appear to be a contradiction in the devic information if you look at the advice as absolute. Most likely, what is meant by the deva is that you start the process with hand digging, then till later. It is not saying you are only to hand dig and never till. If you feel there are contradictions, get clarification by asking questions as to what precisely was meant.

About errors: Errors may surface especially as you attempt to work out contradictions. If after all your efforts to clarify there is still a problem, you simply may have made a mistake in your testing. Go back to the original questions involved and retest.

5. Double-check your procedure by either:
    a. reading it aloud, step by step, and after each step testing if your information is accurate, or
    b. reading the entire procedure, then testing it as 1 unit.

If you choose to do *b* and get a positive, you've saved yourself and your fingers some steps. If a negative, go through the procedure step by step to discover which part is not correct. Once again, ask the original question pertaining to the step. If you get the same answer, make sure you understand your own question. If you only have a vague idea of what you are asking, clarify it to yourself and restate the question. That ought to clear up any problems.

If you straightened out a problem by adjusting the procedure, read the entire procedure through one more time and test it with the deva. A positive will tell you it's correct, and you can start working the soil in the new garden accordingly.

DEVA OF SOIL

When humans open a garden, any garden, a note is sounded within the devic level. One mustn't forget that a garden is a man-made invention. Therefore, the sounding of the note indicating that a garden is to be created must come from humans. When that occurs, the devic level immediately responds by creating the numerous energy units which will eventually be grounded into form.

When a human sounds the note with the intent to work in co-creative partnership with devas and nature spirits, that note is very different in sound, quality and vibration. If I were to use an orchestra as an example, I would say that in the case of the ordinary garden, the note sounded would be that of one instrument. Add to it the intent to co-create the garden with nature, and one would suddenly hear a full orchestra sounding a deep and vibrant multi-levelled chord.

Nature, on all its levels, will respond in kind. The various energy units we on the devic level create when the single note is heard are very different from the units we create when the full orchestra is sounded. So from the instant you sound the note with the more expanded intent, you will set off creation and movement on a far grander scale.

I point this out to help you understand that assisting a garden into full form once you have sounded the broader note requires a comparable expansion of insight, understanding and action. One cannot sound the orchestra, and then respond as if it were a single instrument. The result would surely be frustration on every level.

When we of the devic level "hear" a full orchestral note, we respond as a finely tuned team, and create all the various aspects of a garden reality in balance and harmony with one another. So although that which I would create in the area of soil is completely different from that which the Deva of the Carrot or the Deva of the Garden would create, we are functioning

in complete harmony with one another. The quality of detail which is **SOIL**
reflected in the energy unit drawn together by the Deva of the Garden
regarding what goes into the garden and where must be equally reflected in
all the other related energy units.

Obviously, this includes soil. The potential quality of vibrant life energy
which is part of the makeup of all that is to grow in your garden must
have, as its base, an equal source of life energy from which to draw. This is
one of the dynamics of universal natural law—the balanced interrelation-
ship of energy on all its levels. As you concentrate to expand awareness
around that which is above ground level in the garden, expand awareness
equally to that which is below the surface. As you open to and assist the
expansion of potential above the ground, remember to open and assist an
equal expansion below. The two levels function as a team and your efforts
above ground will be greatly eased and enhanced if the team is kept work-
ing in tandem.

I urge you not to become frightened or overwhelmed by the scope of
what is being said to you throughout this book. If you were to begin a
relationship with nature without any notion of what this meant or where it
would lead, and if you simply followed our insights on a day-to-day basis,
you would not feel overwhelmed at all. The expansion of your awareness
and our partnership would be organic, gentle and smooth. This Machaelle
can attest to for it has been her experience. In this book, you are receiving
the benefit as well as the challenge of insight, overview and past ex-
perience all at one time. By seeing the broader picture, you will have a
sense of direction and not have to summon the exceptional blind faith one
must have to constantly move forward into the unknown. At the same time,
you must deal with the challenge of a quicker personal expansion of
awareness which is inherent in being faced with the broad picture.

It might be helpful to remember, as you deal with the challenge of the
*broad picture, that **you** are the one who sounds the note. This has deep and*
practical implications regarding the timing, movement and development of
the garden environment. You are also a fully functioning member of the
garden team and by the mere fact that you are the one who sounded the
note, the garden has you inherent in its makeup. And you become, on an
energy level, a part of the devically created garden unit. Especially in the
areas of development, progression and timing, your energy is an equal
consideration. If one can see that which is above ground moving in tandem

with that which is below ground, then expand this notion to include the gardener. All three move in tandem. The balance of the garden must include the gardener. You will not see a garden team in which advanced practices of soil management are being required of someone just beginning to move into gardening. So as you consider the broad picture, also understand that where you are concerned, you are a part of that broad picture and its balance. I urge you to move forward in confidence, knowing that whatever the degree of the broad picture you connect with and move into, it is a starting point. The overall timing and movement will establish itself in that starting point, and will grow and expand from there.

This brings us full circle to the notion of working with me as you move to open a new garden. The pattern for that movement was set when you sounded the note of your intent. So although the process Machaelle has suggested may seem an outrageous amount of insight and information to deal with on a practical level, remember it was meant only as a guideline and framework from which you and I can begin our communication and working partnership. As I give you the details of the soil blueprint, you will not feel alien to the information because, as I have pointed out, your own energy is a part of that blueprint. And what you receive will be completely consistent and supportive to all other aspects of the garden.

BUILDING AND IMPROVING SOIL

I'm not going to attempt to teach the fine points of soil. For one thing, I don't feel qualified. I'm learning, too. It is a vast area of study that seems as extensive in levels and activity as the universe itself. There are quite a few excellent books written by qualified people, and if you wish to familiarize yourself with the subject a little more but can't find any books locally, contact the following folks for their catalog and book list:

Mellinger's Inc.
2310 W. South Range Rd.
North Lima, OH 44452-9731
800-321-7444

I'm going to teach you precisely how to build and improve your soil *without* knowing what you are doing. You have the best possible expert available to you—the Deva of Soil. All the information is sitting right there. Your challenge is how to get the information from that level to you, and like everything else so far, you just need to know what questions to ask. So, here we go.

Fertilizer for the New Garden

In the previous section, you determined whether fertilizer was to be added to the new garden prior to planting anything. Most likely it was. Now's the time to find out what's to be added.

It is important to consider right up front what fertilizers are available in your area and which of them you are willing to use. If you are near sources of manure, it will be essential to find out if you can get it delivered or if you have the means to pick it up. It's very nice if you live in an area that has ample supply of chicken manure, horse manure, cattle manure and llama manure—but if no one will deliver and you don't want a half ton of horse manure sitting in the back of your Mercedes SL, then these really aren't available supplies.

An alternative to animal manures is organic fertilizer such as rock phosphate, bone meal, cottonseed meal, granite meal, alfalfa meal, kelp meal and dried blood. I'm steering you away from chemical fertilizers that have catchy names related to the compound in the bag, such as "5-10-5." I know that even in this day and age, it's sometimes hard as hens' teeth to find a reasonable organic fertilizer source, and you may feel trapped into using chemical fertilizers if that's all your local garden center offers. I give you an alternative: Mellinger's, Inc., whose address I just gave, is about the finest stocked organic fertilizing and supply place I've found. (Just for the record, I am not receiving kickbacks from these people. I use them myself, and I've always found them to be helpful. They're convenient because they're set up for mail order. And they service the needs of home gardens, commercial gardens and large farms.)

Once you decide what you're willing to make available to the garden, you're ready to work with the Deva of Soil. One approaches manures from the bagged organic fertilizers differently, so I'll deal with them separately.

Let's say you have chicken, rabbit, horse and cattle manures available. (Either you live in a rural area or New York City and are using Central Park as your resource!)

1. Connect with the Deva of Soil. Test to verify your connection.

2. Read aloud the list you are making available. This states for the deva precisely what it will be working with.

3. Ask if you are to deal with the garden as 1 whole unit or, if its design has sections, each section separately. (This is an either/or situation that gets reworded in a yes/no format.)

4. If you are to treat the garden as 1 unit, ask which manures are to be added:
>   Chicken?
>   Rabbit?
>   Horse?
>   Cattle?

Let's say you got a positive on horse, cattle and rabbit. This means you'll be adding a combination of the 3.

5. To determine how much, consider each manure separately and ask:
>   How much _____ manure is to be added?

Here you are going to have to use some common sense. If you have a small garden, the most reasonable measurement to use in the sequential counting may be bushels rather than tons. If you have a 3-acre commercial garden, the reverse would make more sense. Whatever you use, make a decision, inform the deva what measurement you are using, and begin your sequential count. In order to get accurate information, it is vital that the Deva of Soil be clear as to what measurement you have chosen.

Do this for each of the manures indicated.

6. Next, ask:
>   Are the manures to sit on the ground as a mulch?
>   Are they to be worked into the soil?
>   If so, how deep? (Do a sequential count in inches.)

Okay. If you are using manures, you now know how much of what kind and how it's to be worked in with the soil.

HINT: Suppose you are to get 2-1/2 tons of chicken manure and have absolutely no idea how much in actual volume that is. More likely than not, your chicken manure supplier will know. If he has tons of it to offer, he's been hauling this stuff around the farm a bit and has a fair idea of volume and weight. So don't panic until you talk to your supplier.

If, by chance, your supplier looks at you funny when you ask for precisely 2-1/2 tons, and says something like: "Lady/Mister. How many scoops of this front-end loader do you want dumped into the back of your Buick station wagon?" Still don't panic. Assume he already thinks you're crazy and just excuse yourself. Go to the Buick and pretend you're doing some figuring on a piece of paper. Instead, connect with the Deva of Soil. (Test your connection.) Look directly at the front-end loader in question (you're keying the precise measurement of the loader to the deva), and ask:

How many loader scoops of chicken manure does my garden need? Then do a sequential testing. Let's say you get 8 scoops. That would be the equivalent of 2-1/2 tons. It also means you've grossly underestimated the volume of 2-1/2 tons, and you're going to have to tell this guy you want 8 scoops but will be back tomorrow with a borrowed pickup truck.

Organic Fertilizers

Again, the first thing to do is decide what you're willing to make available to the garden. If you're using a local garden center as your source, the decision is pretty well made for you. If you are planning to order the fertilizer, you'll probably have a wider selection to work with. In either case, choices will have to be made, and like everything else, I let nature do its own choosing.

For those of you who don't know, let me explain that catchy chemical fertilizer name I gave you earlier. "5-10-5" refers to the chemical analysis of what's in the bag: 5 percent nitrogen, 10 percent available phosphoric acid, and 5 percent water-soluble potash. These represent the major elements most commonly deficient in soil. Since I'm recommending you use organic fertilizer, you normally won't have the benefit of pre-mixed bags and will have to create the mix yourself.

Just for the record, let me distinguish between organic and inorganic or chemical fertilizer.

ORGANIC FERTILIZERS are substances produced by animals or derived from plants or natural mineral deposits.

INORGANIC FERTILIZERS include manufactured or synthetic products, and by-products of steel mills and factories.

Now, I know I promised you wouldn't need to know what you are doing, but I thought a little bit of explanation would help.

To work with organic fertilizers well, you'll need to have an acceptable source for nitrogen, phosphorus and potash, plus a soil balancer such as lime. Every organic supplier I know has a catalog that lists what it offers for each of these. For example, under phosphate sources you may find rock phosphate, colloidal phosphate and bone meal. Each source has different properties, and which to use depends on the makeup and needs of the soil. This is where I let the Deva of Soil take over. With this said, I'll set up the procedure for you.

1. Have your list or catalog ready. In case you want to have an idea of what we're talking about here and are having trouble making a list or don't have your catalog yet, I'll give you one catalog breakdown of organic fertilizers and additives from which you can work now.

PHOSPHATE:
    Rock phosphate
    Colloidal phosphate
    Bone meal

POTASH:
    Sul-po-mag
    Greensand
    Granite meal

NITROGEN:
    Fish solubles
    Sugar beet waste
    Dried blood
    Cottonseed meal

LIMES AND BALANCERS:
    High calcium limestone
    Dolomitic limestone
    Humates
    Gypsum
    Sulfur
    Epsom salts
    Oyster shells
    Aragonite

2. Connect with the Deva of Soil. Verify your connection. Then state that you would like to determine what is to be added to the new garden. (Keep in mind that this information will help with your soil building program before you approach the specific needs for planting time.)

3. Begin the questions:

Does it need nitrogen?

Phosphorus?

Potash?

Balancer?

Whatever you received a positive on is the area you'll need to test further. If you need to add phosphorus, read aloud the list of available phosphorus sources. The deva will choose the one that best meets the soil needs.

Continue through the list of needs and identify the best sources you are to use. (I hope you're keeping a record of all the answers you're getting.) When finished, you'll have the combination of organic fertilizers to be added to the soil of your new garden. You've just let the Deva of Soil guide you through a very tricky and sometimes complicated garden issue. Congratulations!

HINT: If your list or catalog includes other items that are considered soil amendments (conditioners and organic fertilizers), read them aloud and ask if any of these are to be used, and if so, ask if it is in addition to or in place of what has already been identified.

4. Determining quantity: At this point, the garden can be approached as a whole unit rather than specific rows to be used by specific plants. For each of the nutrients you are adding, ask:

How much _____ (fertilizer) does the garden need?

Begin a sequential count in pounds. Unless you're dealing with a tiny garden, I suggest you start the count in increments of 10 (pounds). In large commercial gardens, we may be talking tons.

HINT: Let's say you've been told your 30-by-50-foot garden needs 86 pounds of rock phosphate, 450 pounds of greensand, 62 pounds of cottonseed meal, and 5 pounds of high calcium limestone. That's all fine and dandy, but now you have to figure out how to spread this stuff evenly over that garden. Some suggestions: Buy a small spreader and figure out how much per square foot each fertilizer is to be spread, set the lever appropriately, dump the fertilizer in, and start walking. The spreader will solve the problem for you. Or, divide the garden into manageable sections, do some quick math and divide the number of sections into each amount of fertilizer (which tells you how many pounds per section is to be spread), then broadcast by hand that amount into each section.

5. You're finished with this particular soil process. Close the session with the Deva of Soil.

Determining the Fertilizers Needed at Planting Time

Each year, after I have gotten the information from the Deva of the Garden where everything is to be placed, I have a session with the Deva of Soil to determine what, if any, fertilizers are needed for each row to prepare for planting. I approach the garden row by row, section by section. To expedite the process, I made a fertilizer chart. Across the top, I list all the fertilizers I make available. Down the left-hand column, I list all the plant varieties row by row.

Here's the list of fertilizers I have on hand for the Perelandra garden. I got this list by reading to the Deva of Soil a larger catalog list of fertilizers I could make available. The final selection was made by the deva.

Bone Meal
Rock Phosphate
Greensand
Nitro-10 (a nitogen additive)
Lime
Cottonseed Meal
Alfalfa Meal
Kelp
SeaMix (for foliar feeding)
Liquid Minerals (for foliar feeding)

I've included a blank fertilizer chart in the back of the book for you to photocopy and use. It really does help to expedite things and I find it interesting to keep a record from year to year as to what each plant variety needs and where in the garden the fertilizers are being added. Because the garden environment is continuously changing, the soil building, and the plants themselves healing, I find the needs are never the same from year to year. The record allows me to observe part of the overall soil building process.

By now, you probably have a clear idea of how to proceed with this process. But just to be sure, I'll describe it.

1. Get the chart ready. If the garden is divided into sections, I suggest you make 1 chart for each section, identifying the section at the top. (You're not using the master chart provided for you in this book before making a bunch of copies, are you?)

2. Connect with the Deva of Soil. Verify your connection.

3. For each plant variety in each row, ask:
    Does _____ (plant) in row _____ need any fertilizer?
By identifying the row, you are making sure you and the deva are referring to the same position in the garden. It is essential to maintain this clarity in order for the deva to give you an accurate readout.

If you get a negative for everything, move on to the next row.

If you get a positive, ask:

Does it need _____?

Read the list of fertilizers, testing each as you go along. (It helps to check the box under any of the fertilizers that test positive. That way you won't have to clutter your mind trying to remember.)

4. For anything that tests positive, you'll need to determine how much. To do this, I first ask:

Is the fertilizer to be added:

Per each plant? (For vegetables such as broccoli that have a lot of spacing between them.)

Per 3 running feet? (For rows such as beans).

I use 3 feet because when I'm in the garden applying the fertilizer, it's easy to pace off a row in 3-foot increments. Choose whatever pacing distance is comfortable for you.

Next question:

How much _____ (fertilizer) will I need per plant/three feet?

For the sequential count, I use measuring cups:

1/8 cup?

1/4 cup?

1/3 cup?

1/2?, 2/3?, 3/4?, 1 cup?, and upward.

So, for a row of snap peas I might test that I am to add, per each 3 feet, 1 cup bone meal and 1/2 cup cottonseed meal. And for brussels sprouts, per plant, I might have to add 1/3 cup alfalfa meal and 1/4 cup cottonseed meal.

HINT: I add the fertilizers to be mixed in the soil around a week or 2 before planting. This gives the soil and the fertilizers time to make one cohesive unit before I plant the transplants or seeds.

In a row where there is interplanting (like green beans mixed with radishes), and each need a different fertilizer, just add whatever is needed to the entire row.

Because in this fertilizing process you are only dealing with the specific row area that is to be planted (not the space or paths between the rows), you will need small amounts of fertilizers (which will save money), and a set of measuring cups.

5. For each plant variety needing fertilizer, ask,

Is this fertilizer to be:

mixed into the soil?

top dressed*?

6. Go through steps 3 and 4 for each row and plant variety that tested positive for fertilizer. Be sure to double-check your results.

7. This completes the planting fertilizing process, and you can close down the session.

Here's an example of what your information can look like. (C = cup.)

1985 Perelandra Garden Fertilizing: Strawberry Section

1. Chives: per clump	1/3C cottonseed meal
Leeks: per 1 ft.	1/3C cottonseed meal
Marigolds	OK
2. Red Okra: per plant	1/4C bone meal
White Petunias	OK
3. Yellow Sn. Beans: per 3 ft.	1/2C alfalfa meal, 2/3C kelp
Red Basil: per plant	1/8C cottonseed meal
4. Brussels Sprouts: per pl.	1/3C alfalfa meal, 1/4C cottons. meal
White Petunias	OK
Celery: per plant	1/3C alfalfa meal
White Petunias	OK
5. Carrots: per 3 ft.	1-1/2C alfalfa meal, 1/2C cottons. m.
Green Peppers: per plant	1/3C alfalfa meal
Red Basil: per plant	1/8C cottonseed meal
6. Snap Peas: per 3 ft.	1C bone meal, 1/2C cottonseed meal
Corn: per 3 ft.	1C alfalfa meal, 1/2C lime
7. Corn: per 3 ft.	1C alfalfa meal, 2/3C lime
Sw. Banana Peppers: per pl.	1/3C alfalfa meal
Anaheim Peppers: per plant	1/2C alfalfa meal

If you are like I was in the beginning, none of the results are going to make sense. If you are like I am now and know something about fertilizing and what has been advised in gardening books and magazines regarding what should be applied to which plants, some of your results will look *outrageous* to you.

For 14 years I have fertilized according to the advice of the Deva of Soil. The first year was a real act of faith—probably the gutsiest leap into the unknown I've had to take in this gardening process. Everyone I showed the results of the testing to that first year and who knew anything about fertilizing said I was crazy and I was going to burn out the garden. (Too much fertilizer actually overwhelms and burns the roots of the plant, causing death.) I wasn't nearly as reluctant to make a mistake in the positioning process as I was to burn out an entire garden in the fertilizing process.

Finally, during her visit to Perelandra that first year, I showed Dorothy Maclean the charts. (Dorothy is one of the co-founders of the Findhorn Community and has worked with the devic realm for over 25 years.) I told her about my reluctance and pointed out some of the more outrageous results of my testing. She looked at me and said, "Why are you even questioning this? Do it."

Well, that was the boot in the butt I needed, and the result was as amazing as the information was outrageous. Everything that should have died was healthier than I had ever seen it. The entire garden was noticeably vibrant and healthy. And those fertilizing experts around me just shook their heads in disbelief.

I can't say the fertilizing information has gotten any less outlandish, only that it works—and now seems logical! I find working with the Deva of Soil a magical experience on one hand and a highly technical experience on the other. Like working a huge computer. I enter all the necessary data—10 broccoli and 8 yellow marigold plants are going into row 6 of the strawberry section—and the deva deals with all the variables and gives me the exact fertilizer readout. Since adding the Deva of Soil's input to the overall garden process, the garden has visibly and invisibly strengthened and stabilized many times over. It's as if I added the bottom half of the support system—the soil balance. That's why I feel I can't urge you enough to incorporate the devic fertilizer information into your garden process.

A FINAL HINT: I suggest checking with the Deva of Soil early in the season each year to find out if the garden needs to be fertilized as a whole unit before doing any specific plant fertilizing. If so, use the process I've given you for fertilizing the new garden.

DEVA OF SOIL

I wish to continue with the imagery of an orchestra—in particular, the concept of orchestration. As a plant germinates, grows and develops, it passes through a series of stages that, when linked together as the full life cycle, create a fine orchestration of movement, sound, pattern, light, intake, release. It crescendos and decrescendos. There are periods in the orchestration where the dynamic is that of a peaceful, still, summer lake. At other times, there is an explosion of life vitality of such magnitude that one could liken it to fireworks in the sky. Just as one might sense the orchestration to be almost silent, there is suddenly a reverse and another swelling to a majestic crescendo.

The entire orchestration is created within the devic level of each plant and is part of the blueprint. Once the Deva of the Garden has worked with you to position the various plants into the planting pattern, the blueprint energy of each plant, including its orchestration, begins to fuse into position within the garden itself. It is that fusion which enables me to get an accurate picture of what the soil will have to supply to each plant.

Usually, when humans consider fertilizing plants, they look at it as feeding for the purpose of facilitating growth. In one sense, this is accurate, but it is much too simplistic. We of the devic level see the soil activity as not just a support system but a comparable and fine orchestration in itself which, when played out, interweaves in harmony with the orchestration of the plant. The two orchestrations, one sounding from above, the other from below, touch and intertwine in a way which creates one larger, fuller and more complex orchestration. When a garden is devically designed and positioned from above and devically prepared from below, the coming together of the two orchestrations occurs prior to seed and plant making contact with soil. This is one of the major benefits of such a garden. The orchestrations are already in place, interwoven, and playing out in perfect timing, and it is into this harmonious environment that seed and plant physically unite with soil.

As you have probably guessed, the information I give you during the various fertilizing processes is given in light of the soil's orchestral response to the specific plants. When a necessary element is missing from its makeup, there will be certain points where the soil will be unable to link appropriately, creating a sudden narrow and limiting shift of the dynamic and dimension in the orchestration. The plant will be temporarily left to move through that point partially or entirely alone, depending on what is missing. Dare I say that the rug has been temporarily pulled from under the plant.

I'd like to make a distinction at this point. The fertilizer information given for a new garden or when the overall health of the garden soil is considered responds to the orchestral development of the soil itself. The information given after the planting pattern is established modifies the basic soil orchestration to enhance and allow the fusion of the soil and plant at the location where they will meet.

If you could physically hear what I have been describing, you would hear one orchestral dynamic in the garden even if absolutely nothing was growing in it at the time. This would be the music of the soil playing out in its unique timing. Add to the garden all of the plants and suddenly you would hear not only the original music of the soil, but a most intricate, multi-levelled, multidimensional, balanced orchestral piece into which the music of the soil would now be interwoven. It is this full orchestration which is released into the universe and it is this which is sought by the universe.

Tying Up Loose Ends

I have specifically dealt with the use of organic fertilizers and animal manure in this issue of soil building and improvement. But there are other approaches and practices which you may already be doing or feel inclined to do. In particular, I am thinking about compost and green manure. In both areas, I know next to nothing because they are not practices I use. I mean nothing negative by that. It's just that out of the grab bag of soil building and improving options, we must make the combination of choices that addresses the individual needs of our garden, and compost and green manure are presently not part of Perelandra's needs. I'm going to approach these 2 practices from the vantage point of knowing almost nothing about them and let you see how I use the devic processes I've been describing to help me get direction as to how to incorporate something new into the garden.

Composting

First I'd connect with the Deva of Soil and ask if composting is to be part of the present soil building practices. If yes, then I'd arm myself with an easy, concise book or pamphlet on composting and compost pile management or look at an organic supply catalog which quite often has incorporated in its section on composting a list of conditions and variables that must be considered for successful composting. With any new addition, I let what is already known about the practice be the starting point for asking questions of the deva involved. This gives both the deva and me a mutual framework from which to build. Very often I'll end up with a new practice that resembles the old tried-and-true one, but is slightly altered either in timing or by some steps being eliminated or replaced. In short, nature has upgraded the old process.

I am told that the variables to consider in composting are the moisture content, the carbon:nitrogen ratio, aeration, temperature and activation. I would address each one of these areas with the deva and find out precisely what size pile I should begin with, how much of what (the "what" being those ingredients identified in the information I was using) should be added to achieve the carbon:nitrogen ratio, how much water should be mixed in, how often the pile should be turned for aeration, what the optimum temperature should be, and if anything extra needs to be added to encourage microorganism activity. I would *not* assume any pre-existing data (literature and common knowledge) is to be used in my compost pile. As far as purchasing special tools and supplies, I'd go right down the list of options in the store or catalog and test. The positive results will give you the combination of supplies suggested by the deva. I would also ask where the pile should be located and get some guidelines as to how to set it up. I know that there is a direct relationship between maintaining all the variables in balance with how one works the pile—the turning, watering, layering, etc. That requires a sensitivity to timing and I would look to the Deva of Soil to give me direction in timing, perhaps checking weekly if anything

Because we maintain a constant blanket of mulch, there is continuous composting action going on directly in the Perelandra garden. For whatever reasons, nature prefers this composting approach for Perelandra rather than maintaining compost piles outside the garden and hauling it in.

needs to be done to the pile. I'd do everything that was suggested to me and observe what is happening in that pile in order to learn.

One more area I'd question would be when the resulting material should be introduced into the garden, what condition the material should be in, and what process should be used to work the new soil in with the soil already there.

Green Manure

This refers to a fast-growing cover crop of legumes or grasses that is planted in spring, summer or fall (depending on the effects desired), and that conditions, fertilizes and mulches soil.

Again I'd check with the Deva of Soil to make sure this practice is to be incorporated. Then I'd read through a concise source of information about green manure and use that as my framework to ask the Deva of Soil questions. I'd use exactly the same process I used with composting—different questions, of course—and move right through this new area with the deva as my guide. Most organic suppliers have green manuring mixtures; I would read the list to the deva and let it make the choice as to the best mixture for my garden.

HINTS: In any new practice you introduce into the garden, assume that the initial information is the starting point of a building process. Also, I check with nature annually regarding all of the practices that I have been upgrading in order to best facilitate the soil building process. I do this annual checking with the nature spirit level.

HOW TO WORK THE SOIL

PAN

In each garden, there is a crew of nature spirits assisting the process of soil building and improving. The emphasis of their work is the fusion of the soil building pattern into the soil, and assisting the unfolding and movement of that pattern. When humans work the garden soil, they are more likely to interweave with the activity of the nature spirits in the area of unfolding and moving of the soil building pattern.

Now, outside the garden reality, where nature is expected and allowed to move naturally through its processes, nature spirits work in an unhampered manner and unfold dynamics that are quite unlike that which must be unfolded in the garden environment. They are related but different. The garden environment is one area where man and nature come together with mutual needs that are interdependent for a successful conclusion. It is not only appropriate, but vital that man and the nature spirits work together in the garden, and not at odds with one another—and this especially holds true with working the soil.

As has been stated by the Deva of Soil, a pattern of timing and rhythm regarding the soil is formulated on the devic level. This pattern is received by us of the nature spirit level and it is this that we seek to assist into perfect fruition within the soil's cycle. Because we are speaking of the soil within the man-made environment known as a garden, that pattern has inherent in it the co-creative and active partnership between man and the nature spirit level. That partnership is built right into the soil pattern. The specific practices and dynamics need to be unlocked from the nature spirit level, taken into consideration, and appropriately acted upon by man.

Quite often, we observe humans working the soil from the heart, but it is a heart connection based on sentimentality, not appropriateness. Sentimentality springs from heartfelt conclusions that usually have nothing to do with pertinent facts. I'll give you an example. We see humans struggling mightily to cultivate tough, heavy soil using only poorly designed hand tools. The results are usually mediocre, and don't really allow the soil to fully respond to the growth process of the plants. Despite this, the human will continue to struggle physically with a hand tool. We sense the determination to stick with the struggle based on personal feelings about motorized tools being a disruption to the natural process both in function and sound. We of nature have not been consulted on this issue, yet humans continue to struggle under the assumption that we have somehow spoken in protest.

On the contrary, we of the nature spirit level look to the celebration of appropriate technology. After all, appropriate technology is the celebration of man and nature come together in creativity resulting in a useful device which allows a task to be accomplished perfectly. We relate to movement, and we appreciate fine, well-assisted movement in process. We look to humans teaming with the perfect tool and working with us in an efficient manner for the purpose of unfolding that soil pattern.

Don't get me wrong. I do not for a moment say that the hand tools which have gone through centuries of fine development are to be tossed aside. If I am encouraging humans to respond without sentimentality regarding power tools, I also encourage them to respond likewise regarding the multitude of fine hand tools. The key is to choose what is appropriate, what is necessary to accomplish the task at hand perfectly. I dare say that the indication that the proper combination of choices in both tools and soil work practices is the amount of joy and contentment the human feels in his heart as he performs any specific task.

And this brings me to the second and equally important issue around soil work: Intent and attitude. Behind all human action in the garden comes an infusion of the intent and attitude held by the human at the time of the action. This is one reason why appropriate technology is such a vital issue. If someone is insisting on using an inappropriate tool to do a tough job, he will most likely experience frustration, pain, anger, resentment, impatience.... All of these emotions are infused right into the soil through a conduit—the tool being held at one end by the human, the other end touching the soil. At that point, we of the nature spirit level have a new ingredient to deal with as we attempt to go about our work of fusing and unfolding the pattern. We now have the reality of the emotions grounded by the gardener, the impact of which must be dealt with. I urge you not to underestimate the impact of human emotions, both positive ones as well as negative ones. They are a dynamic force that must be recognized. Out of ignorance, humans leave the resulting problems up to the nature spirit level to deal with.

*I am fully aware that what I am now saying is not new. It's been said before—this thing about working in the garden with a positive attitude. **I've** said it many times before through quite a few people. But the issue still remains, and what I have said bears repeating. I strongly urge each human to concentrate on combining the appropriate tool to each specific task and choose the tool within the range of appropriateness that, when used, makes his heart sing. Once accomplished, we will eradicate a major stumbling block in the soil building and improvement process. This will, in turn, positively affect every level and aspect of the entire gardening process and environment.*

10

PLANTING AND FERTILIZING RHYTHMS

SPRING PLANTING RHYTHM

I believe it was the 1981 garden season when it dawned on me to ask if there was a spring planting pattern I should be following that was different from the accepted, well-charted planting times. You know the information I'm referring to. Plant onions early March. Beets and carrots early April. Cabbage family gets planted in mid-April, etc., etc. I received a resounding "yes."

The next question was how to get the information. I knew where to get it—from the devic level. But I had to devise a way of shifting it from that level to mine. I designed another chart! (I've included a blank of this chart in the back of the book so that you may reproduce a bunch of copies, and use it yourself.) Briefly explained, I listed the 4 planting months—March, April, May, June. Then I broke down each month week by week. March: week #1, week #2, week #3, week #4. Armed with the new chart and the list of plants to go into the garden, I was ready to work with the devas again. Here's what we came up with.

1. Have new chart, pencil and list of garden plants ready. Make sure your plant list includes which are to be planted by seed directly into the garden and which are to be transplanted.

2. For the sake of overall clarity, state that you are opening this session with the devas for the purpose of receiving the planting rhythm you are to use in the garden. Taking time to make this statement, either to yourself or aloud, makes sure everyone involved knows what is going on.

3. Connect with the deva of the first vegetable, flower or herb on your list. Verify your connection.

4. Ask:

    a) What month is _____ (plant) to be planted?

Then test each month sequentially. The positive response identifies the month.

    b) What week of this month?

Test each week sequentially and where you get a positive, place the name of the plant in the box on the chart.

Do step 4 for the entire list. The only change in this process occurs when you get to a plant that is to be transplanted. There, you'll have 2 questions to ask:

    a) When is it to be planted in the indoor flats? (Identify month and week.)

    b) When is it to be transplanted into the garden? (Identify month and week.)*

5. When you've completed the list, you'll have the spring planting rhythm.

I've included the 1985 Perelandra Spring Planting Rhythm chart to give you an idea of what it can look like.

Coding used in this chart:

    fl = plant in flats

    g = plant seeds in garden

    tr = transplant time

    (vegetable) 1 or (vegetable) 2 = succession planting

    [(vegetable) interpl] = plant in ratio and pattern with a specific inter-
        planting

** I color code my chart according to the following breakdown:
1. start plants in flats,
2. plant seeds in garden,
3. plant transplants in garden.
This makes it easy to quickly differentiate between the 3 when I refer to the chart.*

1985 Perelandra Garden Spring Planting Rhythm

March

#1	#2	#3	#4
Celery (fl)			Mustard (fl)
Green Cabbage (fl)			Tomatoes (fl)
Red Cabbage (fl)			
Broccoli (fl)			

April

#1	#2	#3	#4
Kale (fl)		Leeks (g)	Lettuce (g)
Cauliflower (fl)		Beets (g)	Snap Peas (g)
B. Sprouts (fl)		Carrots (g)	Celery (tr)
Marigolds (fl)		Spinach (g)	
Salvia (fl)		Zinnia (fl)	
		Broccoli (tr)	
		Onions (g)	

May

#1	#2	#3	#4
Green Beans 1 (g)	Zucchini 1 (g)	Watermelon (g)	Lima Beans (g)
Okra (g)		Cucumber 1 (g)	B. Sprouts (tr)
Nasturtium (g)		Cantaloupe (g)	Tomatoes (tr)
Green Cabbage (tr)		Squash 1 (g)	Zinnia (tr)
		Yellow Beans (g)	
		Red Cabbage (tr)	
		All Peppers (tr)	
		Mustard (tr)	
		Kale (tr)	
		Cauliflower (tr)	
		[C's Onions(g)]	
		All Marigolds (tr)	

June

#1	#2	#3	#4
Corn (g)	Corn (g)	Cucumber 2 (g)	
Gr. Beans 2 (g)	Gr. Beans 2 (g)		
Squash 2 (g)	Squash 2 (g)		
Zucchini 2 (g)	Zucchini 2 (g)		

HINT: You'll probably be very surprised at the crazy information you've gotten. Most likely, it will only vaguely resemble the old planting-time charts you've been relying on all these years. I guess it would seem superfluous if I said I am strongly recommending that you follow the new planting rhythm. After all, I'm strongly recommending that you follow all devic information you receive in the processes I have outlined in this book. But this particular one is especially fun to see work out. It's one thing to acknowledge that the devic information takes into consideration all sorts of variables. It's quite another thing to actually see how those variables such as soil temperature, weather and moisture come together. The spring planting rhythm gives you an opportunity to watch these things unfold most clearly.

Not long ago, I was explaining the planting rhythm process to someone in my area, and she asked, "When do you put in your tomato plants?" I told her the last week in May. That's a solid 4 weeks after the majority of people in my area begin the tomato sweepstakes (i.e., the race each year utilizing every trick ever devised by mankind in order to be the first in the neighborhood to have a ripe tomato). She looked at me a little funny and said, "Oh. That's late." Then she asked, "Well, when do your tomatoes come in?" I could tell she was expecting me to say something like the second week of October. Instead, I told her around August 1st. She couldn't believe it. I put my plants out a full month "late" and begin harvesting the same time as she does. That's part of the fun and magic of the new planting rhythm.

NATURE SPIRITS AT PERELANDRA

We wish to point out right here that the planting rhythm not only takes into account the obvious physical variables which Machaelle has listed, but also those which are the higher rhythm and timing that have become part of the energy unit from the devic level. When you utilize the planting rhythms, you work in tandem with us on the nature spirit level as we unfold the garden energy into form in the spring and carry out all the rhythms and timing throughout the entire growing season. Let's just say that when we work together in this, you facilitate our keeping the orchestration of the garden synchronized. When you plant according to arbitrary timing, you tend to move into the garden in a timing and rhythm all your own that has nothing to do with what is really to be played out. We end up having to work around, under, in between, behind, and through you in our efforts to move with the higher patterns. This can become very challenging. Machaelle's success in this area serves as a validation to you of the ease with which a garden can achieve its goals when the orchestration is kept synchronized on all levels.

FERTILIZING RHYTHM

Not long after I instituted the planting rhythm information, I questioned the possibility of a similar rhythm being present in the area of fertilizing. Seemed reasonable. This time I got a qualified "yes."

If there are any perennials in the garden (as there are at Perelandra), the spring or fall fertilizing did have a specific pattern. To discover this, I used a planting rhythm chart and went through the perennials one by one with the devas and identified which month and week I should fertilize. I can see that with these plants and bushes, my more precise fertilizer timing is more in sync with the growth cycle.

I don't go through this process with the annual plants that are added to the garden. Nature suggested that I add the fertilizer to each row or hill a week or 2 prior to planting. As I mentioned earlier, this gives the soil and fertilizer time to commingle and become one homogenous unit.

As I am planting or fertilizing or working the soil on a week-to-week basis, I do keep one eye on another rhythm—the moon cycles. And that leads me to the next section.

MOON CYCLES

Planting and working the soil according to moon cycles has been practiced for a long time. The Native Americans were very aware of the benefits of paying attention to the moon cycles, especially when planting. It's a well-founded tradition among organic gardeners and farmers. I treat the moon cycles not as gospel tenets which dictate my movements, but rather a source of free, beneficial energy which, if possible to use, can enhance the gardening process. In short, if the best time to plant a row of beans is tomorrow (according to the moon), but it's been raining for 3 days

Update on this process: I still make the astrological calendar, but nature and I have added a new twist. Now I look at the planting rhythm chart and what's to be planted each week: Then, working with the Deva of the Moon and the deva of each variety, I find out exactly which day of that week it's to be planted. This spreads the planting work out rather than condensing the planting days into a 1- or 2-day moon-cycle period.

Once I get this more precise planting rhythm, I then compare it to the almanac's moon cycles. I learn a lot this way. For one thing, I've learned that nature seems to know more about moon cycles than we do. Sometimes nature scheduled planting during some pretty odd moon-cycle times. If there seems to be a conflict between the moon cycle calendar and nature's more precise planting pattern, I always opt for nature's pattern.

If you don't care to do this comparison, you don't have to do the moon-cycle calendar at all.

straight and the bean row looks like a swamp, I'm not going to plant tomorrow.

Each year I make a moon cycle calendar. I get the information from either the *Farmer's Almanack* or the *Hagerstown Almanack*, whichever I happen to purchase first. I can't imagine an area in the country where one can't purchase an almanac, but just in case there is, and you happen to live in it and wish to set up the calendar, here's an address for you:

The Gruber Almanack Co.

1120 Professional Ct., P.O. Box 609

Hagerstown, MD 21741-0609

Both almanacs I've mentioned include a chart titled something like "Best Days For Planting, Weeding and Harvesting." For the months from March through October, it lists the good, better and best days to plant above-ground crops, plant below-ground crops, weed and work the soil, and harvest. I use my color coding again to transfer this information onto a calendar.

Green = Plant above-ground crops

Purple = Plant below-ground crops

Brown = Work the soil and weed

Red = Harvest

I incorporate one other coding which is broken down for you in the almanac chart:

1 = good

2 = better

3 = best

So, if I look at March 28 on my 1986 calendar and see a green 2, that means that March 28th is a better day to plant above-ground crops.

How do I use this information? Simple. In the planting rhythm chart, you have identified which week of what month is best to plant whatever. In 1986, I was to plant lettuce seeds during the fourth week in April. I looked at my calendar for that week and discovered that April 25th and 26th are coded green and 2 (better planting days for above-ground crops). In my planning, I'll aim to have the row prepared and ready to go for those 2 days and, weather and soil conditions permitting, I'll plant then. If variables make it impossible to plant those days, I make sure the seeds are in sometime during the fourth week in April. This way, I keep the rhythm and timing intact—and, whenever possible, I take advantage of the moon cycles as well. As casual as I am about adhering to the moon cycles, it's fair to say that I'm able to coordinate them about 90 percent of the time.

For all you advanced astrology types out there who wish to have the chart included on your calendar for a full year, I'll break down the information so you can get it from the month-by-month calendar in the almanac. Why would I want this information, you ask, for the months of January, February, November and December when I'm not about to do one thing in my garden? Well, I use the moon cycles in my rhythm, too. If I have to set up a meeting to discuss a new idea and I have a choice of days, I'll choose a day with a green number—a moon day for planting above-ground crops. If I'm planning to subvert something—like another country or foreign despot—I'll choose a day that is coded purple for planting below-ground crops! Also, as with the garden, I tend to keep one eye on the moon rhythms just to watch how the pattern of my year unfolds in relation to the moon. It's kinda interesting.

I checked with nature to make sure the moon information as we have it in this book (which was originally gotten from an almanac) is the correct information for us to use when making a moon-cycle chart. Nature said the information is fine as long as we understand that the moon-cycle chart will be a more generalized breakdown when compared to the day-by-day breakdown we can get devically.

Nature says that when working in a garden, consideration of the moon cycles are important. If you do not have the time or inclination to get the more precise information directly from nature, it would be better to use these more general moon cycles than to skip the whole moon thing altogether.

So, here's how the almanac information about the moon cycle breaks down.

Planting above-ground crops: (green pen = g in calendar below)

    3 - Cancer (best)

    2 - Scorpio (better)

    1 - Pisces (good)

Planting below-ground crops: (purple pen = p)

    3 - Taurus

    2 - Libra

    1 - Capricorn

Working the soil and weeding: (brown pen = b)

    3 - Leo

    2 - Gemini

    1 - Virgo

Harvesting (red pen = r)

    3 - Aquarius

    2 - Sagittarius

    1 - Aries

In the month-to-month almanac information, there is a column where the astrological symbols are given to indicate what the day is. (In the front is a small chart identifying the symbols they use.) For example:

January 5, 1986 = Libra = a *better* day to plant below-ground crops [purple 2 or 2/p in calendar below]

JANUARY 1986

Sun	Mon	Tues	Wed	Thurs	Fri	Sat
			1/b	1/b	2/p	2/p
2/p	2/g	2/g	2/r	2/r	1/p	1/p
3/r	3/r	1/g	1/g	1/r	1/r	1/r
3/p	3/p	2/b	2/b	2/b	3/g	3/g
3/b	3/b	1/b	1/b	1/b	2/p	

This, I sense, is a bit of a surprise for you—communicating with the overseeing nature intelligence of a form that is related to but not on your planet Earth. You must understand that all form within your universe and those realities and dimensions that exist beyond your universe consists of nature energy. The nature energy which humans experience on Earth is but one set of aspects within the broad scope of the reality called nature. The very same dynamics which exist within Earth's form-reality exist wherever there is form, no matter what galaxy, solar system, dimension or level. Just as the human spirit is present in one capacity or another everywhere, so too is nature. Both may be viewed as two fine gold chains whose links serve to connect all levels of the universe, thus giving two distinct energies of continuity within the vast arena called reality. Perhaps what I am saying will help humans to see more clearly that their home planet is not at all isolated from all that is around and beyond them. It is a very active and vibrant participant within the larger picture and its links in the universal chain are essential for holding together all that connects before it and after it.

*The life energy of the Moon has a special connection with the life energy of Earth. One reason, which I quickly point out, is the proximity of the two spheres. But more important is the relationship between the two spheres that has to do with one being **of** the other. As I have said, the Moon is related to Earth but not **on** it. There is a continuous physical interplay between them. Although they would seem to be totally different in physical makeup, they are in fact very related, supportive and stabilizing in dynamic. It would be helpful if those who have seen pictures of the moonscape or studied that part of its nature which forms its crust, would release their imagery and preconceptions for the time being and allow themselves to accept that which is naturally of the Moon to be directly related to that which is naturally of Earth, each physically being the extension of the other, and each physically linked within the context of matter.*

Visualize the two spheres side by side but not touching. The area I wish to call attention to for the deeper understanding of the Moon's role with natural life energy on Earth is the space between the two spheres. It is here that the dynamic relationship between the spheres occurs. The stability of that which exists within nature on Earth and on the Moon is a direct result of the dynamic relationship which travels between them.

Physically, the Moon is made up of natural matter that is, as I have said, related to but not of Earth. The same is true for Earth's natural matter. It is related to but not of the Moon. So, technically speaking, each sphere is an extension of the other. Each holds a dynamic beyond that which exists on the individual sphere. Therefore, there is a bond existing between each sphere's natural form. That bond is important to understand, for it is active, not passive; it emits a driving energy which seeks to maintain connection. One might say that the natural form on one sphere actively seeks to reach out to, connect with, and create an extended reality beyond that which it would have experienced had it remained isolated. It is natural law for related form to resonate to, connect with, expand, and experience a broader reality of itself.

It is this relationship that mankind on Earth responds to when he allows the energy of the Moon to commingle and become a part of the natural cycle of his planet. What you call the moon cycles, which relate to rhythm and timing, are but one aspect of the bonding dynamic that occurs between Earth and Moon. When man expands his attention to include the Moon within the arena of gardens and agriculture, he has become a participant in that part of the bonding dynamic. Simply stated, when broccoli is planted according to the proper moon cycle, the plant reaches out to that part of itself which is based on the Moon, which in this example has to do with timing. Not general timing that can apply to any plant, but the specific timing of the broccoli itself. From the vantage point of the Moon, when broccoli is planted on the planet Earth, that energy which is of the Moon resonates to the broccoli reality and seeks to bond with the form on Earth, thus experiencing an extension of its own life vitality.

To say that the relationship between Earth and its Moon is intimate would not at all be understating the facts. The natural bond between the two which I have described is played out between each planet and its corresponding moons no matter what universe or dimension. It is a strong dynamic, these bonds, and will assist humankind most favorably if he not only recognizes their presence but moves within their reality as well.

Process is always more easily brought to a successful conclusion when natural law is allowed to function unimpeded.

11

PLANTING PROCESS AND MAINTAINING THE ENERGY OF THE YOUNG GARDEN

DEVA OF THE PERELANDRA GARDEN

The physical process of planting a garden is not the primary issue I wish to address here. What is of utmost importance is attitude and intent. For with attitude and intent in harmony with nature, the gardener will automatically choose tools, processes and movements which will coincide with the overall energy dynamic of his garden. So, I will focus attention, not on the various physical processes one may have at his disposal, but rather on the underlying attitude and intent.

The imagery of music has been utilized well in this book when describing the energy dynamics of the garden. I will continue with this imagery, but shift it to that of dance. If one is to sense the placement, pattern, rhythms and timing as a complex orchestration, then it would be logical to extend this to include dance. For when the nature spirits and the gardener move into the garden environment for the purpose of facilitating the fusion of spirit into form, and they are being responsive to the multi-levelled orchestration which has been co-created by the gardener and the devic level, they are truly moving in dance.

I have specifically chosen dance because in order to participate fully in dance, one must lift his spirit, center his senses, focus his thoughts—in essence, he must strike an attitude that will allow him to hear the music all the way in his soul and move in accordance with that music. It is this attitude I wish to suggest for one who wishes to move into the garden in harmony with what is happening there.

For now, I will address the spring garden since there is a special atmosphere present there that changes once the garden is fully planted and growing. You will recall that all plants and minerals are placed in a precise pattern of balancing vibrations that when translated into sound create a complex and subtle pattern of harmonizing notes. You will also recall that the individual growth patterns of each plant emit a pattern of vibratory sound which weave together creating the overall orchestral movement. The spring planting rhythm is in direct response to this orchestral movement. Each plant with its specific timing, rhythms and patterns moves into the garden environment in right timing, thus introducing its various sounds exactly on cue.

We on the devic level approach the spring cycle of the garden in the spirit of a building process and pattern. We do not start the spring in full orchestration. We start carefully, precisely, and introduce a few sounds at a time. We allow those sounds to commingle and fully develop their weave in the orchestration before introducing the next related series of notes.

Young plants and seedlings, as with babies, do not respond favorably to loud, full-bodied orchestration. It is simply too much for their systems. Machaelle once likened the early spring planting process to the Leboyer Birth Method. We on the devic level read from this method gentleness and softness on every level—full consideration for the open sensitivity of the moment. With this understanding, I would say that this is exactly the atmosphere of the early garden during the planting process and the very atmosphere that is part of the devic design. Consequently, why would we encourage full-bodied orchestration in the spring?

Instead, we begin with a gentle, awakening music. Don't misunderstand. It does not begin weakly, but rather simply. And it gradually builds until eventually all the plants' tonal patterns are fully interwoven into one full-bodied orchestration.

The building process does not begin when you as gardener start planting. On the contrary, each garden's orchestration begins in what you term "late winter" when we in nature sound the first note of spring. By planting time, the orchestration has been building for some weeks but still can be characterized as simple, gentle and soft in every way. It is important that these young plants be fully enveloped by gentle but stabilized notes. To envision this quality as protective would not be inaccurate. Each young transplant and new seedling is fully encased in perfectly harmonized and gently patterned sound which supports and protects it as the new plant acclimates and begins its intonation.

You probably thought that I forgot about this issue of the dance. I have not. In order to understand your participation in the dance, you must understand the atmosphere created by the music. You already have the pattern and rhythm of the dance. This is contained in your devic charts. But it is the atmosphere of the music that will now give to you the attitude and intent with which you will move in the garden. Attitude and intent are realities which for humans are based within the heart and mind. This dance which I am trying to describe begins within the heart and mind of the gardener, and is automatically translated into appropriate movement. This is not a fox trot that can be taught to you step by step.

When a small boy is forced to learn the fox trot for reasons known only to his parents, he will move through the steps with the attitude of detachment. He can learn how to go through the steps, but his mind and heart are elsewhere—and his dance shows it. It is not unusual for those of us within the realms of nature intelligence to sense or observe a gardener moving through the spring planting process—or any gardening process for that matter—in the same detached spirit as the small boy being forced to fox trot.

If you wish to see that boy move in spirit and true dance, simply place him wherever his mind and heart are. Likewise, if you wish to join in the early spring dance, bring along your mind and heart. Through them, the music will move and you will naturally move with it, both within and outside yourself. And you will be most surprised at the ease and grace in which you, your tools, and your young plants and seeds join in effortless movement. For remember, within that movement, carrying and supporting you, is the encompassing energy of the orchestration.

12

SUCCESSION PLANTING

I do very little succession planting at Perelandra. Some years back nature suggested that I concentrate on establishing one full-season garden with one set of spring rhythms and timing in order to learn the intricacies of such a garden. This move freed up the garden considerably in that I didn't have to throw seeds and plants into the ground early in order to get their production time completed, thus making space available for later plantings. The timing and rhythms that I have described up till now have been my primary focus. Through the recent years, succession planting has been incorporated into the planning a little at a time. You will note that on the Perelandra garden plan there are 2 rows for green beans (green bean #1 and green bean #2) and they are planted 5 weeks apart. That's succession planting of sorts. I realize I am not using the same ground for 2 separate, sequential plantings—the strict definition of succession planting—but this is how the concept was first added to the Perelandra garden. A subsequent refinement around this issue has to do with vegetables such as squash, zucchini, cucumber, etc., where several hills or plants are indicated. Rather than plant all hills at the same time, nature gave me information that the planting could be staggered, thus assuring production of that particular vegetable throughout the season and easing its inevitable glut in the kitchen. However, some years nature tells me to put all the hills of a specific vegetable in at the same time. In order to get this information, all one has to do is:

1. Connect with the deva of the specific vegetable in question. Verify the connection.

2. Ask:

> Are there different times in which the individual _____ (vegetable) hills/plants are to be planted? (Test.)

If the result is negative, for some reason all the plants should go in at the same time. If the result is positive, then go on to the next step.

3. Refer to the patterning information you did on your garden (back in Chapter 6) so that you'll know where the individual hills or plants are to go. If you have, for example, 4 hills of zucchini planned, label each hill position A, B, C and D, and ask:

> Does A get planted first? (Test.)
>> Second? (Test.)
>> Third? (Test.)
>> Fourth? (Test.)

The positive response is the order for planting A. Do the same for B, C and D. You may end up with something that looks like this:

A = second	or	A = second		
B = first		B = first		
C = fourth		C = third		
D = third		D = second		

(Two second plantings and no fourth one)

HINT: Following this particular rhythm has given me the chance to observe and appreciate the wisdom of the devas to no end. To complete a garden season and have a manageable production throughout is truly magical to me. I enjoy watching such variables as temperature and rain (or lack thereof) interweave with these succession planting rhythms. It's clear evidence to me that somebody sure knows what they're doing—and it's not me because all I'm doing is following instructions!

4. Once you've gotten the order of planting, all you'll need to do is refer to the planting rhythm chart and identify which week each successive hill or plant is to go in.

But we still haven't dealt with the issue of planting fall lettuce where the spring spinach once grew: using the same ground for an extended growing period for 2 separate vegetables. Garden greens usually fall into this situation. It just so happens that built into the planning of my garden is, at least, a partial answer to the problem. The spring planting rhythm is such that spinach and lettuce are planted for spring and early summer production, while kale and India mustard are planted for late summer and early fall production. (I didn't have anything to do with that timing.) If I cut the loose leaf lettuce plants even to the ground in the spring, I'll get a second production off the same plants in the fall.

If you'd like a fall planting of anything, ask the Deva of the Garden if it is in keeping with the rhythm of the garden to do a second planting. If you get a yes, check to make sure the fall spinach is to go where the spring spinach grew, or if there is to be a little bit of jockeying between the available spots. Then do a fertilizer check, and add what is called for to the row in preparation for the second planting. Also, identify the week for planting the seed. In this way, you're assured that you are maintaining the overall garden rhythm.

13

MAINTENANCE

I have to be honest here. Once the garden is planted and the summer 8 to 12 inches of straw mulch have been spread, I have very little to do except sit around and watch it grow—and shift nets!* Because of the mulching, I don't water or weed. Because of the work I've done with the nature intelligences, I don't deal with repelling insects. I've learned that if I just sit back and allow nature to live out its rhythm—which, after all, is the very issue I attempt to facilitate with all that spring information and those charts—the whole garden maintains a life-giving balance that requires no repelling or interference from me. And except for a request here and there for a mid-season pick-me-up, I don't have to fertilize—that's already been done. So I watch and learn. And shift those nets.

If I see a row being consumed by insects, I ask the deva of the vegetable involved if there is something I should do. Remember, the whole garden is approached from the direction of energy balance, and it's possible that something unexpected in the overall picture has changed and has impacted this particular row. Also, it's quite conceivable that I made a mistake in translating the information, and that's what is causing the problem. If the response to my question is a devic no, I stand back and let whatever is happening happen. And I watch. If I get a yes, then I'll continue asking questions to determine in what area help is needed: fertilizing, thinning,

* Since 1989 nature has added nets to my garden landscape. They are not used for insect repelling, which was why they were developed by some enterprising person to begin with. In my garden they are used for shading. We have 3 different weights of netting that shade anywhere from 50 percent to 15 percent of sunlight. At first I didn't understand why we were using them. But I soon noticed that even the sun-loving plants under the netting that shaded 50 percent of the sun were growing and producing as if they were in full sunlight. This didn't make any sense. After 3 seasons of putting nets on and removing them when nature told me, I realized that this was a research project for developing ultra-violet-ray protection for gardens as the thinning of our ozone layer causes problems for plant health.

In each row, the different weight nets are laid loosely over metal hoops. This allows easy row access for insects. Right away, I noticed that the frogs, lizards, snakes and salamanders also have easy access and love the protected environment the nets give—and reptiles love insects! We were told to put a reptile pond in the garden area the year the nets were first used.

I have included information in Supplies and Resources on where to get nets, in case the deva of your garden recommends that nets be used. I suggest that you not use them unless recommended by nature.

* *The* Perelandra Garden Workbook II *contains processes that are especially helpful during the maintenance time. It also has a chapter and a process for working with nature on troubleshooting anything that is going awry during the growing season. For ordering information, see the form in the back of this book.*

** *Because the intent of the Perelandra garden is research, nature schedules in the year's devic plan various projects for us to work on together throughout the growing season. This is how all the processes in both* Workbook *and* Workbook II *were developed. Sometimes the research requires me to deal with a sudden problem, even sudden croaking of plants. I say "sudden" because, until the time the actual research is to be done, the plants involved are in fine shape. More often than not, the plants return to their original healthy state once the research is completed. It's not exactly the normal way to garden, but it adds an element of surprise and interest!*

(and for those of you without mulch) watering, aeration or weeding. Once I establish which direction I'm to move in, I'll ask specific yes/no questions designed to eliminate what isn't needed and identify what is.*

About a row being consumed by something other than yourself: In the earlier years, I would sometimes lose a row—and nature told me to go ahead and let it happen. I've since learned that this is part of the healing and building process that goes on. A garden environment heals gradually and organically. Its healing processes build on top of one another. This concept adds stability to change, and healing is real change. If our body were to suddenly completely heal, if all that was off-balance were to magically move to a position of total balance, we would experience spasm on all levels. We would not have given ourselves a chance to integrate all the steps of the change on any level—physical, emotional, mental or spiritual. In order to affect stable change in healing, each step has to be integrated and the next step built on top of that. After all, each step in deterioration, imbalance and poor health was integrated and that downward spiral had a building-block action. Certainly the same concept but in the reverse direction would be true for the upward-spiraling healing process.

I'm saying all of this so that you won't be tough on yourself or the garden, especially in the beginning. I've been working with the nature intelligences since 1976, and each season has built on top of the previous ones. Then, as I mentioned earlier, in early 1985, the garden reached a level of health that allowed everything (insects included) to become life-giving with all else in the garden environment. In short, in the general garden where I am not doing specific research work with nature on some new process,** I don't lose rows. I'm not going to say that I'll never lose a row again. That would not only be dumb, but it would not take into account any future healing the Perelandra garden has before it that will require new process and change. It's just that at this point, it's stabilized.

One maintenance process I do practice is thinning. In the beginning, I did not assume I understood thinning or even the ruling logic behind it. So I got devic direction. As I watched the row in question grow, I kept tabs with the deva on thinning. Basically, I'd connect with the deva and ask, "Now?" Invariably, I'd get a no. The logic that I had learned from reading traditional organic gardening material or from other gardeners was not what was playing out in my garden. Once I got the go ahead, I'd ask for the preferred spacing between plants by 1) asking that question, and 2) doing a sequential testing using inches until I got the desired number. This, too, surprised me. Either it was further apart than I had expected or closer together. Either way, it still wasn't jiving with the traditional logic.

I made it a point to follow these instructions. At first, it was just to see what would happen if I followed these crazy suggestions. Once I saw that the vegetables thrived, then I changed my attitude a bit. Now I follow these instructions because they work. In time, my sense of logic around the thinning issue changed, and I took on a new logic that correlates more closely with what I've been taught by nature. When I consider thinning, I'm operating from this new logic, and I tend to open the question to the deva right at the time thinning is to take place. It's become an exercise in verification.

On issues you might be facing that aren't part of the Perelandra garden, I'd recommend the same approach I used for uncovering a new logic in thinning. Especially for watering and weeding, there might be a different way of looking at them that we've overlooked by our dependence on established thinking. I have no judgment regarding watering or weeding. If they are to be part of your garden process, then my support is with you. But if either are to be practiced, then once again I encourage you to allow the deva and/or nature spirits involved to refine and upgrade the practice wherever needed.

Okay. The next question is how to find out who to connect with in order to receive the proper information. With most maintenance, you connect with the nature spirits tending the area/plant in question.* Maintenance questions are not architectural by nature. They address issues of action and interaction—the plant life cycle in process. The patterns and rhythms have already been set on the devic level. Maintenance focuses on the day-to-day unfolding of those patterns and rhythms. For example, when thinning spinach, connect with the nature spirit tending the spinach. Use the same 4-step procedure** you used for getting devic information. Nature spirits connect with us just as easily as devas. For watering needs, consult the nature spirit of the specific vegetable in question. By identifying precisely which plants need watering, you may be able to conserve water rather than approach the job with one massive watering that takes care of the entire garden whether some plants need it or not.

*In the first edition of the Workbook, I suggested here that you continue to get your information devically. I did this because you can get this information devically, and I thought it would be less stressful on you if you did so. I figured you'd find it easier if you just continued working as you had up to this point (devically), rather than concentrate on learning to work with nature spirits. Well, my good intentions only caused confusion. Even Pan tried to warn me by pointing out in the original session in this chapter that maintenance is actually a nature-spirit thing. If you are confused about what you are supposed to do regarding maintenance, disregard the first edition of the Workbook and follow what's suggested here—work mostly with the nature spirits. The first edition wasn't wrong, it's just that this is better.

** The basic 4-step procedure is listed in Chapter 6. Remember, this is the test I mentioned in Chapter 6 to see if you would remember where the steps are listed.

For weeding, I'd consult with the Deva of the Garden for a general approach to weeding in your garden. This is an overall blueprint issue. Should you be vigilant, moderately vigilant, a little on the loose side, or let the garden become a complete combination of its weeds and the vegetables? (The latter is a recognized gardening approach that emphasizes natural interplanting.) Once the general approach is identified, then related specific information can be gotten from the nature spirits of the individual plants in question.

There's one other area of maintenance which I have approached with a light and delicate touch throughout the growing season. That's the mid-season pick-me-up kind of fertilizing. I have used manure tea and foliar feeding.* Every 2 weeks or so, I go through a list of the vegetables or use the garden chart and connect with each deva to find out which plants need a little shot. Because of the earlier fertilizing, this mid-season maintenance is not a huge issue. As I said, I practice it with a light and delicate touch. If you are using manure tea and you discover that broccoli is in need, just ask the nature spirit "How much should I spray?" and do a sequential count in quarts or pints, whatever is appropriate for the job. Also ask how much you are to dilute the solution for foliar feeding. I ask if I'm to spray lightly, "mediumly" or heavily. My basic attitude is to assist the plants by giving them what they need rather than blindly gorging them with the equivalent of 4 Thanksgiving meals.

Foliar Feeding: An efficient method for fertilizing plants by mixing a liquid solution and spraying it on all the leaf surfaces.

PAN

In the spring, nature spirits concentrate their efforts on translating the plan of the garden into form. That is, once planted according to the devic blueprint, the garden is the true physical manifestation of the energy that coalesced into one overlighting plan on the devic level. What you see before you is manifestation in its clearest example. Energy has been fused into form.

When the garden is fully planted, the nature spirits enter a new phase of focus. Machaelle has aptly called this maintenance. From our point of view, maintenance means the carrying through of the growth patterns of all in the garden throughout the entire growing season. If one were to see these two focuses in terms of horizontal and vertical, one could say that the spring focus is vertical. The primary flow of energy movement is vertical—

that is, energy is manifesting vertically into form. The second focus is primarily horizontal. The form has been made manifest, and now its pattern of growth is to be assisted. The various patterns of growth are a part of the overall patterns that manifested into form. So it is no longer a matter of reaching up, as it were, to receive energy patterns. It is simply an issue of reading these patterns which exist within the form energy and assisting their unfolding.

If you are at a loss as to who to consult regarding maintenance, you may request to be connected with the nature spirit involved with the plant or the process in question. That part of the blueprint is, as I have stated, already accessible to the nature spirits, and any of them will be most glad to give you a readout. You may connect with the nature spirit exactly as you have been connecting with the devas. And you may receive answers to your yes/no questions using the same tool of kinesiology. You need not know precisely which nature spirit to consult by name, only that you wish to connect with the nature spirit involved with the question you are raising. You'll be connected with the right one immediately. Machaelle frequently connects with us and we on the nature spirit level sense that when she is in the garden, involved with the dynamics of doing and motion, she feels her proximity to us and addresses maintenance issues to us right on the spot.

14

FURRED, FEATHERED AND WINGED GARDEN COMPANIONS

In 1981, nature told me the following: *The garden is inclusive, not exclusive.* Well, that struck me deeply because I had become accustomed to thinking that if you do A it will produce B which will, in turn, exclude problem C. And problem C usually referred to something furred, feathered, winged—or slimy. In short, that part of nature which falls within the realm of the animal and insect kingdoms. This insight was for me a 180-degree turn in mindset, and I spent the entire summer repeating it to myself often. I wrote it on the garden-shed blackboard so that every time I hung up my tools, I'd see it. Gradually, as the summer wore on, I could tell that my attitude was shifting from the mindset of exclusion to that of inclusion.

The very first difference I noticed was inside *me*. I began to sense myself move through the garden without a feeling of burden. Then I began to identify that the burden had been made up of worry, concern, anger, frustration, a sense of injustice—and it had all been directed to those of the animal and insect kingdoms. Now I walked through the garden with the attitude that bugs, birds, rabbits, frogs, snakes and slugs were all supposed to be there. They are a legitimate part of the garden environment, and when we consider a *balanced* garden environment, all of these creatures must be taken into consideration. To exclude or ignore their well-being would make it impossible for us to create a balanced garden environment.

The second change I noted was, I'm sure, a direct result of the first change. I noticed an increase in numbers and activity from animals and insects, and a corresponding decrease in what we gardeners would call "damage" from these creatures. A baby rabbit lived for awhile amongst the herbs in the center ring of the garden. I had to be careful when harvesting because of the increased number of snakes. (I'm not sure who was more startled when we met—me or them.) A skunk moved into the space under the shed. Wasp nests were being built everywhere. Tommy the Turtle joined the garden and each year since, he has returned for the summer. He begins in the strawberry patch and migrates from row to row throughout the season. (I know it's Tommy, because he has only 3 legs.) For 1 season, a groundhog joined us everyday at 2 P.M. He climbed up in a tree near the garden and would just watch. He'd stay about an hour and then leave. Never came into the garden. I called him the garden's guard groundhog. The general insect population grew to mammoth proportions. Bats and birds began swooping in each day from every angle. Yet with all this action going on, I didn't notice any additional loss of plant or produce.

Since beginning my adventure in co-creative gardening, I have tithed 10 percent of the garden back to nature just on general principle. To be frank, I don't believe nature has ever fully taken in that tithing. If they're taking 10 percent, I'm not noticing it. Now what I observed was that where animal or insect and plant interfaced, it was with the softest of touches. At the same time, I felt an air of aggression that had hung over the garden gradually dissipate and eventually it disappeared altogether. What I realized was that I had removed my attitude of aggression toward the animal and insect kingdoms when I changed my attitude and this, in turn, changed the collective attitude with which those kingdoms interfaced with the garden. They no longer had to fight for their life. They could exist within a natural environment without fear of reprisal. Plus, it set into motion the creation of a new balance—one in which the quantity and quality of activity increased many times.

Whenever the question of what I do about various "visiting pests" comes

The Perelandra garden is bordered on two sides by a large woods. And it's surrounded by rolling, open farmland which is used primarily for livestock grazing. There are a lot of wild animals living in the woods and traveling through the fields. The garden is wide open to wildlife visits.

up at workshops, I explain what I have done to change the interaction of animals in the garden. People are usually disappointed by the answer. In my answer, we humans are the issue, not the animals. People want to hear that the animals are the problem. (It's part of that old exclusion mentality.) They also would prefer that I give them some specific easy-to-follow process. Then, once accomplished, the wildlife would be forever banished. The point is, I have done nothing except change my attitude. That's it, folks. As I changed my attitude, the wildlife changed its activity in the garden.

With the increase in animal and insect activity, I received information regarding certain adjustments I needed to make in the garden area. A substantial portion of the field just off the east side of the garden was declared a woods edge and has developed an overgrowth of grasses, cedars and brambles for the protection, housing and breeding of small animals and birds. A birdfeeding station complete with birdbath was added in the garden itself. In 1990, we put in a reptile pond. To maintain a safe environment for reptile breeding, we do not stock the pond with fish. Also, there are special wildflower areas positioned around the garden area. And we have 2 large fields—about 16 acres total—that are left alone each growing season to develop into wildflower meadows.

The garden is fenced for the purpose of keeping out the neighbor's herd of horses and cattle. They managed to move through the garden a number of times and have proven beyond a shadow of a doubt that even when they walk along the various spiral paths and stay out of the planting area itself, they still do extensive damage just from sheer size and weight. They're just not appropriate garden companions! The fence excludes nothing else. Deer jump it with ease and grace and lope on through to the other side, jump that fence and head on into the woods. Rarely do I find any evidence of their having been through, save a plop or two.

To give you a further idea as to how my attitude has changed, I can say that I move throughout the garden area with the specific intent of not doing anything, leaving anything around, or setting anything up that might damage or injure an animal or bird. I store my tools in a way that they can't cut or damage. I dispose of old seeds carefully because they have been treated or inoculated, and I'm not sure what effect this will have on wildlife. I check the fence from time to time to make sure it is easily and

*If you have insects or rodents living in a building and would like to urge them outside, don't write me to ask what to do. I will only say that you must ask nature, specifically the nature intelligences directly involved with the insects or animals in question. Often it is simply a matter of making the connection with nature and **clearly** stating that you need them to be outside and why. Wildlife considers a building just another part of the landscape, not a human's home. You'd be surprised how often a clear request will do the trick. To put it simply, they just didn't know they weren't welcome and will be glad to honor your request once they understand.*

Sometimes you will need to do more, and nature can give you this information. You may need to eliminate something that is attracting the animals or insects, or supply something that will make a suitable alternative for them in a different location.

The key is to be clear and concise with nature about your requests, and to act without hesitation and in a clear manner on any information that nature gives you.

safely negotiable by all but the cows and horses. I try to stake and rope needed areas clearly so that a passing animal or bird won't get hung up. In essence, I put considerable effort into providing a safe environment for all. This is another way of demonstrating that the garden is inclusive, not exclusive.

I fear I may be sounding as if this has been an effortless, rosy process, this change of attitude. That would not only be untrue, it would be unfair to give that impression. The change has been gradual and the lessons constant. As my old attitude unravelled, I was surprised to see how much the sense of exclusion had pervaded my thoughts and actions.

In 1985, I was observing the early spring beauty of the garden. A very large flock of robins had been around for days. In fact, the size of the flock was so big that I spent considerable time each day watching its movements and interaction with the garden area. Eventually, I felt real concern for the earthworm population. The concern grew. I worked to keep my thoughts in check, and concentrated on trying to learn through observation what was really occurring. I trusted that all was well, but I couldn't see evidence of this. One day as I was watching, a robin not more than 10 feet from me bent its head, yanked one of my prized earthworms out of the ground and gobbled it in less than a second. I was livid and yelled something like, "How dare you eat my earthworm!" Had I had any weapon in hand, I'm sure I would have gone after that robin.

Well, it was obvious that my attempt at containment had just collapsed, and I knew I was going to have to get some kind of insight on what the robins were accomplishing (besides devouring my earthworms) in order to rebalance my thinking.

I opened a combined session on March 23, 1985, with the Deva of Perelandra, the Deva of the Garden, the Deva of the Soil, the Deva of the Robin, and Pan. (I figured someone in this group could give me answers.) I asked that all these intelligences speak as one, homogenous voice so I wouldn't have to try to deal with 5 separate voices, each saying something different.* Then I requested insight on the increased robin activity in the garden area.

The following session is what I got:

* If you're not sure who to consult about a problem, you can 1) ask Pan who to consult and then connect to the appropriate consultant, 2) connect with several intelligences you feel might be involved and ask that their information come as 1 unit. Then test the yes/no answers as you normally would.

The second option is also particularly helpful if you have a series of questions within one related topic that cover areas that are overseen by different devas and/or nature spirits. Here you can set up a simple "meeting" with all of them, requesting they create one information package for you to test.

Better yet, open a coning when a meeting is called for. To learn about conings and how to activate them, see Chapter 18.

The increased robin activity relates to the overall improvement of the health of the garden. Your concern has been the possible imbalance in the earthworm population that might be caused by the increased robin activity. You are not looking at a negative in action, you are looking at a positive in action. Rest assured that there are more than enough earthworms to go around! The soil is not being depleted of earthworms. In fact, the soil is being enhanced by the opening up, scratching and aerating created by the robins.

We could leave your insight at this—our assurance that all is quite well in the Perelandra garden. But we'd like to deepen your understanding since you have taken the time to observe the robin activity and ask us about it.

We'd like to point out a phenomenon which exists within the chain of life that few understand: that is the increase of intensity in life energy when there is full purpose existing within the chain of life. In the case of the robin/earthworm interaction, the attention the robin is paying to the earthworm is enhancing the earthworm's sense of life energy. Being used as food for the robin, of course, adds to the earthworm's experience of purpose. That increase in purpose creates a higher life energy, a more intense life energy, and encourages the earthworm population to multiply. It multiplies not only for its sense of self-survival, but also in response to a sense of purpose beyond itself.

The energy that is created by the interaction between two participants in the grand chain of life is extremely powerful. It encourages life quality with the individuals—a fine sharpening of skills and sensitivities which can be directly related to the challenge of survival, or as we see it, the natural interaction within the chain of life. The species becomes stronger when these skills and sensitivities are sharpened. This is fairly well understood by man in his use of the phrase "survival of the fittest."

*What we are emphasizing here is not this aspect of the phenomenon, but rather the heightening of energy when participants are fully interacting within the chain of life that, in turn, enhances the drive to reproduce, to continue the species, to maintain full participation within the chain of life. This second aspect of the phenomenon relates directly to **purpose**—understanding one's purpose individually and as part of the whole. To use your* *example of the earthworm/robin activity: The earthworms at Perelandra are not only responding to the balanced environment when they multiply but also the increase in activity provided by the birds, etc. (in this case, the robins). The earthworms at Perelandra have the drive to multiply. Their sense of life energy and quality is very high. Their participation in life is one of excitement, purpose and immediacy.*

The flip side of this issue would be the garden where birds are kept out while at the same time, earthworms are purchased from outside the garden environment and introduced into the soil. If we were to describe the quality of life energy among the earthworms in this situation, one could use the word "sluggish." The level of purpose is minimal. The earthworm's response to its own life is also minimal. In this type of garden it would be safe to say that the gardener's overall understanding of energy and its relationship to form is minimal—the quality of life energy among his earthworms reflects this just as all other aspects in the garden would reflect this.

In 1981, you were given the insight that the garden is inclusive, not exclusive. That insight directly relates to what we are talking about here. By including all members of the chain of life who belong within the balanced garden environment, one encourages and enhances the quality and intensity of life energy within that chain—and within that environment as a whole. Your robin activity is a sign of this enhancement. So, do not fret over what appears to be a massive assault on your prized earthworm population. See the robins with new eyes, and celebrate with us the acting out of the high intensity and level of life energy that is inherent in the Perelandra garden. The robins, the earthworms, the garden, and you are the better for it!

A note on balance: The Perelandra garden reflects balance on many levels. The activity it calls to itself will be of like reflection—balance. Just as there is out-of-balance activity evident in out-of-balance gardens with or without the gardener's direct assistance to promote this imbalance, there is balanced activity called to and reflected in a balanced garden—with or without your direct assistance. In essence, as long as you keep your focus on striving for and maintaining the overall balance of the garden and garden area, you can rest assured that the activity called to it will also reflect balance. You've already seen this in relationship to how insects interact with plants. Why would this not work in the very same manner in relationship to how birds interact with earthworms?

Now when I see a robin in the garden, I just say to myself he's giving purpose to the earthworms.

INSECTS

The relationship between the gardener and his insects deserves its own section. As you have probably gathered, my relationship on a direct level is quite nonchalant. I concentrate on getting the garden in the ground in the right position with the correct interplanting and ratio and from then on, I let nature take its course. The insects move in and out creating an intricate pattern that seems to magically weave into the larger fabric of the garden whole. It's extraordinary to observe.

One of the problems in showing this kind of garden to others is that in a day's visit, they see only 1/365th of that weave. They may see the garden right at the time when the cabbage worm is present on the plants and not realize that if they returned a week later, what they assumed would be disastrous would not only no longer be a threat but would no longer even be present. In that short period of time, birds, wasps and various other creatures will have feasted royally on the abundant cabbage worms, and the plants are left to continue their growth without missing the tiniest of beats.

Having watched this amazing process year after year, I have been able to change my attitude about bugs from a focus on what they attack, weaken, damage or destroy to a focus of the gift each insect offers to the countless other members of the garden. This, in turn, has allowed me to see the insects' *right of relationship* to the plant kingdom. It may sound odd, I am sure, but I see the insects as not only an integral part of the environment, but also as a crop and part of the garden's harvest. They feed many! I encourage their health and vibrancy as I would anything else in the garden. And I look to the garden to draw to it and support a balanced and full population of insects which, in turn, helps to support the overall life of that environment.

Now, on a practical level, this has meant that I have had to learn to co-exist with the insects in new ways. If I am going to welcome them into my garden environment, I certainly can't operate in a way that ignores insects' needs. The birdbath is also a water source for insects as much as it is for the birds. The reptile pond has a lot of insect activity and has, in turn, encouraged the addition of quite a "herd" of dragonflies throughout the entire garden area. (Dragonflies are very big on eating insects.) I welcome dandelions as part of the grassy areas because they are such a good source of nectar in the early spring. I will keep a row of green beans growing long after it has completed its bean production if the bean beetle process is at a critical stage, and more time is needed to successfully complete their cycle. In the herb ring I was told to plant costmary, an herb I personally do absolutely nothing with. (I've heard it is used for medicinal teas.) Each year I dutifully fertilize it, and early each spring it becomes completely covered with a billion aphids. About a week later, an equal number of ladybugs appear in the costmary. Not long after that, there are no aphids, and the ladybugs have scattered about the garden. So, I've decided that the costmary in the Perelandra garden is actually a ladybug feeding and breeding ground.

I don't remove insects by hand. I try not to interfere with their process at all. If in the process of some pruning I must disturb an egg case, I will try to work around the branch in question or tie the pruned branch to another located in a similar environment.

As soon as the warmth of early spring hits, there are wasps everywhere looking to start nests. For the most part, this is not an issue as long as the nests are not in an area where my presence throughout the summer will be deemed a direct threat. Once the larva are laid, the adult wasps become aggressively protective. This seems reasonable to me. I've seen human parents get aggressively protective when their child is being threatened in any manner. So, I'll respect this in the wasps and make an agreement not to have nests where my presence is seen as threatening—like the front doorjamb to my garden cabin or heavily traveled areas in the garden shed. After the agreement is made, Clarence or I will keep any nests out of those areas *before* larva eggs are laid.

When I planted the outer ring of the garden in rose bushes, I wondered how the Japanese beetles would react. I pictured every beetle within a 600-mile range being drawn to the rose ring of the Perelandra garden. Since I don't spray or discourage them in any way, they have total freedom. Well, I do have Japanese beetles. But the number, in light of their freedom is astonishingly low. And they don't *attack* the rose ring. They move rather gently around the ring in a pattern that allows all the rose bushes to blossom fully at different times within the Japanese beetle season. I've also learned that if I allow the beetles to remain on the rose flower they have chosen, they will stay with that flower until it is fully eaten before moving on. They seem to have a memory of the flower and although they may fly around during the day, they will return to that particular flower in the afternoon and stay there for the night. Of course, I am not certain that it is the very same beetles returning to a specific rose. But I am sure that when a rose is hosting beetles, it remains the sole host on the bush until fully devoured. More often than not, the beetles move on to another bush rather than to another rose of the same bush. So if I don't bother them, they take one or 2 roses on the bush while I get to enjoy the other 10 roses on the same bush. The bottom line is that there are Japanese beetles with my roses, but they are nowhere near a problem. They seem to be a positive part of the rose environment.

I have found that garden insects function as quick dispatchers of communication. If I see a plant or row suddenly overwhelmed, or seemingly overwhelmed, with insects, I'll open to the appropriate deva and ask if the plant balance is off. For example, I may find that a particular rose bush is covered with aphids. When I have inquired, I have been told not to panic, just do the monthly fertilizing as planned and that will rebalance the bush. Once I do the planned fertilizing, the aphids leave the bush within 24 hours. Another example: One year we had a shift in timing with broccoli which occurred right after the transplants were placed into the garden. Slugs took over and it wasn't long before the plants had leaf and stem damage. I connected to the Deva of Broccoli and asked if I was to replace these damaged plants with new ones. I was told no. Then I was told to mound dirt to a level above the stem damage, water with liquid seaweed and mulch with oak leaves. I was also informed that the broccoli timing had shifted and that the slugs had facilitated the shift. If I followed instructions, the present plants would re-form and continue their growth cycle in the new rhythm. Needless to say, I did follow instructions, and the plants responded exactly as I was told they would.

In essence, when I look at the role of insects in the garden, I assume balanced interaction. I don't assume that the garden has suddenly come under attack from marauding hordes of alien insects bent on destruction, and then respond with an attitude of doing battle to reestablish my control. Instead, I assume communication and service. At these moments, I'm usually at a loss as to what is occurring, so I'll connect with the nature spirit or deva in question to get direction and insight into what is happening and if I am to assist in any way. In my experience, being asked to assist as I was with the broccoli is rare. Usually I am told there is a change, and all is under control. Then I simply stand back and watch a new rhythm take over.

In 1992, I added something else specifically for the insects—an Insect Sanctuary. This is a direct result of what we have been doing with the Insect Balancing and Insect Triangulation Processes.* Nature then explained that the Insect Sanctuary (which we lovingly call "Bug Boulevard") is not an area for attracting or housing insects, such as the meadows and wildflower areas. The Sanctuary is where insect healing and balancing work is done, and how the Sanctuary is laid out and designed stabilizes and enhances that activity. The nature spirits tending the Insect Sanctuary are not only working with the plants in this garden but also with the healing and balancing of all the insects present in the Perelandra garden environment. In short, some of these nature spirits work primarily in the area of insect healing and balancing. The Insect Sanctuary is their base of operation and the location from which nature and I work together in this area.**

* For more direct co-creative work with insects, I recommend the Insect Balancing Process and the Insect Triangulation Process. Both are energy processes and are explained in the Perelandra Garden Workbook II.

** To set up the Insect Sanctuary, I worked with the Overlighting Deva of Insects for the placement, design and layout. My sanctuary is a 5-foot-by-60-foot flower, vegetable and herb garden with a slate slab in the center. If I am to give any flower essences to the insects, I place the mixed solution in a glass bowl on the slate slab and the appropriate healing nature spirits take over from there. (Flower essences are discussed in Chapter 16. Working with them regarding insects is discussed in Workbook II.)

I don't wish to mislead you into thinking that from the very moment I stepped foot into the garden with this new attitude of co-creation, the insect world responded in complete and total balance. As the garden went through its healing processes, the insect population adjusted accordingly. Again, they functioned as communicators as to just how far along we were in the healing process. It has taken me 17 years to discover the pieces of the puzzle I have given you in this book and to put them into place. (It won't take you so long since you have the book!) Each time I added a new piece, the garden, including the insects, adjusted and struck a stronger balance. I say this in an effort to help you when things appear discouraging and to urge to have patience. If you stick with the process, you're going to come out at the other end, and your garden will be as friendly and life-giving as mine.

OVERLIGHTING DEVA OF INSECTS

Within the devic level you will find devas who respond to specific and individual natural form, such as the Deva of the Cabbage Moth, and devas who function from an overlighting position which encompasses patterns and processes of entire kingdoms. In this case, I overlight the insect kingdom and wish to give you insight into some of the patterns and purpose which can assist your needed change of consciousness in this area.

Without realizing it, Machaelle has touched upon the overall intent of the insect world in its relationship to humankind. I am speaking here of communication. When the nature kingdoms need to draw human attention to a situation, it will first dispatch large numbers of insects to interact with humans. This may sound ridiculous to you, perhaps even a bit too contrived a notion, but consider this: If nature wished to turn human attention from a focus centered around human cares to a situation occurring within nature that is a result of misguided interfacing between man and nature, what better way to jolt and shift the human attention than through a sudden intrusion, even invasion, from the insect world. From our point of view, it is this world of nature which can be dispatched without creating instantaneous panic. Consider how you would feel if suddenly you were beset by a stampeding forest of trees! Or a massive herd of wild beasts! The latter, of course, has been experienced within the human community and perfectly illustrates my point. There would be panic, mass confusion, fear, destruction, and in the case of stampeding trees, shock. This is not the communication I wish to stress here. What I speak of is the communication of sounding an alert, of drawing human attention to nature. It is the insect world which can interface with the human world without creating an immediate destructive result from either party. They can touch humans, pester humans, continuously draw human attention to themselves—and eventually, if successful, draw human attention to a critical situation that is occurring in his environment.

If one were to consider the state of natural balance within a specific area, it would be a wise move indeed to observe the state of the insect world within that area and the impact of the insects not only upon the rest of nature but on the human population either in the area itself or residing nearby.

It is true that when nature is out of balance, that imbalance is reflected throughout all kingdoms represented in the specific area in question. Therefore, it would be reasonable to assume that it is nothing more than simple logic I am imparting to you. But I am saying more. Yes, the insects would naturally reflect an environment's imbalance. Even more importantly for you, it is the insects who first telegraph this imbalance to humans and they do this long before the natural form within that environment visibly shows the signs of the imbalance. If the communication lines between the insect world and humankind were to be consciously accepted by man and allowed to operate on the level in which it is intended, the threat of ecological imbalance would be communicated long before a specific area begins the reflective process of sickness, destruction, and eventual removal of natural areas from the planet. If man were to sensitize himself to that which the insects are attempting to telegraph, he would be able to reclaim areas to levels of ecological balance far more easily than he can now imagine possible.

Where insects have interfaced with humankind to such a degree that disease within the human community results, it is not correct to assume that this is a vicious attack by nature. The disease which occurs within the human population is in direct proportion to the seriousness of the imbalance occurring in nature, of which man is a part. They are related. And the key to the natural imbalance is how the disease manifests within the human body. Again, although extreme, the insects are functioning as carriers of communication. In the area of disease, they are manifesting the very problem they wish to communicate symbolically in this microcosm within human form.

It might help you to consider what I am saying more fully if I remind you that the human form is natural. It embodies all three kingdoms—plant, animal and mineral—and integrates them into one functioning unit. Keeping this in mind, it is easy to see how nature can reflect in microcosm in the human form exactly what is occurring in macrocosm in the environment around him. All the kingdoms of nature are represented in the human form and available to us at all times. Conversely, the human form reflects the balance of the surrounding natural environment, and that is not only a communication from us of nature, it is the sign of celebration. Man and nature reflecting in balance and in tandem.

If man is to sensitize himself to the communication of the insects, it is important that he view them as messengers of a problem and not the problem itself. When dealing with human disease or nature disease, the insects in question may be conquered or controlled by man and his technology, but the disease itself will not be eliminated until the underlying reason is addressed. In areas where insects appear to be out of control or troublesome, I suggest you draw back and look at the larger environmental picture for the answers you seek. If you are still having difficulty identifying the real problem, look at precisely how the insects are interfacing with human or natural form and there lie the clues you'll need for the answers in the overall picture.

In instances where massive ecological imbalance is being demonstrated in drastic, life-threatening ways either within nature or the human community, understand that this is not a situation where nature is deliberately attacking man out of independent outrage or anger. Humans are not innocent victims being ravaged by some outside, powerful source. Such willful actions are not the way of nature. Where they interface, man and nature are in partnership and have been since mankind joined the life cycle of the planet. Up until now, the partnership has been one of cause and effect on both sides. What is critical at this point is for us to join in a new partnership of co-creativity. Again, remember that the human body is the direct link you have with the natural world. The only way to sever that link is to completely remove spirit from form. But while the link remains, mankind must expect that what occurs in the natural world will be demonstrated in kind within the kingdoms in question contained within human form. This is natural law. What occurs in form resonates in kind throughout all corresponding reflections of that specific aspect of form.

15

THE SOLSTICE AND EQUINOX CYCLE

Annually, there are 4 important dates that are especially linked with nature. They are: fall equinox, around September 21st; winter solstice, around December 21st; spring equinox, around March 21st; and summer solstice, around June 21st.

Technically, the equinox refers to the 2 days of the year in which the sunrise and sunset are 12 hours apart, giving equal hours to day and night. The summer solstice is the longest day of the year, and the winter solstice is the longest night of the year.

I observe these 4 days as nature holidays and use them to take time out, step back, and remember the specific nature process that is related to the equinox or solstice in effect that day. Through the years, nature has taught me the following about each of the 4 days.

FALL EQUINOX

In nature, this is the new year, the day that begins the next year's cycle. It is the day when the call goes out for the new cycle to activate and begin its formation processes on the deepest of energy levels. At Perelandra, at the precise moment of the fall equinox I, as creator of this garden, initiate the call by saying aloud,

I request the next cycle and wish to assist its full unfolding.

For this, I usually make a small gesture—such as lighting a candle. Nothing hinges on this. It's only an option.

NOTE: When I say "precise moment," I mean the precise time of the day the equinox or solstice occurs. For example, 1986's fall equinox was on September 23rd at 2:59 A.M.* There is a strong release and surge of dynamic energy within the forces of nature at this precise time that is above and beyond the energy of the day itself, and I choose to link what I am initiating with the enhanced energy. The time for the equinoxes and solstices can be gotten from the almanac, and in most areas they can be gotten from the local newspaper or TV weather report.

It took a while for me to rearrange my thinking about the beginning of the new year not being January 1. And it was a little difficult to still be looking at the growing garden of the present cycle while at the same time calling in the pattern for the next year. But as I moved through the rest of the equinox/solstice cycle, I soon learned how appropriate this shift was.

IMPORTANT: I have incorporated another dimension into this little ceremony, and that has to do with my personal cycle. Each year at the time of the fall equinox, I also call in the next step in my own evolutionary process. I make the commitment to receive and act on that cycle, and I activate this commitment by consciously including it in the ceremony. I have learned from nature that all that exists on planet Earth is grounded fully and completely in form and physical action through the energy of nature. That energy commingles with the human dynamics of thought and creativity and serves to fuse into these dynamics the matter, means and action necessary for grounding. It is the natural law of the planet. It is called involution/evolution balance. The energy of nature (involution) links with and energizes the creative, forward-moving spirit of humankind (evolution) to create one cohesive, efficient unit of life energy. I have seen this principle demonstrated often in areas outside the usual nature environment. It seemed reasonable to me that my personal process would be greatly assisted if I formally and consciously participated in the fusion process between it and the nature energies. My logic was verified by nature and for

** Yes, of course I gripe and groan about an equinox or solstice that hits at such an ungodly hour. I'm not **that** crazy! But I observe the moment anyway. I feel the benefits far outweigh the inconvenience.*

a number of years now, I have combined my personal cycle with the nature cycle. I continue the cycle by including my personal process in the winter solstice, spring equinox and summer solstice celebrations.

I can't give you hard evidence that there has been a drastic change in how I move through my personal cycle each year. However, I feel that there has been an enormous amount of clarity added to the process, its purpose and direction—and this could certainly be attributed to my conscious participation in the fusion of nature energy through the vehicle of the equinox/solstice cycle. It's like the pieces of my life and the direction I am taking within this year's period are appropriately energized and enhanced 4 times, and the result is that those pieces fall into place smoothly, even effortlessly—and I experience clarity.

It is also important to point out that I do not predetermine or speculate on either the garden's direction or my own at the time of the fall equinox. For both, I clearly put out the call for *whatever is to be* and I leave it at that. I'll say, "I call in my next personal cycle." For many people, this is hard, if not impossible, to do. They want to speculate about what's coming for them. They *know* what's in store. Personally, I never speculate about my future. I haven't the vaguest idea what's in store. If I did, it would probably scare the bejeesus out of me anyway. In my mind, to speculate on, predefine or predetermine the direction would put me in the position of second-guessing or even manipulating the garden or myself into a direction out of pure desire. I don't want my will to be the guiding force in this. I want to do what I am to do—for both me and the garden.

WINTER SOLSTICE

This is the celebration of the devic level and its role as architect. It is at this moment that I can feel the next natural cycle come together on the devic level and form one balanced, cohesive unit. It is also the moment when I can sense the energies of my cycle as a unit, as well.

For the ceremony, I have a more elaborate setting. This is around Christmastime and to give nature its fair share of the season, I set up what I call a Life Table. On it, I create a nature setting of greens, nests, nuts, berries, and birdfeather ornaments. I also include several jars of canned fruit or vegetables from the latest garden season and handmade crafts to

** You would connect with the
deva of your garden.*

*** A very simple process. I
talked about it in Chapter 2. All
you do is ask to be consciously
connected with your higher self.
You may feel a sense of energy
sweep through you which will
signal that you are now connected. If you feel nothing,
verify its connection by testing,
trust that the connection has
been made, and draw the card.
Believe me, that connection is
there for you.*

symbolize the creative coming together of man and nature. For the winter solstice, the Life Table candle is lit and at the moment of the solstice, I focus my attention on the devic quality of life—the creation of the blueprints.

Just after the solstice moment, I draw 2 cards from the Aquarian Tarot. For the first card, I connect with the devic level (the Deva of Perelandra*) and request that this card symbolize the spirit of the next garden cycle. The second card pertains to my personal process and I link with my own higher self for this one.** I then place the 2 cards on the Life Table. They give me the first glimpse at the direction of the 2 new cycles.

NOTE: I do not even attempt to do the garden charts I talked about in Chapter 6 until *after* the winter solstice. I feel that then the architectural blueprint is complete and its information is accessible to me.

SPRING EQUINOX

For this one, I concentrate on the nature spirit level. At the equinox moment, I sense the transfer of the entire garden reality in energy from the devic level to the nature spirit level. I also sense a shift in the overall dynamic of the garden from one of planning to one of action. Although I may already be working the garden in early March, I use this particular day to consciously recognize that vital devic and nature spirit interaction.

For my personal cycle, I feel the very same dynamic as with the nature cycle: the transfer of energy and the shift of intent from planning to action. I usually start to see my personal direction start to unfold in clearer, more tangible ways after the spring equinox.

Regarding the ceremony itself, it's another simple moment at Perelandra: the lighting of a single white candle and the conscious focusing on the matter at hand at the exact moment of the equinox.

SUMMER SOLSTICE

This is the time for celebrating the result of the whole natural process—the devic pattern successfully and fully fused into form with the active assistance of humans and nature spirits. It is the celebration of the coming together of all levels and I experience it as a celebration of joy, sunshine and laughter within all realms of nature.

To prepare for this one, I link into the nature spirit level via Pan, and am told 1 or 2 colors that best carry the vibration and intent of the specific summer solstice being celebrated.* I then buy ribbon and make a bunch of bows combining the colors, if more than one, in each bow. I place the bows at key spots around Perelandra: the garden focal point, at the edge of the Elemental Annex, my office, the reptile pond, the barn, the mailroom, the UPS station, all the other various Perelandra offices, our family areas—and on anyone or anything that happens to pass when I'm putting these things up! This visually unites Perelandra for the solstice. I leave the bows up for the week following the solstice day and carry the intent and celebration of the day throughout the week.

*You can get the colors by linking with Pan or the nature spirits of your garden, requesting that you be given the appropriate colors, and kinesiologically testing a list of colors. The positive results are the ones.

At the precise moment of the summer solstice, I light a candle and sit quietly. I often feel the energy shift at the precise solstice moment, and often I get a visualization. Once I "saw" the solstice energies lower into the garden area, then move toward the center of the garden, form into a stem which grew and grew right out into the universe. There a white lotus opened and showered the universe with solstice energy in the form of sparkling lights that looked like fireworks.

As far as my personal cycle is concerned, by this time I have a sense of what I called in and how I am moving, and it is this knowledge that I celebrate. I've always found this to be a pretty amazing process to see unfold. When I call in the cycle in the fall, I have no idea what I am getting myself into.

This completes the yearly cycle and, in the fall, I start the whole process over.

OVERLIGHTING DEVA OF PERELANDRA

It is important that one consider the power and impact of action when performed within the state of conscious awareness. The recognition of the nature cycle within the framework of the equinox and solstice rhythm is a perfect example of the fusion of action and awareness. In this particular case, we have two levels of the example. First, there is the recognition of the special dynamic energy activated and released during these four days that is directly linked to the annual natural progression of the planet.

Second, by taking a moment out to stand back from the day-to-day process and consciously acknowledge the specific stages of that process, one is able to re-infuse his commitment to the process itself. What I am saying is very similar to the relationship the Christmas or Easter festivals have to the Christian. He may struggle on a day-to-day basis to live out his life within his perceived context of Christianity, and his focus throughout the year is on the quality of his response and action within a given moment. The Christmas and Easter festivals serve to allow him to step out of the forest, as it were, where he has been most busy concentrating on each of the trees, and give him the chance to experience the overview of what he is doing. The result is a revitalization of his commitment to the day-to-day process which, in turn, enables him to step back into the forest and once again work with each tree.

The annual solstice and equinox cycle functions much in the same manner for those individuals who choose to participate. It does not matter if one is actively working in some area of nature. The overriding commitment during these times is to the natural process between spirit and matter which exists throughout the entire planet. Of course, if an individual is actively working in a natural environment, the participation during such a moment translates fully into his personal sphere of interaction and directly enhances that work process in every way.

The equinox and solstice cycle has existed on the planet since the present establishment of the patterning between the planet, its moon and its relative positioning within the solar system. I say this to remind you that cycles such as this go on around you whether they are recognized by humans or not. The elements of the planet which are already naturally aligned to such cycles receive the beneficial energies these cycles contain. Humans who have no conscious awareness of the equinox and solstice cycle also receive benefit by the mere fact that they are on the planet at the time of these shifts and releases, and by the fact that they are directly linked to the three kingdoms in nature through their physical body.

The energy contained within and released during the cycle, as Machaelle has described, relates to the natural process on all levels. If left alone, if not consciously recognized, that energy is released and results in a general recommitment to that process on the planet. But when humans enter the picture and add to it their free will in the form of a conscious choice to actively participate in the moment, they empower that moment many times

*over. This, in turn, empowers that commitment not just within the in-
dividual but within the planet as well.*

*To make the point further, anytime an individual fuses conscious aware-
ness to heretofore unconscious action, he empowers the action many times
over. Awareness is a vital dynamic within the broad picture of reality. It is
not some empty personality trait, as many humans seem to feel. It is a
reality itself with its own power and it can be used for the benefit or detri-
ment of humans. It is an aspect of human reality which can be directly
linked into the world of nature, thus benefiting both. And it is another example of co-creative partnership.*

*So, as the individual consciously links his awareness into already exist-
ing natural cycles, he empowers that cycle to the degree directly propor-
tional to his level of awareness. As his awareness broadens and deepens,
the cycle is that much more empowered, and energies released permeate
the planet and all that exists on the planet more directly and clearly.*

*In the case of the equinox and solstice cycle, it is most appropriate to
include the individual's personal evolutionary cycle consciously because
that which is inherent in the process of the personal cycle is precisely that
which is being recognized, energized and released in the equinox and
solstice cycle. If one did not recognize this similarity, there would still be
beneficial input into one's personal evolutionary cycle. You see, by definition the latter is already a part of the former. Their dynamic process is the
same. In order for one's personal process to become physically accessible
to him in every way, it must move through the natural laws of the environment in which the individual operates. How one demonstrates his process
and progression depends on the level or dimension of reality in which he
exists. Therefore, when on Earth, one demonstrates his process in physical
action and form. The key to physical action and form on the planet Earth is
nature. The framework of the process within nature that relates directly to
the translation and fusion of energy or spirit into matter or form is contained in the annual cycle of the equinox and solstice. Therefore, when one
consciously includes his personal cycle with the nature cycle, he is in fact
taking a specific dynamic (his personal cycle) which is already a part of
the whole (the equinox and solstice cycle) and bringing it to the fore, thereby spotlighting it and empowering it many times over in those areas that
are related to the whole. This same will occur for whatever part of the*

whole an individual wishes to define consciously and spotlight. Simply by bringing it forward in awareness, the individual empowers it with the prevailing dynamic of the moment.

16

HARVESTING

Now comes the moment of truth. You've done everything possible to keep the garden in balance, and it has rewarded you mightily. The aforementioned volume of food for Philadelphia awaits you.

My experience in the harvesting process has been a sense of joy and celebration for a job well done. At special times, I can feel all of nature around me, on its various levels, literally celebrate not just the health and balance of the garden, but the resulting incredible production as well. When I approach gardening, it is with my sights set on creating a balanced, healthful environment. I don't consider production. That automatically takes care of itself. So there is always this odd moment of surprise when I realize the green bean row has produced a whole slew of beans. It may sound terribly naive, but I think this probably illustrates best how changed my thoughts, focus and intent are around gardening.

There are days in the moon cycle that are best for harvesting. If I have a choice, I'll use those days accordingly. But really, when vegetables are ready and ripe it's harvest time no matter what day it is. I move into the garden with an attitude of continuation. In fact, the garden process is only half complete. The primary goal of a garden, unless it's for research, is to grow food for human consumption. At this particular point in the process,

This sounds a little pollyannaish, actually. It is more accurate to describe my early years in the garden. Now I function primarily in the role of researcher. Except as tangible evidence that we have maintained a good balance, I'm not that interested in the size of the harvest. The problem is that we usually get a boatload of produce which, as my research work has increased, I tend to grouse about. I have to stop and harvest all this stuff. (I know—some of us have real problems!) I have given most of the harvesting work over to my assistant. She gets all excited about it and carries on the tradition of those early years.

I must admit, most gardeners don't have this problem!

only the food-growing part has been accomplished. Next comes the human consumption process.

I'm making a rather obvious point out of this for a reason. I have met many people who are developing their sensitivities around nature and get caught in a quagmire of sentimentality at this point. They've experienced "talking" to and working with the intelligences of nature, and consider harvesting a head of broccoli akin to decapitation. Along the way, they have somehow forgotten that the intent of the garden is to grow food for eating. That's why gardens were invented. This intent is incorporated in the overall energy dynamic that is initiated and activated on the devic level. All that is for the purpose of consumption carries within its pattern harvesting. Not to harvest is to cut the process short and not demonstrate in action this particular aspect of the devic blueprint. The goal of the food is to be integrated with, enhance and improve human form. In simple terms, the plants know this, expect this, and harvesting does not come as a surprise to them.

Now from our point of view, consider the following. The physical body is the vehicle through which a soul interfaces with the planet. The soul has within its makeup endless potential, and connects with all of reality and truth. In order for that soul to demonstrate its full potential through form, it must have at its disposal a form that in quality is on a par with the soul. A lesser-developed physical form simply cannot maintain its stability and efficient level of functioning while being infused with the intensity of energy streaming from the soul operating on a fuller capacity. The soul adjusts to the level of the body, and functions on planet Earth in a limited scope that is relative to and on a par with the quality of the physical development of its form. It would be quite accurate if one looked at his own body/soul relationship as being in true partnership. As the soul moves through its evolutionary cycles and seeks to expand its conscious presence within form, it will require that the quality of the form be improved to a comparable level. In essence, they move through evolutionary process in tandem. This is another example of involutionary/evolutionary balance—the body having all the matter, means and ability to act in order for the soul to express what it wishes, whenever and however. There is no sense of limitation between the 2.

With the food harvested from the co-creative garden, the gardener, through eating, has the opportunity to incorporate and integrate the very shifts and changes that go into the garden itself in order to create a balanced environment. So, suddenly the balanced and healthful environment that is reflected outside you in the form of a garden can be fully realized inside your own body environment. The body itself—its cells and molecules—adjusts to the new quality and makeup of the food fuel it is now receiving. The obvious result, besides good physical health, is the development of a vehicle that can support a broader infusion of energy from the soul which then allows the individual to operate on a more expanded and aware level.

Back to harvesting. On a practical level, I harvest with the intent of doing it cleanly, precisely and with care for the parent plant involved. That's the motivating intent behind my movements. I choose between sharp tools or dexterous hands, depending on which will best facilitate my intent. And I try to move with a sense of celebration, not mutilation and murder.

PAN

The word "celebration" is most appropriate when we of the nature spirit level consider what humans refer to as the harvest. I also add to this part of the garden cycle the concept contained within the word "bridge," for whenever any element of the nature kingdoms directly interfaces with and is integrated into any other life form or element, that which is integrated serves as a bridge between the two and makes available the life essence of each to the other. Harvesting consciously initiates this dynamic, which is then brought to completion through ingestion.

And this brings me to the third word I would use in describing the dynamic intent contained within the act of harvesting—"service." The overriding intent of a garden is service. Without this, there would be no need to create such an environment. Prior to harvest, the gardener is of service as he works to assist the garden into balanced form. During this period, the garden serves humans in return by creating an environment that shifts and heals all it touches and enfolds. This is true healing service. But the garden's full capacity to serve begins with the harvest. At this point, the human experiences through harvest and ingestion the full notion of serving on all levels. And the partnership that was formed from the very instant he set foot upon the planet is celebrated by man and nature on all levels. Those humans who work with nature in the spirit of co-creativity have *acknowledged and successfully demonstrated the link they have with the nature world both physically **and** spiritually, and nature has responded in kind by producing appropriate food fuel for the physical support of the human spirit on the planet.*

COOKING

All of my friends turned to this section of the book first just to see what I would dare say about cooking. Let's get real here! The truth is, by the time I tend the garden (do the research involved) and get it to the kitchen, I've had it. Even though I now have help in the garden, I've still had it. My personal connection to the process stops at the kitchen door. The process itself doesn't stop, but my attachment to it definitely severs. I know in my heart that to take this food and joyfully and lovingly prepare it continues the quality of the process that was begun way back in February when I started the charts. And I know that there are folks out there who are completely taken with the joy and art of fine cooking. Thank God they exist. I'm not one of them. For this book, you'll all have to use your imaginations to bring the co-creative garden food cycle to its wondrous conclusion in a meal. I am simply not going to be much help to you in this. Aside from what Clarence prepares, I personally ingest the food by munching and grazing the garden directly. It's one of the perks of being the gardener. When I'm hungry, whatever is the closest edible thing tends to go into my mouth. That's about the height of my culinary interest. So, let's move on.

I would like to introduce to you an additional way to harvest a garden. This is the use of the vegetables, herbs and flowers to make what are known as flower essences. By incorporating essence production into your harvest routine, you will add another dimension of the garden's healing service. Already you experience the healing interaction from creating and working in a balanced environment. And there are, of course, the benefits from eating what is produced in this environment. With flower essences, you create your own collection of body-balancing agents to be taken orally and used throughout the year by you and your family for specific healing, rebalancing and stabilizing—not only on the physical level, but on the emotional, mental and spiritual levels as well.

Let me be more specific. The human body has within and surrounding it an electrical network. When we experience health, this electrical network is balanced and fully connected. When something in our life or environment threatens that balance, the electrical system responds by either short-circuiting or overloading. That imbalance in the electrical system immediately impacts the central nervous system. The body then goes into high gear in an effort to correct the imbalance. If our body does not succeed, we physically manifest the imbalance. We get a cold or a headache, or our allergy pops up again or another migraine belts us. Or we get back pain or our neck goes out again. Or we become seriously ill.

Flower essences work directly with both the electrical and the central nervous systems. By taking the correct essences, we immediately balance the electrical system, stabilize the nervous system and stop the domino effect that leads to illness.

If we don't take the essences and wind up getting sick, we can still take the essence(s) which will then stabilize and balance the electrical and nervous systems while the body gets on with the business of fighting off the problem. By assisting this process, flower essences drastically reduce our recovery time. In short, by using the essences, we are not asking our body to pull double duty by working to heal us systemically *and* rebalance our electrical and central nervous systems.

Flower essences have been used in wholistic healing practices in one form or another since man and medicine became a united force. In the 1930s, an English physician named Dr. Edward Bach developed a set of 38

This is a good thumbnail sketch of flower essences and how they work. For more information about the essences and how to use them with humans and animals, I recommend my book, Flower Essences: Reordering Our Understanding and Approach to Illness and Health. *(Order form is at the back of this book.)*

essences which he used to treat the underlying emotional patterns that were the cause of physical disorders and disease in his patients. This set of essences and his books are still available and used widely throughout the world today. Since Bach, several groups and organizations have continued flower essence research and developed additional essences. Perelandra is one of them. I have listed the addresses of some of the other companies in Supplies and Resources.

To further explain the flower essences and what they do, I'll give you an excerpt from a session I had with Universal Light in 1984 on a topic he referred to as horizontal healing.

UNIVERSAL LIGHT

The effect of the flower essences on form (we use "form" to indicate all form, not just human) is directly related to a universal principle: the healing process that occurs on the horizontal level. Although we may not have flower essences per se on other levels of reality, in other corners of this universe, the principle of horizontal movement, or connection, within the same level of reality remains.

To explain: Flower essences are form, are essences of form—flowers—released into another substance which is also form—water—and then given for the healing and balancing of form within a human, an animal, another plant, or even rocks. There is a strong healing quality between like and like. Edward Bach understood this when he shifted from the traditional homeopathic concept (of negative and positive—in other words, two negatives creating a positive) to that of the flower essences (of two positives, or like connecting to like). On a personality level, one finds a healing experience when he relates to a person of like mind and feels, during this communication or interchange, a sense of ease, balance, healing, and understanding. Similarly, the flower essences relate to the body or to form— one might say they are of like mind; they are horizontally connected and related.

Many flower essence practitioners and many people who use flower essences feel that the essences are successful because they respond to the soul, respond beyond the level of form. To put it bluntly, this is not true. Man understands neither the level of form nor the expansiveness within his *own level. Flower essences respond from the level of form to the level of form and are highly successful for that reason. The same holds true in any natural healing process. The mountain woman or mountain doctor who heals through the use of plants, the witch doctor in Africa who heals through the use of plants and minerals, and the Native American who uses plants, minerals and crystals have all drawn from their "brothers" (form, nature, and this includes flower essences). They have found a "friend of like mind" who is able and **eager** to come to and into them for the purpose of healing, balancing and reestablishing stability.*

To continue:

OVERLIGHTING DEVA
OF FLOWER ESSENCES

I am part of what might be called the healing devas, in that I am a part of a group of overlighting intelligences in nature who focus specifically on the various healing dynamics within and throughout the kingdoms of nature on planet Earth.

When the human soul chose to inspirit physical matter on the planet, we of nature consciously accepted a partnership with humans that related to the development of their physical form and all matters relating to what may be best described as the upkeep and maintenance of that form in every way. In present-day terminology, you may say that we have a "contractual agreement" with you humans which was initiated prior to the human soul coming to the planet, and was fully activated the very instant the first souls entered the planet's atmosphere. Nature has been completely at your disposal as you took on matter and developed your form. All that comprises human form is extracted from the three kingdoms of nature.

But form development and its maintenance through food, shelter and clothing are only a part of our agreement. In light of the universal law of horizontal healing, we also took on the responsibility to rebalance the human form during times of dysfunction. So in these areas we have the overlighting healing devas who establish the patterns in nature that respond to human form in healing ways and integrate those patterns into the specific blueprint of individual plants, animals and minerals to be recognized, unlocked and used appropriately by humans. I will say to you

HARVESTING

now that there is contained within nature a pattern of healing which responds and relates to every specific dysfunction within mankind. It is an ever-changing area of service, in that when specific diseases or dysfunctions are eliminated or released as part of the human experience, we devas who work in this area release the complementary healing pattern that has been held in custodianship within nature. Conversely, when humans introduce and take on a new dysfunctional pattern, we respond immediately and infuse the appropriate balancing pattern within the blueprint of one or more members of the kingdoms of nature.

What you call ecological problems, that you now face play directly into the very area of service of which I have been speaking. Simply put, we devas infuse the specific healing patterns in nature on its corresponding devic level. Those patterns are fully integrated. As humans have disassociated themselves from the life balances of nature and moved into a consciousness of manipulating nature solely for their own ends, they have interfered with the successful fusion of that blueprint into its form. Consequently, the healing patterns, although still available, have become clouded, unfocused, and less accessible to humans.

This brings me full circle to the enormous benefit that lies before those who consciously work to create a garden environment with the attitudes and intent described in this book. By working the garden with a mindset of co-creation rather than manipulation, one establishes an environment which is raised to a level of life above and beyond the ecological messes surrounding it. This, in turn, allows for the healing patterns to be fully present and a part of the specific forms within the garden environment. The unlocking and understanding of those patterns will be clear and complete, and the appropriate form in which the patterns are released will be developed.

It is not an exaggeration (although many will perceive it to be) to say that at some point in the future, the medical world will look to those who have established co-creative gardens to supply the pattern-infused solutions to be used within their own medical arena. These solutions will be recognized for their power, potency, and their ability to quickly get to the heart of a matter in order to return the human to balanced form. Do not underestimate the power and clarity that will be released from each co-creative garden as it establishes its position of balance.

To address the issue of flower essences: We healing devas look to the

196   PERELANDRA GARDEN WORKBOOK

plant kingdom as the primary recipients for the infusion of specific healing patterns. This is because the plant kingdom responds to and resonates with the central nervous system* in humans. All disorder and dysfunction are reflected in the nervous system, thus making accessible the problems to the plant kingdom. The scope of the nervous system in its various levels of function is no smaller than the universe itself. It is, in the body, the bridge which directly connects and fuses the soul to its form. Since the soul is linked to the universe at large, it is essential that the nervous system have, in form, the same capacity. Eventually, as soul and form balance, the nervous system will operate coequally with the soul and translate all that is accessible to the soul into and through the body. There will be no separation between the human soul and his body.

As I stated earlier, humans borrowed from the three kingdoms in nature that which was needed for an appropriate form. For the central nervous system, he borrowed primarily from the plant kingdom. And, as I have also stated, it is the plant kingdom which we primarily utilize for the infusing of the blueprint into human healing patterns. As can easily be seen, it is most appropriate for mankind to look to the plant kingdom for these healing patterns.

It is especially appropriate for the individual and his family to draw from the garden environment flower essences from those specific plants which are useful in aiding and assisting their physical balance. Consider the following: It has been said that the co-creative garden environment shifts, balances, and enhances all that its energy envelops. This includes, of course, those individuals connected with the garden. As it reaches new levels of balance, the garden literally shifts and raises all that it touches to a level relative to that which it is now on itself. The process is continued, but in a different manner, when the food is eaten. Now, those connected with the garden are being affected by its energy from without and within. The physical form is receiving an enormous amount of input from this environment. Aside from the heart influence of the individual, it is the overriding healing impulse received by the body. To continue that impulse in the form of flower essences derived from the very environment in which I speak, is to move along the healing path without missing one step, one beat.

I bring another consideration to your attention. The individual is drawn at specific times throughout his life to live in the location that best serves

The Overlighting Deva of Flower Essences is including the electrical system as part of the central nervous system.

his higher purpose. This is a truth. It does not discount human free will which allows him to override his inner knowing and establish himself in an environment based on willful desire. When the soul fuses into form it implants its own higher pattern into the nature energy in the body. At this time, like a computer readout, the individual takes on an awareness as to what environment he must be part of in order for his higher purpose to be fully stabilized and supported in form. This includes the environmental conditions and the food he must have as well as the healing patterns contained in specific members of the nature kingdoms which must be made accessible to him. At various times you will observe individuals, or sense within yourself, a compulsive drive to move or change locations. This is that inner awareness coming into consciousness and, quite often, you will feel the healing power of the new location as soon as you enter it.

Do not misunderstand what I am saying to mean that in a highly mobile society, the individual must strive for permanent roots or a series of long-term roots, or he will loose his opportunity to have needed access to important healing and stabilizing patterns. Remember that I said it is the higher purpose of the individual which fuses with nature thus creating the awareness of appropriate environmental needs. If his higher purpose includes the scenario of many homes in quick succession, roots in many corners of the world, it will result in his desire to move around the planet in directions that place him in the environment which offers physical support and healing at specific times.

Now, people who are drawn to gardening respond to this inner impulse in a very concrete manner. Without realizing it, they create their garden from those plants and minerals which hold the very healing patterns they personally need. Don't forget that the garden is designed on the devic level in the spirit of full environmental balance. It is precisely that balanced energy to which his inner soul/form awareness resonates, not an ecologically imbalanced or damaged image of this balance. When they expand their gardening awareness to include the production of flower essences, they release from fully inspirited and empowered plants these healing patterns, thus enabling them to enter a new level of personal healing. This is, in fact, a continuation of that which has already begun when they responded to the inner soul/form resonance, settled into a specific location, and established their co-creative garden.

I cannot resist giving you a glimpse into the future, for you see the relationship of humans to their movement around the planet is directly con-nected to this notion of their responding to environments which hold for them the very healing patterns they have needed. Humans are presently experiencing much mobility, a great desire to move around the planet, see the world, live in different cultures and environments. At this time in his evolution, it is important that man physically familiarize himself with the planet upon which he lives, for in the future it will be the planet as a whole, not just one corner of it, that will be the focus of his higher soul patterns and the support for his physical vehicle. In short, humans are rapidly moving into an era of global consciousness. The drive to be physi-cally present in many different countries and cultures is preparing him for this shift, not just intellectually and emotionally, but physically and spiritually as well. As he travels, his body experiences and responds to new natural patterns, not just new cultural patterns. This exposure opens him to the healing patterns needed in order to expand his physical body balance so that it can fully support the expansion of his awareness of himself and the world in which he lives.

You will note that the emphasis in the present is one of physical move-ment around the planet. But the population as a whole is moving into a new era in which movement around the planet will be primarily ac-complished on the inner levels through the development and use of the sixth sense. The physical bridge for this era is already being established through the technology of electronics and computers. These technologies are beginning to supply, through the use of physical form, what will be accomplished in the future through the use of the sixth sense. Countries are linking in ways that were never before imagined. Individuals have instan-taneous connection and communication with others in areas that used to take days of utilizing the best, most efficient transportation modes to reach. Many have noted that the world is becoming smaller. Well, it is not really becoming smaller; it is becoming whole.

Once this shift occurs and humans have instant communication through the sixth sense with anyone anywhere on the planet, the need to physically travel will no longer exist. You will see humans physically a part of one environment while at the same time experiencing total access to the rest of the planet.

This will create a change in how the human relates to the environment for physical support and healing. Remember that now the fusion of the higher purpose into form is still, for all intents and purposes, regional. It requires that the individual enter and experience a specific environment for support and healing. In the future, the higher purpose will be global, yet at the same time it will not require physical presence in every environment. At that time, the individual will be drawn back into establishing stable, long-term roots in an area that gives him his basic natural support. In the beginning, he will need to pull to him the elements of nature from outside areas that will round out the support for his new global balance. It is quite conceivable that the primary source of global balance will not come in the form of imported food, but rather in the form of flower essences made from ecologically balanced, co-creative gardens throughout the world. The high quality of nature support derived from the plant essences resonating to the greater sensitized human central nervous system will be the most desired form of global natural interchange. And the multitude of co-creative gardens then in existence will link in a new way and respond in global service to human healing.

MAKING FLOWER ESSENCES FROM YOUR GARDEN

Identifying Which Plants to Use

Well, you've decided you'd like to dive into this flower essence stuff—or perhaps just get your toes wet. The problem now is to find out which plants from the garden you are to use. This can be an overwhelming moment if you are faced with a hundred different plant varieties. There's a way out of this, trust me.

1. Make a list of every plant (flower, herb and vegetable) in the garden.

2. Connect with (simply by requesting) the Overlighting Deva of Flower Essences. (Test your connection.)

3. Ask:
   Which plants from the garden hold the healing and balancing patterns that would be best for me and my family (my group, my community) to experience in the form of flower essences now and over the coming year's cycle?

I have carefully set up this question so that the deva knows to identify only those plants that apply to you in your *current* situation or growth. This way, you won't be faced with making 60 essences, only 5 to be used the first year. Each year, I recommend that you open to this deva and identify more flower essences as they are needed.

4. Read through the garden list, testing each plant. The positive responses are the ones you now need in the form of flower essences. (In case you haven't already done it, make a list of the ones that got the positive responses.)

Preparation of Flower Essences

The following brief description will give you a basic idea of the process. Flower petals (or in some cases, leaves) are gathered at a certain time of the day, floated in a bowl of water, and exposed to sunlight for a specific amount of time (this is where the energy is released from the petals and stabilized in water). The tincture is then preserved in brandy (this keeps slimy, green things from growing), and is now ready to store away in a cool, dark place indefinitely. A quart of any 1 flower essence will probably be enough for one family's use till the children are grown and have their own garden for essence making. They are administered 1 drop at a time— not a teaspoon, but 1 drop. That's how powerful and efficient they are.

In 1984, I developed the Perelandra Rose Essences.* At that time, I received rather precise instructions from the Deva of Flower Essences on how they were to be prepared. Since then, I've developed and produced additional sets of flower essences from the garden.** Each time I've checked these original production instructions for any changes, and each time the process has remained unchanged. So, I pass along to you these instructions and the deva's comments given to me at the time I got the original information.

* The Perelandra Rose Essences (set 1) are 8 flower essences, each produced from specific roses grown in the garden, and used to stabilize and balance an individual's body/soul unit as he proceeds from day to day. As we move forward in daily process, there are mechanisms within us which are set in motion to facilitate our periods of growth. The Rose Essences address these issues.

**I have included information about the additional sets of Perelandra Essences in Appendix C.

Directions for Co-Creative Flower Essence Preparation

Tools and Ingredients:
> Scissors
> Long tweezers
> 2-qt. clear glass batter bowl (with a handle but with *no* colored
> measurements marked on the side)
> Glass saucer or plate
> Untreated or distilled water
> Quart canning jars and lids
> Brandy

Best time for selecting flowers: 8 A.M.–10:30 A.M.

Choose flowers that are about one day from being fully open.

DEVA OF FLOWER ESSENCES: At this time you have the flower on the up-swing in energy, just before it releases its full potency to the environment. By harvesting the flower at this stage, you will allow it to release its full potency to the water, instead of the environment.

Clean with hot soapy water all utensils (including scissors and tweezers), the bowl and the saucer or plate, 2 quart canning jars and lids. Do not touch the inside surface of the bowl or jars after washing. This will assure that your energy will not commingle with the essence.

1. Connect with the Deva of Flower Essences and determine how many flowers are needed to convert one quart of water to a full essence solution. Usually this will be just 1 to 5 flowers, depending mostly on size and potency.* With tiny flowers, you'll probably need more. Ninety-five percent of the time you will be working with the flower of the plant only. If you sense that some other part of the plant is to be used, ask the deva if this is one of the times you are to work with the plant's leaves (or any other part of the plant that has tested positive for you to use). If so, ask how much to use and test.

* Ask the Deva of Flower Essences how many flowers you are to use when making an essence tincture. This will help assure potency.

2. Concentrate on making one essence at a time. Collect the flowers (or leaves) *without touching them* with your hands. Catch the flower on the glass saucer as you cut if it is difficult to get a long enough stem for holding. Touching the flower (or sniffing) will disperse and change the energy you wish to use for the solution. Do not make a full circle around

the garden collecting a bouquet of flowers for all the essences you wish to make. It is important that the different flowers not be commingled.

3. In your work area, most likely the kitchen, ask the deva if you are to remove the petals from the flower. If so, remove them with scissors or tweezers (whatever method is most efficient without touching the petals with your fingers), allowing the petals to fall onto the glass saucer. If you are to keep the flower whole, cut off all its stem while lightly holding the flower with the tweezers.*

* I remove the petals for all the Rose Essences I produce and I leave most of the flowers intact for the Garden Essences I produce.

4. Fill the large batter bowl (or glass casserole dish) with 1 quart of untreated or distilled water.

5. Using the tweezers, place the flowers on the water's surface—whole flowers and petals float. Lift the petals one by one from the glass saucer, shaking off all stamen, and place them in the bowl of water so that each petal touches the water's surface.

6. Place the uncovered bowl, water and petals in a sunny spot in the garden where it won't be disturbed. At Perelandra, I've set up a table in the garden for this.

DEVA OF FLOWER ESSENCES: The direct interaction of the sun's energy with the petals and water plays an important part in the essence-making process. Since sun is important, I suggest that essences be made on a sunny day!

7. At this point in the process, open to and connect with the nature spirit level. Request to be connected with the nature spirit who will be assisting you with flower essence production. (The connection will occur immediately.) Verify your connection. *Without touching the bowl,* place your open hands on each side of it and ask this nature spirit *to release the full healing and balancing patterns of this flower to the water.* Allow about 15 seconds for the process to complete before removing your hands. You may feel the pattern being released from the flowers.**

** This is an important step and the one that makes your flower essences fully co-creative. It also gives your essences full, clear potency.

DEVA OF FLOWER ESSENCES: The release will be done electrically, then stabilized into the water by its interaction with the sun. The release of the essence by the nature spirit will occur instantly. The stabilization process will take:

> *3 hrs. on a full sunny day to 4 hrs. on a partly sunny day*
> *6 hrs. on a cloudy day (but avoid if possible)*

Although the nature spirit level can stabilize electrical energy into form instantly, it is preferable, in this case, that the seating of the essence into form be done in "form timing" not "energy timing." Stabilizing via form timing will more fully resonate horizontally to other forms for healing.

NOTE: If bugs falling into the water becomes an issue, a one-layer covering of white gauze will protect the water without interfering with the sun's interaction with the water and flowers. No extra time need be added to the stabilizing process.

(In the beginning, I thought I would have a bug problem. We have countless squads of them in the garden, and I assumed at least a squad or 2 would nose-dive into these inviting bowls of floating flowers. So I armed myself with a bunch of white gauze. And the odd thing is, I've never used it. For whatever reason, bugs simply steer clear of the bowls. I like to think it has something to do with the quality of the essence-making process being used!)

8. After the allotted time, bring the glass bowl—making sure you touch only the handle or the outside of the bowl—back to the kitchen work area. With clean tweezers, remove the petals from the bowl. Remove any foreign matter from the water with the tweezers, being careful not to touch the water with your fingers. It will not effect the potency or clarity of the essence if metal touches or is immersed into the solution as long as that metal is clean. It will compromise and alter the tincture if your fingers touch it.*

* At this stage, you have what is called a flower essence "tincture."

9. Fill 2 quart canning jars (for each quart of tincture you've made) to just under the 16-ounce mark with brandy. The ratio of brandy to flower essence solution is 40-percent brandy to 60-percent tincture or 50-50 percent. There should not be more than 50-percent brandy added to the tincture. The brandy is used as a preservative. In simple terms, it keeps slimy green things from growing in the essence tincture. With the proper amount of brandy preservative, the essences may be stored indefinitely at room temperature.

10. Fill the remainder of each jar (up to the 1-quart mark) with the flower essence tincture. Put the clean lids and bands on securely and label each jar and lid with the essence name. You might wish to include the date.

11. At this point, you are finished and may store the jars. It is suggested

that they be stored out of sunlight. Also, as stated above, they may be stored indefinitely and maintain full potency because they are preserved in brandy.

OPTION: At Perelandra, I have one more step which I'll share with you in case you'd like to do something similar. I place the quart jars of preserved and sealed essences in the center of the Perelandra garden for a final shift and stabilizing process. There, each jar is set inside the copper genesa crystal, which cleanses it and shifts its energy up "a spiral" and enhances it with tensor energy (commonly known as pyramid energy) and clear quartz and topaz energy. All parts—the flower essence tincture, brandy, tensor and mineral energies—are coalesced into one stable, fully-balanced unit. Since this is an energy step, sunshine is not necessary. I leave the jars in the genesa crystal for 1 hour. (As instructed by the Overlighting Deva of Flower Essences.) I've also been advised not to place more than 8 quart jars at a time in my 2-foot-diameter genesa crystal.

This step (or any other energy step) should be done on the same day the flower essence tincture is made. And I recommend that you first clear with the Overlighting Deva of Flower Essences any additional steps such as this that you might be considering before you add them to the process. Additional energy steps are not always appropriate, and you need to find out what's good for your flower essences.

Suggestions from a Seasoned Flower Essence Practitioner

I suggest you buy from the local pharmacy a 1-ounce or 1/2-ounce dropper bottle for each different flower essence you make. Transfer tincture into these bottles, label them, and use them for your day-to-day needs. That way, if you contaminate the tincture in any way, you can pour it out, clean the bottle and refill it from your quart stock. Since you are only using the flower essences a drop at a time, it is most unwieldy to try to use them directly from the quart jar, and in the case of contamination, you won't loose the entire quart of tincture.

The easiest way to transfer the tincture that I have found is with a turkey baster. I have been told that it is important to store the tincture in glass containers, but it is okay to transfer the tincture from container to container using clean plastic utensils. It was also suggested to me in the original instructions that for the transfer of the tincture to small bottles, the same

* For the entire set of utensils, bowls, plates and jars I use in the flower essence process, I make it a point to use them for this only. I do not use the batter bowl in the kitchen or the baster for that night's turkey.

** Just to be sure, I suggest you check with the deva to make sure you're adding the right amount of tincture drops to your concentrate bottles.

spirit of cleanliness and care not to contaminate either human to essence, or essence to essence is to be continued.*

You can purchase small bottles (dram, ounce or 1/2-ounce) of essences. The flower essences you buy in sets are tinctures that have been diluted once again to create what is called a *concentrate*. For the Perelandra essences, a 1/2-ounce dropper bottle is filled with brandy (distilled white vinegar for those who are allergic to brandy), and 10 drops of the quart-jar essence tincture are added. (That's 10 drops tincture per 1/2-ounce bottle.**) This is considered a *concentrate* of the flower essence and labeled as such. If you wish to conserve your tincture supply, you may also make concentrates in the small, pharmaceutical dropper bottles.

Ten drops sound outrageous—especially since we live in an age when such drastic, hard-hitting things are done to us in the name of health. The no-pain-no-gain mentality. But our electrical system operates completely and efficiently with the lightest of touches—a feather touch. To illustrate the point even further, at the time of use, you may choose to dilute them further by putting a couple of drops in 8 ounces of water. Full essence power is still maintained.

OVERLIGHTING DEVA OF FLOWER ESSENCES

In order to understand what Machaelle refers to as "the lightest of touches," let us add some additional insight. We refer you back to the principle of horizontal healing—like healing like. The vibratory healing pattern that is released from the flower petal to the water is on the electrical level. We of the devic level could have chosen for that pattern to release into the water on any vibratory level as long as it related directly to form, to the physical reality of all life on planet Earth. We chose the electrical level for two reasons: One, the most efficient level in which to address imbalance in form is on the electrical level. In the human body, the central nervous system with its network of nerves allows instantaneous access to the body as a whole. In essence, a complete system or network was already in place and, to be frank, could not have been more potentially efficient. Two, there are many more people inhabiting the planet than there are numbers of individual flowers. Sheer logistics became a consideration in the original decisions on the method of imprinting human healing patterns through the vehicle of plant flowers. If we were to release the pattern on a purely physical vibration level, you would need to use one flower per dose of essence. Considering the present population, it would not take very long to eradicate plant life on the planet once the idea of flower essences caught on. Due to its properties, the electrical vibration level allows the pattern to infuse into a water solution at such a high concentration that the essence may be diluted many times over in order to be made available to the population as a whole without damaging the ecological balance of the planet.

DEFINITIONS

Well, there you are with perhaps 6 quart jars of flower essences staring at you, and you say, "Now what?"

There is this little issue of identifying the specific balancing pattern contained within each essence so that you'll have an idea when to use them and why. Flower essences aren't used like traditional, drugstore-type medicines in that you do not have jars labeled "For colds and flu" as you would have on the drugstore shelves. Flower essences work with the electrical and the central nervous systems by addressing the underlying causes that may be physically manifesting in your body as a cold or flu. So, one can't say that flower essence X is for colds, because the underlying cause of the cold from one person to the next can be quite different. Having a cold only means that this is the way you physically process the imbalance created by the underlying physical, emotional, mental and/or spiritual issue.

This brings us back to the issue of identifying the healing pattern in each flower essence. The best way I know to get you started and give you an idea of how the definitions sound is for you to read the definitions of the Perelandra Garden Essences. These essences were developed as a result of this book—in fact, as a result of this chapter. I asked the healing devas, including the Deva of Flower Essences, to identify a list of plants from the Perelandra garden that would be presently helpful to everyone in general and could be defined for you in this book. This way, if you wish to make your own essences from these plants in your garden, you would already know their patterns. Also, I included the numbers of flowers nature told me to use when making my essences.

In this column, alongside the longer definitions, I include what I call the "short definitions." I realize not everyone can translate these long definitions from nature but, once you see how they were condensed into the short version, I feel certain you'll be able to work with nature to nail your own short definitions. If you get the more manageable short definitions, you'll be doing just fine.

NOTE: *Both the long and short definitions are intended for your private use only. They are copyrighted and are not to be used in a public or commercial manner without written permission from us at Perelandra.*

BROCCOLI: *For the power balance that must be maintained when one perceives himself to be under siege from outside influences. Stabilizes the body/soul unit so the person won't close down, detach and scatter.*

CAULIFLOWER: *Stabilizes and balances the child during the birth process.*

BROCCOLI: *Power. Several of these flower essences will deal with the state of power. It is one of the most sought after states today and perhaps the least understood. Consequently, individuals who relinquish their personal infinite power take on the trappings of surface finite power in their misguided attempts to rediscover and reconnect with their infinite power. Infinite power is a complex issue in that it denotes balance on all levels and in every way. Therefore, you will see coming to the foreground in the area of flower essences those flowers which address various avenues and aspects of power. The movement into a future on the planet rests heavily on humans coming to terms with this broad notion of power.*

The balancing pattern contained in broccoli focuses on the power balance which must be maintained when the individual perceives himself to be under siege on any or all of the four levels of his being. (By levels, we mean the physical, emotional, mental and spiritual or universal.) [Referred to as "PEMS."] The source of the siege is perceived to be from outside rather than from within. The potential here is for a strong reaction of self-protection. In an attempt to isolate and contain the level from which the threat seems to be occurring, there is a sudden closing down and detachment from any or all of the four levels. This renders the individual powerless, for he has scattered himself to the four winds. The essence of broccoli stabilizes the body/soul unit during this intense time, thus enabling confrontation of the perceived siege as a fully functioning and balanced body/soul unit. Broccoli Essence will be especially useful to those going through deep emotional wrenchings such as separation or divorce, those suffering from hallucinations (or mental illness that includes hallucinations as part of its pattern), and those experiencing what are perceived to be frightening sixth-sense incidents, experiences or expansions.

Use five flower clusters (one head of broccoli, if left on the plant, creates many flower clusters) to one quart of water.

CAULIFLOWER: *In the future, the essence of cauliflower will be known as "the birth essence." Whereas the Perelandra Rose Essences deal with transition and transformation on all levels throughout one's life and death process, the essence of cauliflower holds the stabilizing patterns specifically for the experience of birth. Many of the dysfunctional patterns an individual experiences throughout his entire life cycle are fused into the body and soul during the process of birth. These patterns are a result of the body/soul balance being thrown off-center due to the child's refusal to maintain conscious awareness during birth. The essence of cauliflower supports and stabilizes the awareness of both the higher, expanded soul and the conscious child-soul as the two move through birth. With these two levels stabilized in process, the body/soul unit of the child maintains its balance, thus eliminating what could crystalize into the child's body as a dysfunctional pattern.*

The Cauliflower Essence will not prevent the child from experiencing the kind of birth which is keyed into the evolutionary pattern from its soul level. It will, however, assist his ability to maintain full awareness and to focus on purpose as he moves through birth.

THE CAULIFLOWER ESSENCE BIRTH STABILIZING PROCESS: The mother should begin this support of the child's process as soon as contractions begin. One or two drops of Cauliflower Essence taken every two hours will provide the necessary internal environment for the child. By concentrating her attention on the baby at the time she is administering the drops to herself, the mother will "telegraph" the vibration of the essence directly to the child. If possible, continue the two-hour rhythm right up to birth. At the first opportunity after birth, place one drop of Cauliflower Essence directly on the lips of the newborn child and another drop two hours after birth. (Two drops of essence concentrate may be diluted in eight ounces of water. Two drops of this solution placed on the baby's lips will be tasteless.) Administer one drop concentrate or two drops water solution each morning for the next two days. This will conclude the Cauliflower Essence Stabilizing Process.

Use three clusters of flowers per quart of water.

CELERY: Restores the balance of the immune system during times when the system is being overworked or stressed. This essence is particularly helpful during long-term illnesses caused by viral or bacterial infections that overpower and can eventually break down the immune system altogether. The essence of celery holds the balancing support for the immune system during such times.

Use six young leaves (not the outer mature leaves) per quart of water.

CHIVES: Power. Chives Essence reestablishes the power one has when the internal male/female dynamics are balanced and the individual is functioning in a state of awareness within this balance. Although the herbal

CELERY: Restores balance of the immune system during times when it is being overworked or stressed, and during long-term viral or bacterial infections.

CHIVES: Reestablishes the power one has when the internal male/female dynamics are balanced and the person is functioning in a state of awareness within this balance.

essence of chives would seem to indicate a leaning towards the masculine dynamic, the flower essence holds the pattern for balance between the two, no matter which is predominant at any given time.

Use three flowers per quart of water.

COMFREY: *Repairs higher vibrational soul damage that occurred in the present or a past lifetime.*

COMFREY: *Healing.* The essence of comfrey repairs higher vibrational soul damage that may be the result of this or another lifetime. It will sometimes be used in combination with other flower essences that respond more directly to the cause(s) of the damage.

Use twelve flowers per quart of water.

CORN: *Stabilization during universal/spiritual expansion. Assists transition of experience into useful, pertinent understanding and action.*

CORN: Traditionally corn has been used for enhancing the spiritualization of Earth and human alike. Specifically, the essence of corn stabilizes the body/soul fusion of an individual during times of spiritual or universal expansion. Rather than focusing on the expansive soul seeking to move through the finite body, Corn Essence balances the individual during those times when his conscious being (which is fully of the Earth, responding to an inner yearning) reaches up and out into that vast universal expansion. Quite often, the individual responds to his yearnings by releasing himself from his physical reality and jettisoning into the universe. This vastly limits the usefulness of the experience in his daily physical reality. Corn Essence assists the individual in holding that body/soul fusion, thus allowing him to translate the universal experience into useful, pertinent understanding and action.

Use one tassel (just prior to it being fully open) per quart of water. The tassel is considered the flower of corn.

CUCUMBER: *Rebalancing during depression. Vital reattachment to life.*

CUCUMBER: The essence of cucumber is to be used to rebalance the individual during times of depression. By this, we mean those times when one feels completely detached from his life and perceives it to be a picture show playing out in front of him, but not involving him. The individual has little or no desire to re-enter the picture. Cucumber Essence strengthens the psyche which allows the individual to move from a state of depression to a vital, positive re-attachment to his life.

Use two flowers per quart of water.

DILL: *Assists individual in reclaiming power balance one has released to others. Heals victimization.*

DILL: *Power.* Dill Essence is very useful to those who have released their personal power to others and as a result live through their day-to-day routine with the attitude of a victim. It assists the individual in reclaiming balance in the area of personal power, thus resulting in a shift in his relationship with those around him.

For unlocking this balancing pattern in an essence solution, use the flower of the dill plant just prior to full opening. Use one full flower head per quart of water.

NASTURTIUM: Vital life energy on the physical level. When an individual is working predominantly from his head, his physical body will atrophy not only within the muscle structure, but in the area of vital life energy as well. This energy, as a dynamic, is directly connected to the muscle structure. Nasturtium Essence assists in keeping that connection and revitalizing the energy itself when necessary. It has a grounding effect within the individual in that it maintains life vitality on the physical level, especially at times when the focus and power on the mental level is pulling that energy to the mental processes.

NASTURTIUM: Restores vital physical life energy during times of intense mental-level focus.

Use seven flowers per quart of water. Although a mix of colors will be fine, it would be best, whenever possible, to use yellow and cream yellow exclusively or as the predominant colors.

OKRA: There are those, and I refer to quite a large group of people, who insist on seeing or translating their reality in the worst possible light. Neither depressed, for they express strong energy, nor just angry, these are people who have lost the ability to perceive beauty and joy on all levels. Okra Essence restores this ability. Now, it may sound like a "frivolous" essence—one given to a grumpy uncle—but these people live in such an all-encompassing atmosphere of gloom and doom that their attitudes challenge their physical health and well-being. Also, they create such a strong negative environment that they draw to them other negativities which exist beyond their immediate environment. Like attracting like. Eventually they create islands of powerful negative forces that dot the surface of the earth. Although not evil, these people have lost the ability to see the positive.

OKRA: Returns ability to see the positive in one's life and environment.

Use one flower per quart of water.

SALVIA (RED): Emotional stability during times of extreme stress. Salvia Essence is very helpful when an individual is plummeted into an extreme, intense emergency situation, either with himself or someone close, such as sudden injury, an automobile accident, a nuclear accident, or the diagnosis of serious illness—those times when one becomes emotionally broadsided

SALVIA: Restores emotional stability during times of extreme stress.

and feels there is nowhere to turn. This essence restores emotional stability which, in turn, allows the individual to think and function in balance as he moves through the most extreme stress.

Use twelve individual flowers (not the full spike) per quart of water.

SNAP PEA: Rebalances child or adult after a nightmare. Assists in ability to translate daily experience into positive, understandable process.

SNAP PEA (GARDEN PEA): *The snap pea is a fairly recent development in the garden pea family, but it carries the balancing pattern that is a part of the overall family vibration. It is helpful in the situation of frightening, tension-provoking dreams—nightmares. It is especially effective with children and those of child-like minds, such as the mentally or emotionally impaired. The essence of snap pea assists the individual with the translation of experience into positive, understandable process. If an individual is prone to frightening dreams, it is because he has not developed an alternative positive pattern for translating stress or fear. He has only this one avenue. Now, we do not mean the occasional frightening dream that all experience from time to time. Rather, we refer to a frequent pattern of nightmares. Snap Pea Essence (or any Garden Pea Essence) supports the individual and allows him to develop alternative, less frightening ways of expressing emotion or experience.*

Because of the support dynamic of this essence, it can also be given to someone who doesn't have frequent nightmares, but who has just experienced one particularly powerful nightmare and is having difficulty pulling out of it. Snap Pea Essence supports and enhances the ability to detach from frightening internal experience.

Use three flowers per quart of water.

SUMMER SQUASH: Restores courage to the person who experiences fear and resistance when faced with daily routine. Shyness. Phobia.

SUMMER SQUASH (YELLOW): *Courage. Whereas the Peace Essence in the Perelandra Rose Essence set pertains to the alignment of the individual with the dynamic of universal courage during times of transition and transformation, the Summer Squash Essence stabilizes the person who experiences fear and resistance when faced with his daily routine. The stability given by this essence during such times will restore the sense of calm courage needed to move forward through the day. Especially helpful to those suffering from shyness or phobias.*

Use two flowers per quart of water.

SWEET BELL PEPPER: Inner peace, clarity and calm when faced with today's stressful times. Stabilizes body/soul balance during times of stress.

SWEET BELL PEPPER (GREEN): *Inner peace. Sweet Bell Pepper Essence restores inner balance to the individual who lives and works in a stressful* environment. It helps the person move through stressful situations with clarity and inner calm. In today's society one could say, "Who doesn't have a stressful life?" Humans are presently seeking to understand and integrate ways that will enable them to live a hectic, fast-paced lifestyle while remaining healthy and in balance. Sweet Bell Pepper Essence will greatly facilitate this process, and a single drop in the morning can be as much a part of the daily routine to release stress as exercising and proper diet. This essence both stabilizes the body/soul balance during stressful situations and restores that balance should a situation throw it off. In short, it may be taken as part of the daily routine, before a specific situation that is perceived to be stressful, or after an experience should the individual be caught off guard.

Use three flowers per quart of water.

TOMATO: Cleansing. Tomato Essence is helpful when infection or disease have become seated in the body. It is particularly useful when the endocrine system is involved. This essence both stabilizes the areas of imbalance and assists the body in shattering and throwing off that which is causing the infection or disease. We use the word "shattering" deliberately, because the Tomato Essence does indeed respond swiftly in the body and in a manner that appears, may even feel, to be shattering. If the immune system has been weakened by the situation, one may need to take Celery Essence in combination with Tomato Essence.

Do not overlook this essence for the small scrape or wound that may potentially develop into a minor infection. It will be useful at these times as well, and could be considered as essential a part of your home first-aid kit as the bandaid. It may be taken orally or sprayed directly on a cut or scrape with equal effectiveness.

Use five flowers per quart of water.

TOMATO: Cleansing. Assists the body in shattering and throwing off that which is causing infection or disease.

YELLOW YARROW: Yarrow as a flower essence has been used for protection on the emotional level during times of vulnerability caused by spiritual and psychological growth process. Yellow Yarrow Essence in particular is helpful during these times in that it not only protects one from outside influence during periods of emotional vulnerability, but supports the individual in a way that allows him to soften on all levels so that the integration of his shifts can occur more easily. It protects and at the same time returns one to a state of softness, gentleness. This essence is especially

YELLOW YARROW: Emotional protection during vulnerable times. Its support softens resistance and assists the integration process.

effective for those who respond to their times of vulnerability by putting up a wall—a wall that impedes their integration process.

Use two flower clusters per one quart of water.

ZINNIA: Restores the individual's sense of playfulness, laughter and joy. Zinnia Essence assists in achieving a balanced and healthful sense of priority while allowing the letting go of those things that need not matter quite so much. It reminds the individual of the balance of a child's laughter and joy, and helps him contact the child within for his balance.

Use four flowers per quart of water. Although any one or combination of the zinnia flower colors may be used, whenever possible use pink and/or cream white. The healing and balancing pattern is particularly clear and strong in these two colors.

ZUCCHINI: Physical strength. The Zucchini Essence is especially helpful during times of convalescence after childbirth, illness or surgery, when the body is working to restore physical vitality. It may be taken during an illness as well, for the essence will assist the individual in maintaining as much of his physical strength as possible while going through the illness process.

Use two flowers per one quart of water.

HINT: After making these essences, I discovered the following modifications in the process which gave maximum contact between the flowers and the water. You might find them helpful if you make these flower essences.

CHIVES: Cut the individual flowers from the head. When doing this, be careful not to touch the flowers with your fingers. Or, float the flowers upside down so that the head is partially submerged, and most or all of the petals are touching water.

CORN: Cut the tassel into its individual stems.

DILL: Cut the individual flowers from the head. Use a clean spoon to skim the tiny flowers from the water's surface after the sun process is complete. Or, float the flower upside down so that the head is partially submerged and most or all of the petals are touching water.

SUMMER SQUASH: Using the tweezers, submerge the flower and allow it to fill with water like a cup. It will remain submerged and be fully surrounded by the water.

YELLOW YARROW: Cut the individual flowers from the cluster. Using a spoon, skim the flowers from the water's surface once the sun process is complete. Or, float the flower upside down so that the head is partially submerged and most or all of the petals are touching water.

ZUCCHINI: Fill the flower with water as in a cup in order to keep it submerged.

Getting Your Own Definitions for Different Flower Essences

Trust me. Nothing is going to make me grouchier than getting 10 requests a day from individuals who feel they need to have the essences of flowers or vegetables not listed above, and are sure the thing I want to do most that day is get their definitions for them.

Let me give you some ideas on how to discern the definitions for yourself.

Pay attention to your intuition. If you sense that you are to make an additional flower essence, your intuition is already working just fine. Let it continue to carry you through the process of learning about this essence. The easy route is to sit down with pen and paper, concentrate on the essence you wish to be defined, connect with the Overlighting Deva of Flower Essences, verbalize aloud that you would like the balancing and healing pattern for this essence and simply write down what comes to mind—*without* censoring it. You can check your accuracy in 2 ways. After using the essences for awhile, see if what you are using it for corresponds to the definition. Or, the fast, more direct check is to use kinesiology to verify the definition.

For the sake of clarity between you and the deva, it is good to set up the following specific framework:

1. Connect with the Overlighting Deva of Flower Essences. (Verify your connection.)

2. Ask that the balancing and healing pattern be given to you for the specific flower essence.

If you are getting definitions for more than 1 essence, be sure to work with only one at a time. Place the jar or bottle of essence in front of you. This will clarify to the deva which essence definition you want. When the process is completed, put that jar to one side and place the next one in front of you. Then be sure to ask again for the healing and balancing pattern for this second essence.

3. Picture the plant and its flower in your mind. That will be your starting point for the Deva of Flower Essences. It's important now that you not censor or edit your thoughts or impressions. Release your thoughts to the deva. It will lead you to a single thought or through a series of thoughts, impressions, visuals or sensations—whatever works best for you. Devas are very efficient about these things and will interface with you in whatever ways you are willing to receive them and their energy. From this, you will get an idea of the balancing pattern the flower essence holds.

I'll give you an example: For cucumber I pictured the cucumber plant and its flowers. Immediately I was struck by the clear yellow color of the flowers and the word that came to mind was "sunshine." Then I felt the sensation of a sunny disposition, which immediately led to a sensation of the opposite—depression. This gave me the direction of the definition and I was off and running with the more precise and complex translation which you have read.

4. Once you get a sense of direction, ask the deva if what you are perceiving is correct. It would be best if you verbalized your perception. Then test. If you get a positive, you've got it! Write it down before you forget it.

5. Once you are finished, close the session by disconnecting from the deva.

If you can't seem to get a handle on the definition, just use kinesiology to test yourself for your need of the flower essence. Take the flower essence whenever you receive a positive test result (thus indicating you are in need), and pay attention to how you are feeling and what is happening around you at that time. Then pay attention to how you feel after you take the flower essence. Once you use it several times, you'll be able to sense a pattern in your life or attitude that will give you the direction for the definition. You'll be functioning as the investigator putting together all the clues. As long as you test for need, you can rest assured that your inner balance is requiring this particular flower essence, and can take a drop with the confidence you are doing the right thing. Set up another session with the deva and get the definition. You'll have something to write down now.

WHEN TO USE FLOWER ESSENCES

Reprinted from Flower Essences: Reordering Our Understanding and Approach to Illness and Health.

Sometimes it is very easy to know if you need flower essences. You're sitting in a chair, eyes watering, nose running, sneezing, coughing, achey all over—in general, you look like one of those cold-remedy commercials on television. Take a hint and test yourself for the essences. In fact, any time you are sick or feel something "coming on," you can take that as a sign to test for flower essences. However, there are plenty of other times in our lives when we could test ourselves for flower essences. The following is a general guideline to give you ideas about when to test.

1. Definitely test when you are not feeling well. This can mean anything from a slight change in your energy level, to feeling something coming on, to when you are just plain sick. Concentrate on feeling the subtle warning signs that your body gives as an indication that the balance is now off and your electrical circuitry has shorted. Also anytime when you catch yourself feeling emotionally or mentally low. For example, you realize you are staring at the TV for 4 hours every night and not caring what you watch or even seeing what you're watching. Or you have no interest in anything going on around you. You can't hold your attention on anything. You just don't give a damn.

2. Test when you are injured or hurt. Test as soon after an accident as possible. I can't tell you the countless burns I've stopped from blistering, the sprains I've stopped from swelling, and the sting reactions I've reversed. An injury is a rapid assault on every level of our being and, most often, our immediate reaction is to either overload or short-circuit. If you want to see vivid evidence of the difference it makes when you use flower essences, treat yourself with essences right after you've been hurt and watch the difference in the healing process. It is amazing to see what we do not need to go through and how fast-paced the recovery and recuperation process can be when the body's electrical circuitry is strong.

3. Test when you are going through obvious change, be it positive or difficult. And maintain the testing throughout the entire period of change and adjustment. Check the kids at the beginning of the school year. Check when there has been a job change or a move to a new home. Check if the family finances suddenly take a nose-dive. Or check if the finances have suddenly turned rosy. Some people don't know how to handle success. Test

during physical changes such as menopause. And test when there has been a change in relationship: separation, divorce, a child "leaving the nest," the last child *finally* leaving the nest, a friend moving away, the death of someone close, marriage to the person you've been waiting for all of your life, or the birth of a baby.

4. Test when you are going through a therapeutic process. By this I mean physical, emotional, mental or spiritual—any situation where you are working with another person for the purpose of making a change, gaining understanding, or improving on something. These frameworks are designed to stir up a great deal. Something as simple as massage, if done correctly, can bring issues to the surface that can suddenly throw us. Flower essences support us as we move through and integrate the process. While in a therapeutic situation, I would suggest testing just prior to each session, and again right after the session.

5. Check for essences when you are faced with challenge—positive or difficult. A big exam. A major presentation. A speech. An important meeting. A contest. A trial. Any situation where the adrenalin is pumping like crazy. Why not check just prior to see if you are about to enter the challenge on all cylinders?

6. And finally, consider testing yourself daily during the first year of using flower essences. I know this sounds like a major pain in the butt, but once you learn kinesiology it only takes 10 seconds to concentrate on the flower essences and test if you need any by asking 1 question: "Do I need any flower essences?" I suggest this because it is how we uncover those patterns we have so cleverly hidden but that tend to get in our way. It also identifies which situations throw us off balance and which don't. In short, this approach to testing gives us a terrific amount of information about ourselves and how we operate on a day-to-day basis. It teaches us to be more sensitive toward ourselves, and brings to the surface our individual patterns. After about a year of this kind of fact-finding mission, you probably won't want to stop because you'll see that it really takes no time at all to test daily, and it really keeps you on top of things. But if you should decide to stop the daily testing, by a year's time you should have enough information logged about yourself to enable you to intuitively stay on top of this balance issue.

The Basic Flower Essence Test

Perhaps the easiest way to choose the flower essences needed is to look at each bottle and select the one(s) which intuitively attracts your attention. Or you can rely on your awareness of your own inner state, and choose among the flower essences based on this awareness.

But sometimes our inner state can be more complex than we realize, and perceiving accurate needs can be tricky. I recommend using kinesiology to identify which essences are needed. Here's what you do:

1. Place a dropper bottle of each flower essence in your lap. (This introduces the essences into your environment.)

2. Ask:

    Do I need any flower essences? (Test.)

If you get a negative, you're fine. Even though you may be experiencing a situation that sounds like one of the flower essence definitions, your balance is holding and you need no additional assistance. Check again later, to make sure you are still in balance.

3. If the result was positive, you need a flower essence. The easiest way to find out which one is to place the bottles one by one in your lap and ask each time:

    Do I need _____ essence?

 The flower essence(s) that tests positive is the one(s) you need.

4. Check your results by placing in your lap just the bottles that tested positive. Ask:

    Are these the only essences I need? (Test.)

If the response is positive and you need only one bottle, go to step 5.

If you get a negative, retest the other essences. A negative means you missed an essence and need to find what was missed. After retesting, ask the question once more.

    Are these the only essences I need? (Test.)

If still negative, keep testing the essences until you get a positive response to the question. This will verify to you that you have all the essences you need.

If you have more than 1 essence, you'll need to check them as a *combination* by placing all of them in your lap and asking:

Is this the combination I need? (Test.)

If you get a negative even though the flower essences tested positive when tested individually, you may need to adjust the combination. This means that when the individual essences that tested positive were put together, a combination was created that made 1 or more of those essences unnecessary. The whole was stronger and more effective than the sum of its parts. Just test each of the combination bottles separately by asking:

Do I remove this bottle from the combination? (Test.)

Whatever tests positive gets removed. Then put the remaining combination bottles in your lap and ask:

Is this combination now correct? (Test.)

You should get a positive. If you don't, test the original combination again to find the correct bottle to be removed, and keep working at it until they test positive as a unit.

5. Take the flower essences that you need, and then read their definitions. The easiest way to take the essences is to put one drop of each essence concentrate on your tongue, being careful not to touch your mouth with the dropper. If you do, wash the dropper well before placing it back in the bottle.

Then ask:

Am I now clear? (Test.)

* Unless you have the book,
Flower Essences, *in hand and can go on to the Peeling Process right away, take the flower essences for which you tested for the amount of time for which you tested (dosage). However, if you have the book in hand, take the needed essences 1 time, then disregard the dosage (the Peeling Process will supercede that dosage); refer to "Peeling" and move right into that process.*

You should test positive at this point, and 99 times out of a hundred, you will. If you test negative, don't panic. You've already double-checked your results, so this test stands as is. A negative result means that you are in need of an additional process. You need to refer to *Flower Essences*, Chapter 8 under the heading "Peeling" for what to do next.* If you don't feel like going on, it's okay. Your body is just telling you that, within the context of flower essence work, you could go on to another process. But if you don't wish to go on, just state this clearly. Your system will automatically shift and put your need on a back burner. When it's more appropriate, when you have *Flower Essences* in hand, when you want to include more flower essence processes in your testing, this need will then come forward. It does not mean you will be hindered in any way. This is an opportunity that is simply being postponed. For now, take the essences you tested positive for and in the dosage that was tested.

If you have tested positive for a bunch of essences, let's say 10 or more, and after all the double-checking you still test positive for them, take them. I know some folks feel it's not good to take more than 3 or 4 at a time, but when using kinesiology you find out precisely what essences make you strong again, reconnect or balance that circuitry, and my feeling is to take what tests positive. I let my body tell me what it needs. If from time to time I break a few established rules about the flower essences, I'll do just that as long as this is what is testing positive for me. This is how I learn both about me and about the flower essences.

However, if you do test positive for a bunch of essences, I will give you one thing to consider. More often than not, I have found that this means a person is structurally out of alignment and needs to see a chiropractor. The essences are temporarily stabilizing the electrical system until the structural alignment is regained. You can easily check this out by asking:

Do I need to see a chiropractor? (Test.)

Many chiropractors have incorporated flower essence testing in their practice, and after realigning you, they will test for whatever new essences are needed. If your chiropractor does not use flower essences, be sure to check yourself right after the appointment. (Actually, it would be a good idea to test yourself after any appointment with the chiropractor or any physician.)

Which brings me to another point: using flower essences with medicine. Flower essences do not interfere with medicine and vice versa. If a physician has prescribed medication, continue to take that medication along with the essences. Flower essences are very helpful in the healing process and work well in tandem with needed medication. Remember that by the time you are taking prescribed medication, your illness is full-fledged and you are in need of that support. You are also in need of electrical support, and that's where the essences come in. So while you are physically healing with the assistance of medication, you are stabilizing yourself electrically.

One thing to be careful about is testing while you are on medication that makes you drowsy. This will interfere with your ability to hold a focus and even make the testing itself fuzzy. So choose a time when you are your most alert to do the testing. One could say that if the medication makes you drowsy, don't operate heavy machinery or do flower essence testing.

About those medicines we prescribe for ourselves—cold remedies, cough syrup, aspirin, antacids . . . This is the area of medication in which you might consider completely changing over to flower essences. For example, instead of treating a cold with a capsule, treat it with flower essences.

The steps I gave for testing are very deliberate and precise, and are designed to verify your test results and catch errors along the way. In the beginning, while getting used to it, I recommend you stick to this approach. When you feel confident about your testing and your ability to focus well, you'll see ways to move more quickly through the process without losing "quality control." For example, you can keep the whole set in your lap, touch each bottle with a free finger, and test down the line, 1 bottle at a time. Or you can keep the box in your lap and simply read the name of each essence, keeping your attention on that specific bottle, and test down the line, 1 bottle at a time. One warning about reading the names this way: It is inevitable that as we grow accustomed to testing, we begin to get a little sloppy. One of the first things to watch out for is the practice we have of saying to ourselves 1 word, the word we've just read, while at the same time focusing our attention on the next word we want to read. For example, you are asking if you need Gruss an Aachen while, at the same time, you are looking at the label on the next bottle, Peace. You've just divided your focus, and in reality, your electrical system doesn't really know if you are asking about Gruss an Aachen or Peace, and you'll get a weak, weird-feeling test result.

For both kinesiology and the flower essences to function at their highest, it is vital that you keep your focus on precisely what you are asking and testing. The act, although cumbersome and time-consuming, of placing 1 bottle at a time in your lap eliminates a lot of the potential areas for split focus. That's why I recommend it until you feel comfortable about testing—which includes feeling comfortable about your ability to maintain focus.

To give you an idea of the time involved in testing, I'd say that in the very beginning you'll be spending about 20 to 30 minutes testing a set of 18 flower essences such as the Perelandra Garden Essences. This includes going through all the steps slowly and cranking your fingers equally as slowly—as it should be in the beginning. Very quickly, after you begin testing and get the hang of what it all feels like, it will take you about 10 to 15 minutes to test 18 essences. Now, I don't mean to sound like I'm boasting (after all, you must remember I've been doing essence testing a lot over the past 15 years), but to give you an idea of how quickly all those steps I've given you can be done, it takes me no more than 2 minutes to do an entire test readout on myself. So if everything feels cumbersome and too damned time-consuming in the beginning, just have a little patience. It'll smooth out with practice.*

* For you folks who are already using kinesiology for working with nature in your garden, you have a head start and your flower essences testing will move more quickly.

Testing for Dosage

This is to find out how many days or weeks you are to take the essences you just tested for.

1. Hold all the bottles you need in your lap.

2. Ask if you need to take the flower essence(s) more than 1 time. If negative, that means, "No, you don't need to take them more than 1 time," and you have already completed the dosage by putting 1 drop from each bottle on your tongue.

(Again, be careful not to touch your mouth with the dropper. If you touch the dropper, wash it well before putting it back into the bottle so that the flower essence won't be contaminated. Children are especially talented at touching that dropper!)

3. If positive, you will need to find out how many days you should take the flower essences and how many times per day. Do a sequential test. With the needed flower essence(s) in your lap, ask yourself:

Do I need these 1 day? (Test.)
2 days? (Test.)
3 days? (Test.)

Do a count until you get a negative response. If you need the flower essences for 3 days, you will test positive when you ask, "1 day?", "2 days?", "3 days?" When you ask, "4 days?" you will test negative. That will tell you that your system is assisted and strengthened by the flower essences for 3 days, not 4 days.

HINT: If you are testing sequentially and you get positive responses up to 14 days, switch your approach and test sequentially in weeks rather than days. This little trick will save wear and tear on the testing fingers. Just ask:

> Do I need them for 2 weeks? (Test.)
> 3 weeks? (Test.)
> 4 weeks? (Test.)

And so on until you get a negative. Let's say you get a negative on 5 weeks. That means you need them for 4 weeks. Now ask:

> Do I need them for more than 4 weeks? (Yes)
> 4 weeks plus 1 day? (Yes)
> 4 weeks plus 2 days? (Yes)
> 4 weeks plus 3 days? (No)

You need to take these essences for a total of 4 weeks plus 2 days.

Daily Dosage

Let's say you test that you need to take the flower essences for 3 days. Now using the same format, ask if you should take the essences:

> 1 time daily? (Test.)
> 2 times daily? (Test.)

And so on, until you get a negative. Most people need to take them either 1 or 2, sometimes 3, times a day. Test until you get a negative response. Your last positive will tell you how many times per day you need to take them.

Generally, flower essences are to be taken first thing in the morning and/or last thing in the evening and/or in the mid-afternoon. If you wish to be more precise with this essence business, test to see if it is best to take them in the morning, afternoon or evening, or any combination of the 3. For example, if I am testing someone who tests for a dosage of 1 time a day, I always check to see if it should be in the morning, afternoon or evening. It is usually in the morning, but I've discovered enough exceptions to that rule to test every time.

For dosages of a number of essences taken several times throughout the day over a period of days, it may be more convenient to add 5 drops of each needed essence to 8 ounces of water (spring water or distilled water is preferred) or juice.* Take 1 sip from this mixed solution each time you are to take the flower essences. (It is more effective if you hold the sip of solution in your mouth for a few seconds prior to swallowing.) You can store the mixture in the refrigerator. If the glass is emptied before you are scheduled to finish taking the essences, just make the same preparation again. HINT: You can test for the precise number of drops of each essence to go into the 8 ounces of water if you like. Just use the same sequential setup as was used to discover the dosage. For each essence, ask:

Do I need 1 drop per 8 ounces of water? (Test.)

2 drops? (Test.)

3 drops? (Test.)

And so on until you get a negative. This testing economizes to the utmost the use of your concentrates. I've suggested you use 5 drops per 8 ounces of water because in my experience, I've never tested anyone for over 5 drops (most people test an average of 3 drops), and I figure right about now you'd appreciate a break in this testing routine.

Dosage Bottles

Suppose you need several essences several times a day, you work away from the home all day, and it's real cumbersome to transport an 8-ounce glass of water everywhere. No problem. When you buy the dropper bottles for the tincture from your local pharmacy, buy a couple extra bottles to keep on hand. Make the solution as needed right in the bottle, adding 3 to 5 drops of each essence and filling the rest of the bottle with water. (Test to see how many drops you are to use for the specific size bottle you bought.) If you are planning to use this bottle for more than a couple of days, add 1 teaspoon of brandy as a preservative (use more if the essences are to be taken for longer than 2 weeks or are exposed to high temperatures) before filling with water. Shake the dosage bottle lightly. Several flower essences may be combined in 1 bottle. All the essences you need for 1 solution should be included in the single bottle. *One dropper full*, about 10 to 12 drops, from the dosage bottle can be put directly into the mouth. (Again, be careful not to touch the mouth with the dropper.)

You are now using your tincture or concentrate to make a solution.

A note on the water to be used in these solutions: Spring or untreated water is best. But if this is unavailable, tap water will suffice. You can also put the drops of essences in juice and refrigerate the solution.

One last thing: If you purchase sets of flower essences from several different producers, there is a question of whether essences from 1 set should be mixed with essences from another set. I let kinesiology answer that for me. If I test for 3 essences, 2 from the Perelandra sets and one from another, I simply test whether it is all right to combine them into 1 solution. If I get a positive result, I mix them. And I tell others that if the Perelandra flower essences test to be mixed with other essences, by all means do it.

A reminder: If you are sensitive to brandy, you may use *distilled white vinegar* as a brandy substitute for preserving your solution. Use the same amount of vinegar as you would brandy for proper preservation. Also, you can dilute the concentrates, 5 drops in 8 ounces of juice or water, and the brandy will be tasteless.

Follow-Up Testing

Often the completion of a situation or process we might be involved in will require a series of flower essences. For example, after doing the basic test, you found that you needed 2 essences for 3 days, 2 times a day. On the day following the completion of this dosage, retest for essences to find out if a new dosage is needed. You may discover that you now need 1 essence for 2 days, 2 times a day. Once this is completed, test again. Keep doing this testing each time you have completed a dosage cycle until you test that no other essences are needed. This means that you are clear, and that either the process has completed or your balance is holding well as you move through the remainder of the cycle.

The issue of follow-up testing is vital to the successful use of flower essences. Frequently I find that people are willing to do the first test, especially when they are not feeling well. They take the needed essences as prescribed and rave about how much better they feel. Then they don't do the follow-up testing, and often the result is that they slip right back into feeling lousy. Just as there are stages in the recuperation period, there are corresponding stages in the flower essences needed. And sometimes the lousy feelings may be completely gone and we think we have come to the end, but we still test the need for essences. This just means we're still in the recuperation period and, despite all evidence to the contrary, it hasn't ended yet. In short, it's important to follow through with the essence testing all the way to the end.

One other thing to caution you about: Let's say you just got rid of a bad cold. You did all the follow-up testing and you finally tested clear—no other essences needed. Everything is going well for about 5 days and then you start to feel the cold coming back. As soon as you get those first signs, go right back to testing the essences. This does not mean you made an error in the previous series of tests. Most likely it means that something unexpected has happened in your life and, while in that vulnerable period right after being sick, it just broadsided you, breaking or overloading your electrical circuitry again. If you move quickly with the essences, you'll reestablish the balance and prevent your getting sick again. However, if you do get sick again, keep testing the essences as you move through it until you test clear.

Keeping Records

This is for the people who want to find out more about themselves. Keep a record of the date, the illness or situation, the symptoms you feel, and the essences needed plus dosage. This is especially helpful during that first year or so of using the essences. Eventually you'll be able to look over the record and see what reactions and types of situations result in what symptoms—what situation tends to be the underlying cause of our headaches, or our lower backache, or our sinus trouble. It's another way of discovering personal patterns. If we know that whenever we got a sinus headache we tended to need Zinnia Essence (reconnects one to the child within; restores playfulness, laughter, joy, and a sense of healthy priorities), we can reexamine our life in light of the priorities we choose and our somber attitude, and make some changes that would strike a better balance for us. This would then break the personal patterning that results in sinus headaches. So besides using flower essences to pull us out of each sinus headache, we can use them to begin eliminating the sinus headache cycle altogether.

Surrogate Testing

There may be times when you feel that someone else could be helped by flower essences but does not have them available or is unable to test himself—a child, someone ill, a troubled friend. You can help that person by testing for the essences using a kinesiology surrogate technique which is also quite simple.

1. *Test yourself first* and take any needed flower essences to make sure you are clear before testing anyone else.*

2. Physically make contact with the person you are going to test. Have him place a hand on your knee or touch your foot with his foot. Focus on the person for a few seconds. This touching and focusing connects his electrical system to yours. Test your connection using the kinesiology technique, asking (aloud or to yourself) if you are fully connected to this person's electrical system. If negative, spend a few more seconds focusing on the individual. If either of you is being distracted, move to a quieter room or quiet the environment you are in. Encourage the other person to keep his mind focused on the hand (or foot) which is touching you. A wandering mind will cause fuzzy test results.

3. If the test for your connection to the other person was positive, you are ready to test for the flower essences. Place the bottles (or box of bottles) in your lap and ask:

Does he/she need any of these flower essences? (Test.)

If positive, place each bottle 1 at a time in *your* lap and ask if that flower essence is needed. A positive test response indicates that this particular flower essence rebalances the other person's system and makes it strong. (Remember, you have already cleared yourself of any need for the essences prior to starting the surrogate testing.) Double-check your results by placing the needed bottles in the free hand or lap of the person, and ask again if these are the flower essences needed.

If negative, make sure your connection with this person is still positive. Ask:

Am I fully connected to this person's electrical system?

If not, go back to step 2, refocus on the person, and do the testing over again.

If you are connected, retest the other essences to find what was missed. Ask again:

Are these all the essences needed? (Test.)

If the response is positive or only 1 bottle is needed, go on to step 4.

If negative, you're still missing an essence. Keep retesting the other essences until you get a positive response to the question.

For a combination, place the combination bottles in the person's free hand or lap,** and ask:

Is this the combinition he/she needs? (Test.)

If negative, adjust the combination by removing any unnecessary essences. Test each bottle separately by having the person hold it and asking:

Is this bottle needed in the combination? (Test.)

Whatever tests negative gets removed. Check the new combination by asking:

Is this combination now correct? (Test.)

Continue working with the combination until it tests positive.

4. When the needed flower essence(s) has been determined, test for how many days/weeks and how many times a day, using the same yes/no testing procedure you used on yourself. *It is important that you remain physically connected with the other person throughout the entire testing process.*

5. Administer the flower essences needed either directly on the tongue or in a glass of water. Or, fix a dosage bottle using the dosage mixtures described in *Dosage Bottles* (page 225). Test to make sure the person is now clear. Rarely will you get a negative on this.*

6. An important component of the effectiveness of all flower essences is understanding. Therefore make sure that whenever possible the person you are working with knows what flower essences are needed and how they are each defined.

FROM THE "LADY! GIVE ME A BREAK" DEPARTMENT

I am very aware that you are going to have your hands full for awhile working the concepts and ideas presented in this book into your garden process. Also, the garden should go through a few years of its healing process before flower essences are made from its plants. So, if you would like to incorporate the flower essences mentioned in this chapter into your life now, I've gone ahead and developed them from the Perelandra garden. I have included ordering information in the back of the book for these 18 flower essences and the other Perelandra Essences that are also developed from the Perelandra garden and described in Appendix C.

A final hint that might make learning all this stuff about flower essences a little easier: The *Perelandra Garden Workbook II* incorporates flower

* If you do, you'll need to get the book Flower Essences, *and check Chapter 8, the section on "Peeling," for what to do next. Unless you have the book on hand, let the person take the solution for the tested period of time. Then either get the book yourself, or let the person know they need to get the book and do the next step—the Peeling Process. Peeling is an easy process. If you don't wish to go further with this and the person doesn't want to go on, it's okay. Just make a clear decision about this. A choice not to go further just means the person will automatically put his or her need for a peeling process on the back burner until a more appropriate time. As with you, if you get in this situation because of the testing, it does not mean the person will be hindered in any way. This is an opportunity that is simply being postponed.*

HARVESTING essences in all of its processes. Learn to use the essences now and you will breeze right through *Workbook II*.

17

PUTTING THE
GARDEN TO BED

By early fall, the Perelandra garden begins to recover from the hot, dry summer days and it takes on a breathtaking beauty. I can tell that its energy is moving toward the winter rest time. Everything has a sense of completion—not that intensity I feel throughout the height of the growing season. It's a time that feels very similar to an older person who has lived well and is now moving through the later years with an air of wisdom, knowing that there are many things in life one need not get in a huge fluff about.

Sometime after the first hard frost and before the winter solstice, I "sit down" with the devas of the garden and soil, and ask for their input about the overall approach I'm to take and what specifics they'd like to see done. Usually, I till in all the dead plants, make sure my stake markers are well set in the rows, spread a little straw if needed, prepare the rose bushes for the winter, and clean and oil my tools. I also prepare the bird station with suet feeders and place a heater in the bath so that they'll have access to water throughout the cold days.

I do not attempt to keep portions of the garden producing all year.* I know that with a little care and attention, certain cold-weather plants can go on well into the winter. But I have sensed that this rest period of the

In 1992, nature and I experimented with some new heavyweight netting over the winter. I planted kale, spinach, lettuce, beets and carrots, covered the rows with the netting and watched. The seeds germinated and wintered over successfully. But, in the spring, nature suggested that for winter greens we should erect a greenhouse instead of using winter nets in the garden. We now have a greenhouse—style, specifications, location and setup approved by nature.

cycle is as vital to the garden environment as any other period throughout the year. And quite frankly, by this time I need a rest also.

When I put my first co-creative garden to bed, I had a most moving experience. For a week, I assisted the nature spirits as they gently removed the energy of each vegetable from the garden environment. It was a very intense time for me. Sixteen years later, it is still an intense time but in a different way. Nature and I are more like old, close friends who have worked together a long time and don't have to say much to one another. We just know what to do and how to put this garden to bed together. It's a nice old-slipper feeling. Now, rather than concentrate on each plant variety, we now move as a team working with a sense of the garden as a whole. Our combined focus is to shift the garden to its point of rest.

When we are finished, the garden is different but equally as beautiful as it had been throughout the growing season. Its shape is accentuated by the clearly delineated paths and the annual vegetable sections lying under a blanket of straw with nothing sticking up but the bamboo stakes marking the circular rows. It is clearly at rest.

DEVA OF THE PERELANDRA GARDEN

It is appropriate for me to point out here that within the original blueprint of each year's garden is the energy patterning for that garden's completion. How Machaelle puts her garden to bed is her response to that patterning. What is worth noting is her precision and clarity in action. And this is what I would emphasize to those of you who feel drawn to participate in this part of the blueprint.

Now, I should point out that since the garden is by definition a creation between humans and nature, it is quite reasonable to assume that all aspects of the blueprint have built in the dynamic of teamwork between the two. This includes the closing-down portion of the blueprint as well.

However you wish to respond, keep in mind the two words I have already mentioned: precision and clarity. Move with this intent and attitude and allow the energy of these two words to permeate your motions. If you do, you will complete the task in the very same spirit as the garden began so many months before when you translated the blueprint onto the charts. And, equally as important, you will set the tone for the coming garden.

The closing down of the garden is primarily an exercise in energy, in that what is being done establishes an overall dynamic of attitude and intent for the benefit of the garden environment as a whole. It is not working directly to benefit form during growth, such as fertilizing the soil or transplanting appropriately. Its purpose is to infuse attitudinal energy into that environment which serves to stabilize the rest period and, as mentioned above, set the tone for the coming cycle. Your physical movement that is permeated with the attitudes of clarity and precision, coupled with the resulting winter changes and preparations that you will actually do, are the two ways in which this important attitudinal energy is infused into the environment. It is an energy infusion through the vehicle of purposeful action.

If left on their own, nature spirits move each growth cycle through to its completion. But in any situation where humans and nature work as a team, it is vital that the teamwork be maintained throughout the entire cycle, including the process of "putting to bed." There are dynamics in this portion of the devic blueprint that are uniquely human and are to be responded to in a human manner. Nature spirits cannot do this for you.

There are no precise steps to follow in order to accomplish your role in this part of the cycle. More than anything, it is an expression of the human heart and soul translated into precise and clear action centered around the many things a gardener may do that will reflect a sense of completion. Just know that we of the nature spirit kingdom work right alongside you, focusing on our part of the task which we weave in and out of your motions, and that together, we will successfully put the garden to bed.

18

ENERGY PROCESSES FOR THE GARDEN AND, COINCIDENTALLY, THE PLANET

There are 3 energy processes I'd like to introduce to you for consideration as part of your gardening practices: the Energy Cleansing Process, the Battle Energy Cleansing Process, and the Soil Balancing and Stabilizing Process. Let me be honest. These processes are vital to the health and well-being of your garden. Now, I don't want to make you nervous, but they're vital to the health and well-being of the planet, too. So, I don't just want you to consider doing them. I want you to learn them, do them and incorporate them into your life.

As far as learning is concerned, you've already laid the foundation for this as you learned to work through nature with the processes in the previous chapters. You have the basic tools in hand. Now you'll just be applying them differently. The concept of directly working with energy to improve and balance form's condition may be a bit foreign to you, but this whole book has probably been foreign to you! So, enter this chapter in the spirit of just forging on. The key here is to follow the directions and steps just as they have been written, whether you feel, see or hear anything or not.

I have placed these 3 processes late in this book because it was important for you to get a feel for working with nature, and to develop those tools before you tackled the energy processes. However, once you learn them, you'll actually be doing them (or checking for the need to do them) right at the beginning of your garden planning time. The best way to handle this is to do the needed processes back to back. They are designed to link together well this way. These processes will clear the board, so to speak, before you get any devic information. Then, as you go through the growing cycle, you'll need to check with the deva of your garden to see if any further energy cleansing or soil balancing and stabilizing is needed. Because of the state of today's ecology, you will most likely need to do these processes regularly throughout the season. As I said, you'll need to check with the deva of your garden to find out how often. I suggest that for now you concentrate on the first round of doing these processes; then, after a week or 2, check back with the deva and ask which of the 3 processes you'll need to do again and how often (monthly? weekly? bi-weekly? etc.).

If, during the growing season, your garden is doing fine and then suddenly it has a problem that's raging out of control, check with the deva to see if any (or all) of the energy processes need to be done. Then do what's needed as soon as possible. You will be amazed at how fast a problem can turn around for you.

When beginning the co-creative process on a new piece of land or for a new garden, you most likely will find that the land needs all 3 energy processes. Again, the best way to handle this is to do all 3 processes back to back. The Energy Cleansing Process releases the surface emotional energy present in the area, and prepares for the deeper releases brought about by the Battle Energy Release Process. Then it is important to move right into the Soil Balancing and Stabilizing Process to strengthen, balance and stabilize the land. All 3 processes operate as a package and lay the foundation for any work, environmental or energy, that will follow.

When working with the energy processes we need to create a different setup with nature. It is called a coning. I hardly touched on the coning concept in the first edition of the *Workbook*.* At the time, nature and I

* In Behaving *... and the first edition of the* Workbook, *the Energy Cleansing Process and the Battle Energy Release Process are set up without the use of a coning. Obviously these 2 processes work without it. Early on I worked without the benefit of coning. However, once you read the section on coning in this book, I feel certain you'll see why working these processes in a coning is preferable.*

were just into the coning research and how to best apply it to the co-creative work. Now I'm going to touch it big time. To do this, I am including the chapter from *Workbook II* on coning.

CREATING AND WORKING IN A CONING

For the environmental processes described in the earlier *Workbook* chapters, we generally work with one specific nature intelligence at a time in order to get the information we need. For example, we'll work with the deva of a garden to find out what seeds are to be planted in what rows. We'll work with the Deva of Soil to get information regarding fertilizers. For the energy processes, we need to expand from working with 1 nature intelligence at a time to working with a team in what is called a coning.

A coning is a balanced vortex of conscious energy. The simplest way to explain a coning is to say that it is a conference call. It is as easy to create and activate a coning as it is to connect with a single nature intelligence. But, with a coning, we are working with more than 1 intelligence simultaneously.

The reason a coning is needed for energy-process work is because of the greater stability, clarity and balance it offers over working with 1 nature intelligence. When getting environmental information, it is efficient and appropriate to work with the 1 intelligence involved. A coning is unnecessary. However, with the energy processes, we are working with larger concepts involving many different facets and levels of nature. Consequently, it is far better to work in a team comprised of all involved in the area we are focused on.

A coning, by nature, has a high degree of protection built into it. Because of the larger scope of the work in the energy processes, it is important to define exactly who and what are involved in that work. All others are excluded by the mere fact that they have not been activated. In essence, a coning creates not only the team but also the room in which the team is meeting. It is important, when activating a coning, to discern between those team members who are a part of the work to be done and others who are not involved. The coning is created and activated by us—the human team member. Only those with whom we seek connection will be included.

Members will not "slide" in and out of a coning on their own. This adds to the exceptional degree of protection contained within the coning.

I have said that a coning also offers balance and clarity. A friend of mine who began to use a coning whenever she did multi-level healing work was quite impressed at the difference the coning made in both the quality of her work and the process she went through during her work. She said that when she began to do her work while "in coning," she felt as if she was sitting in a beautiful, sunlit room with the windows open and a lovely warm breeze softly blowing in. Before she learned to use a coning, she would just "connect in" with various "helpers." She said, in comparison, it was as if she was sitting in a room with no windows and struggling to get a full breath of air. What she was describing was the contrast she felt with the balance and clarity the coning gave her.

Any combination of team members can be activated for the purpose of simultaneous input. But this does not constitute a coning. A true coning has balance built into it. By this I mean a balance between nature and the human soul. In order for us to experience anything fully, we must perceive it in a balanced state; that is, it must have an equal reflection of the soul or spirit dynamics (evolution) combined with an equal reflection of the form/nature dynamics (involution). I see this balance in the shape of a V.

INVOLUTION:
NATURE
Matter
Means
Action

EVOLUTION:
SOUL/SPIRIT
Direction
Purpose

For anything to function well in form, it must have within it a balance between the involution dynamics and the evolution dynamics, or nature and spirit. The extent to which we achieve balance between the involution and evolution dynamics depends on our willingness to allow nature to partner with us. A focus that is primarily involutionary results in a person or situation that is form-oriented with little or no purpose or direction. This is essentially form and movement without soul or spirit. A focus that is primarily fixed on evolution results in an airy-fairy situation or person that has no effective order or organization and no means of action for implementation. To have soul and spirit effectively, efficiently and fully activated into form and action, one must have a balance between involution and evolution.

A coning is set up for the purpose of activating a team for specific work—in this case, the energy processes. It is therefore important for the successful completion of the work that a balance be maintained between the involution dynamics and the evolution dynamics within the coning itself. We do this by setting up a basic coning, which I call the "4-point coning," that lays a balanced involution/evolution foundation.

NATURE: Involution
1. *Devic Connection*
2. *Nature Spirit/Pan*
   Connection

SOUL/SPIRIT: Evolution
3. *White Brotherhood*
4. *Our Higher Self*

As a foundation, the 4-point coning maintains the necessary balance between (a) involution or nature, through the connection with the devic and nature spirit levels and (b) evolution, through the connection with the White Brotherhood level and the higher self of the person or persons working in the coning. We human souls supply the evolutionary dynamic only. *We cannot supply the involutionary dynamic.*

A note about the White Brotherhood: The White Brotherhood* is a large group of highly evolved souls who are dedicated to assisting the evolutionary process of moving universal reality, principles, laws and patterns through all planes and levels of form. They hold the major patterning and rhythms being utilized for the shift we are all going through from the Piscean to the Aquarian era. They are part of a balanced coning because they support and assist in assuring that any work conducted from the coning maintains its forward motion and its connection to the new Aquarian dynamics. For the purpose of a coning, we do not need to link with an individual in the White Brotherhood. In fact, it is preferred that we simply link the coning with the White Brotherhood *generally*, as if we were calling into their "office building," but not being connected to a specific office.

* Several people have written to me questioning—and sometimes complaining—about the name "White Brotherhood." They want to make sure this isn't some white supremist/sexist organization before working with them. Trust me, the White Brotherhood is neither. It includes males, females and souls beyond both persuasions, and they can outdo us any day when it comes to color.

*The name "White Brotherhood" has been used for this group for centuries. We did not coin the name here at Perelandra. It was coined by those folks on the Earth level who first began to consciously work with this group. It is not a name the group chose for itself. It is a name **we** chose for it. The words "white brotherhood" maintained the intent and integrity of the group, so it has always been acceptable to them. "White" is used to signify the reflection of all the rays of the light spectrum. "Brotherhood" is used to signify not only the family of all people but also the family of all life. This is why the work at Perelandra is closely linked with the White Brotherhood, because the group includes nature, as well.*

I have not referred you to any books on the White Brotherhood in Supplies and Resources because, from what I've seen, the material on the market is crap. I've not seen anything that bears any resemblance to what I have experienced with this group. I can't refer you to any of it in good conscience.

If you want to know more about the White Brotherhood, why not address your questions to them directly? Open a 4-point coning and state that you wish to learn more about the White Brotherhood. Then ask to be connected to the appropriate member of that "organization." Instantly, someone will join your coning. Ask him/her/it any questions you wish, and make sure the questions are in a yes/no format for kinesiology testing.

A general connection to this level assures that the evolutionary dynamic in the coning is consistent with the intent and direction of the new Aquarian shift.

We include our higher self in the coning to assure that all the work done is compatible with *our* higher direction and purpose. This input is given automatically by the mere fact that our higher self is linked into the coning.

The devic connection assures that the work being done in coning maintains an overall integrity with nature's design and direction in the area in which we are working.

The nature spirit level is connected through Pan. We do this because all nature spirits except Pan are regional, and rather than try to figure out which nature spirit or groups of nature spirits are involved in the work we wish to do, we work with Pan—the one nature spirit who is universal in dynamic and is involved in all of the nature spirit activities. To work with Pan is to maintain consistency in the coning and to give assurance that the nature spirit activity and input is fully covered at all times.

IMPORTANT: To keep you from getting frustrated, I suggest that you read this chapter completely before attempting to open a 4-point coning or doing any of the energy processes. (There are balancing and stabilizing steps listed in these processes plus references to a soil balancing kit that won't make much sense until you read the section on the Soil Balancing and Stabilizing Process.) After you have read the entire chapter, you'll have all the background information you'll need to open a coning and do each process.

Also, at various points in the process I suggest you balance and stabilize yourself with flower essences. If you are not working with flower essences, it's okay. Just skip these steps. (Then give more thought to those flower essences!)

Steps for Opening a 4-Point Coning

Have your flower essences and soil balancing kit handy.

1. State:
   I wish to open a coning.

2. Link with each appropriate member of the coning individually:
   a) the specific deva(s) involved

b) Pan

c) the White Brotherhood—State:

I'd like to be connected with the White Brotherhood.

d) your higher self—State:

I'd like to be connected with my higher self.

If you do not feel a connection occur, that's fine. Allow about 10 seconds for the connection to occur, just as you would when linking with a deva or nature spirit individually for the environmental processes. Then verify your connection (using kinesiology) before going on to the next step.

3. Balance and stabilize the coning. Ask:

What balancers are needed for the coning? (Test your soil kit balancers.)

Work with Pan to shift the balancers that tested positive into the coning just as you would work with Pan to shift balancers into the soil.*

Then ask:

What stabilizers are needed for the coning? (Test your flower essences.)

Again work with Pan to shift the essences that tested positive into the coning.

To fully understand what is done in this step, you'll need to read the section that follows on Soil Balancing and Stabilizing.

NOTE: I have found that although a coning is quite stable in itself, this stability is enhanced if the coning is balanced and stabilized. In this case, we are not working with a specific area of soil. Rather, we are balancing and stabilizing the physical reality of the coning as it relates to the natural environment in which it has been activated. I have found that I operate more smoothly in a balanced and stabilized coning than I do in a regular coning.

4. Test yourself for flower essences to make sure that the process of activating a coning did not affect your balance. Take any essences you tested positive for. You will not need to do a dosage test at this time for these essences because they are needed for 1 time only: while you are in the coning. To test yourself for essences, ask:

Do I need any flower essences? (Test.)

If no, continue with the coning steps. If yes, test the essences.

5. Do the process or work you desire.

6. When the work or process is completed, thank your team for its assistance and close down or dismantle the coning. *Closing down is important.* You do this simply by focusing on each member of the coning separately, thanking that member, and asking to be disconnected. Then verify that you are disconnected from each member by using kinesiology.

7. Test yourself for flower essences again, just to be sure that you held your balance once the coning work was completed. Take the essences that tested positive and, this time, *check for dosage* to see if you will need to take the essence(s) more than 1 time.*

** You'll find that you will need
essences more when you first
work in conings. This is a new
reality and your body isn't sure
what to do with it or how to
process it. In time your body
will acclimate to this new
reality, and your need for essences will decrease. However, it's
always good to check any time
you work in a coning—just to
be sure.*

If you have difficulty closing down the coning, and keep getting a negative kinesiological response to the question, "Am I disconnected from _____?", it is simply because you have temporarily lost your focus on what you are doing. No member of the coning is going to resist a disconnection any more than they would resist a connection. You are the one in command of the creation, activation and dismantling of the coning. All you need to do when you are having a little trouble closing down is refocus yourself on what you are doing, request a disconnection again and test to verify the disconnection. This time you will receive a positive verification.

The above steps are for opening a 4-point coning. There will be times when you will need to work with more than 4 team members. For example, with some work you will need the devas both of a garden and of soil. Also, there will be times when you will want to do an energy process with others (people, that is!). Once the 4-point coning is open and activated, your stabilizing foundation is laid, and you may add any number of team members to that foundation. The "4" in the 4-point coning refers to the 4 levels of intelligences being activated: devic, nature spirit, White Brotherhood, human soul (you). You may have any number of participants within each of those levels. The 4 points as a unit will maintain their coning balance no matter how many participants are activated within the specific levels. So, if you are working with a process that requires the Deva of Soil to be present, and 2 friends, Sally and Herbert, are participating with you during the process, you would:

1. Open the regular 4-point coning: deva of the area, Pan, White Brotherhood, your higher self.

2. Ask to be linked with the Deva of Soil.

3. Ask that Sally's higher self be connected with the coning. Test to verify this connection.

4. Ask that Herbert's higher self be connected with the coning. Test to verify the connection.

5. Balance and stabilize the coning. Then test Sally, Herbert and yourself for flower essences. Take the essences needed, 1 time only.

6. Do the process as you normally would, including Sally and Herbert in the process wherever appropriate. Be careful not to modify or alter the steps in any way in an effort to include them.

7. Once the work is complete, thank the coning team and dismantle the coning by asking to be disconnected from:

> Sally's higher self
> Herbert's higher self
> Deva of Soil
> Then, the 4-point coning:
> > a) All devic connections, one at a time
> > b) Nature Spirit/Pan
> > c) White Brotherhood
> > d) Your higher self

Test after each disconnection to make sure it has occurred.

8. Test Sally, Herbert and yourself again for flower essences. Take those essences and check for dosage for each person to see if the essences need to be taken more than 1 time.

Some Important Points to Remember about a Coning

1. You may include as many members in your team as you like and maintain involution/evolution balance as long as you begin with the regular 4-point coning as your foundation. However, it is best to include *only* those who are directly related to the work being done. Some people get a little crazy about coning activation and add 42 members who might possibly be involved or might like to be involved. If you do, you no longer have a tight, cohesive team. You now have a mob coning instead.

I urge you to resist activating a mob coning for 2 reasons.

a) It is totally unnecessary and does not strengthen or enhance a coning in any way.

b) *You*, as the initiator and activator of the coning, will feel a substantial physical drain as you try to hold a coning with an unnecessary number of members present throughout the time it takes for the process. A coning, although invisible, is a physical energy reality that will interact with you. It may require of you the same amount of output as you would expend if you were trying to hold a deep conversation with 6 people in the middle of the New York Stock Exchange on Friday afternoon. You are going to feel exhausted from this kind of overload. So, the key to "good coning-building" is to be precise about who you request to be on the team. Each member should have an integral role in the work to be done.

You will need only the 1 connection to the White Brotherhood and the 1 connection to the nature spirit level with Pan. The devic level is represented by the deva of the area you are working with (in the regular 4-point coning) and any other deva who is directly involved in the process you are working with. For the energy processes, I will include a list of who is to be linked with in the coning. The other rule of thumb about coning members is that you must include the higher self of anyone who is physically present during the work.

2. Because working in a coning is a physical phenomenon for us, we need to address some basic physical needs.

a) We should not work in a coning for more than *1 hour at a time*. This is especially true in the beginning when we are getting used to working with and in a coning. Your body needs time to adjust to this new dynamic. For the energy processes, this amount of time will more than cover the time needed for any 1 process and will usually give you enough time to do 2 or 3 processes, if necessary. If you need to do 3 energy processes and cannot do them back to back within the 1-hour time frame, close down the coning after 1 of the processes and continue with the others in a new coning later that day or the next day.

b) Activating, working with and dismantling a coning require sharp focus on our part. As a result, we may experience a protein drain. You will know you are experiencing such a drain if you come out of the coning and are suddenly attacked with a galloping case of the munchies. Oftentimes, we translate a protein drain into a desire for sweets. I have nothing against a great big piece of chocolate from time to time. But in this case, you need protein to compensate for the drain. Then eat your chocolate.

HINT: Have a bag of nuts with you while you are in a coning and occasionally down a few. This will avoid or minimize the protein drain while you are in the coning.

Also, I find that while in the coning, I do not perceive the protein drain or any hunger. It doesn't register until after I close down the coning. So I suggest that, if you are not hungry during the coning, don't let that fool you. Still have your supply of nuts handy, and eat a few throughout the session.

3. If you need to take a break during a coning session, do not close the coning and then re-open it. Just tell your team that you need a break for 15 minutes or a half-hour or whatever (don't make it a vacation). They will automatically shift the coning into what I call the "at-rest position." You may feel the intensity of the coning back off a bit when this shift occurs. It will take all of about 5 seconds. Then have your break. When you are ready to resume, announce that your break is over, and the coning will automatically shift back into its previous connection and intensity.

4. Don't get into the habit of activating conings indiscriminately. They are to be used for interlevel work and process, and not for prediction-type information. Your coning members are functioning in a team-like dynamic with you and do not wish to be asked to function in areas where your common sense should be the dominant factor. Opening a coning to ask if you should go on a specific vacation or if it would be good for you to invest money in a certain stock is not appropriate. As far as your team is concerned, such decisions are best left to your common sense and intelligence.

Don't forget: I also suggest that you limit the questions to issues that pertain to the present. Information about the future is reliable only if all issues and elements involved remain *exactly* the same as they were when you asked your questions. In a changing world populated by people with active free wills, this never happens. By the time you get to some future point in time, all issues and elements will most likely have changed perspective and position. Therefore your answers about what to do will also need to change. In short, I'm saying that it's a waste of time and a crapshoot to try to see into the future.

There is something else I would like to explain. Some people use kinesiology to discern issues about themselves. For example, they may wish to know if they are to take a certain vitamin, or if it would strengthen or weaken them to wear a certain color to a certain business meeting. These are questions that can be accurately answered using kinesiology and should not be addressed in a coning. They are to be directed to the individual who wants that information. If I want to know whether I should wear yellow or red for a special occasion in order to enhance my strength and balance, my electrical system has the answer. Either my electrical system is strong when I hold that color or it is weak. A simple kinesiology test will accurately discern this for me.

⋅🙢🙠⋅

THE ENERGY CLEANSING PROCESS

There are all kinds of environmental imbalances and pollution we gardeners have to deal with. All the way through the co-creative gardening process, we have continuously considered the issue of establishing an environment that reflects balance on all levels. The Energy Cleansing Process deals with this on the levels we can't see, and includes thought and emotional energy pollution. These can have quite an effect on an environment. As I've said, everything can be going along just fine in the garden and all of a sudden, out of nowhere, there's a horde of something eating your vegetables. I have learned that when this happens, more often than not, it is because there has been a sudden and dramatic shift in thought, intent or emotion either with the gardener, the family or the community connected with the garden — or the larger community of humankind.

Before you think I'm exaggerating, let me give you some examples.

In one community I visited, a well-established rose bed that had been thriving for several years was now dying—and for no apparent reason. The gardeners looked for all the possible problems and found nothing. The rose bed happened to be right outside the building where the community's garage and vehicle maintenance crew was headquartered. It turned out that they were in the process of some fundamental organizational changes that were not being accomplished too gracefully. In fact, there were days upon days of heated arguments. Nature functions in the role of the absorber when it comes to ungrounded, raw emotional energy that is released by humans. That is a service to us, and it gives us the time we need to learn how to express ourselves emotionally in a completely grounded, full and balanced manner. If it did not, we would be constantly battered by our own raw emotional energy. In essence, by performing this service, nature is buying us time. (More will be said on this in the Battle Energy Release Process section.) At the community in question, the roses were absorbing the emotional energy from the crew, and the energy was winning. The community gardeners had to go to these people, inform them what was happening, and request that they pay more attention to their process of change. In short, the crew responded, and the roses recuperated fully.

An odd example: In my childhood home, we had a philodendron plant in the kitchen for at least 5 years. Now, the emotional environment in that house was not life-supporting or life-giving. At best, it fostered survival. No one talked to anyone else, which taught me the discipline of observation since I didn't spend my time in verbal communication. I watched a lot—including that house plant. I swear to you, I do not recall it ever growing 1 new leaf. It didn't die, but it didn't grow either. As time went on, and I realized what a strange thing it was for this plant to never grow a new leaf, I watched it that much more. Till the day I left, I don't recall ever seeing signs of growth.

The fact is, even though emotional energy is invisible, it is no less tangible in its effect on the world of form than insects, heavy rain or drought. It has a constant impact on the garden environment (not to mention all other components of the environment at large), and can be introduced into the garden by the gardener, the family, or a national or global occurrence that fosters intense or extreme emotional response by the population at large.

In order to maintain balance in the garden, this issue must be faced. And this is where the Energy Cleansing Process comes in. It is a simple process which was given to me by the nature spirits and devas in 1977. It is designed to remove the stagnant emotional energy that is out of time and place in the environment which has absorbed it, and move that energy out of the Earth's environment and onto the next step of its evolutionary journey towards completion.

There will be a time when we humans will understand that part of

*The Findhorn Community is
in Scotland, and was originally
founded on the concepts of conscious partnership with nature
intelligences. I visited this community in 1977, after my first
co-creative year in the garden.*

ourselves we refer to as our "emotional body," and will know how to ex-press ourselves on this level in complete and balanced ways. For now, we are all in transition and learning about these things. So for the time being, we're going to have to rely on such processes and techniques as the Energy Cleansing Process to aid us in cleaning up what we would otherwise leave behind during emotional times.

I am focusing the process on the garden environment, but if you are going to use this process, I'd highly recommend that you include your entire personal environment, of which the garden is a part. Whenever we of the housekeeping department at Cluny did this at Findhorn,* which was where I introduced the process, we not only focused on the huge hotel called Cluny, but we included the entire Cluny property, outbuildings and gardens as well.

Once you get used to doing it, the process takes about 15 to 20 minutes of focus to do well. It is based on the principle that to move energy from point A to point B, all one has to do is visualize the energy at point A and see it move to point B. That's the power of focus. It is the easiest, most readily accessible tool we have for getting such jobs done. Now, this is not a meditation designed to place you in a euphoric state. It is actual work, done with the tools of visualization. During the process you will be work-ing with nature, and the responsibility of focus will lie with both you and nature. You will not be handling this responsibility alone. Your job will be to maintain your focus on what is to happen at each step along the way. Nature will automatically join with you, and move, shift or remove all the energy that is impacted by this process. *Together*, you accomplish some-thing quite tangible.

Preparation for the Energy Cleansing Process

It's important that when you close your eyes, you are able to easily visualize whatever it is you are cleansing. If it's a room, you'll need to visualize the basic shape and layout of the room. If it's a house, you must have a clear sense of the layout of the rooms and the shape of the house. For land, a farm or a community, the distance and shape of the outside boundary is important—plus the relative position of the garden, its shape and size, and any of the outbuildings. For anything larger than 1 room, I suggest that you sketch the layout of what you are working with. Nothing elaborate or detailed is needed. For land, a simple line sketch of the shape of the property with the relative placement of the buildings on the property will do. For a home in the suburbs with a small garden on a small piece of land, make a sketch of the shape of the property with rectangles to locate the house, the garden, and maybe even the dog house, the flower beds and the driveway. Use anything you feel will give you an accurate but simple representation of what you're working with.

A NOTE ABOUT ATTITUDE: It's a very special moment when we become active participants in the rebalancing of our environment, and it should not be done haphazardly or hurriedly. The biggest mistake we can make is to slip into manipulation. If we forget that we are aiming to act responsibly in this thing we call "life," and that we are choosing to participate as equal partners with the life around us, we can very easily slip from a spirit of co-creation (working in a team) to one of manipulation (demanding action on our own). Then we would not be participating in a process of balance and gentleness, but one of force and domination. Consequently, the attitude we have as we enter the energy processes is vitally important to maintaining a sense of balance while going through the cleansing process.

The Energy Cleansing Process

1. Choose and diagram the area to be cleansed. Place the diagram in front of you during the process. Have your flower essences and soil balancing kit handy.

2. Prepare yourself for doing the process. Relax and focus.

3. Open a 4-point coning. Balance and stabilize the coning. Check yourself for essences.

The deva will be the overlighting deva of the land or area you are working with. State:

I would like to be connected with the overlighting deva of this land.

You need not have a formal devic name in mind to make this connection. Just refer to it as the overlighting deva of the land you are working with.

4. See a bright white beam of light above your head. This is the light of the christ.* See the light rays from this beam move down toward you and totally envelop you in white light. State to yourself or aloud:

*If you have difficulty using this word, refer to it as "the evolutionary light" rather than the light of the christ. "Light of the christ," like "White Brotherhood," is another ancient tradition, the terminology of which has only recently come into question. It was originally used to describe the **evolutionary dynamic** contained within us all, and originally did not refer to the religious figure, Jesus Christ.

I ask that the light of the christ (evolutionary light) aid me so that what I am about to do will be for the highest good. I ask that this light help me in transmuting the ungrounded emotional energies released by us humans, and that I be protected fully during this process. I welcome your presence and thank you for your help.

5. See a second beam of light, a green light—the light of nature (the *involutionary dynamic* contained within us all). See the light totally envelop you, commingling with the white light. State:

I ask that the light of nature aid me in releasing and collecting the energies absorbed by the nature kingdoms, tangible and intangible, animate and inanimate. I also ask that the light of nature aid me so that what I am about to do will be for the highest good. I welcome your presence and thank you for your help.

6. State:

I ask that any inappropriate, stagnant, darkened or ungrounded energies be released from this intended area. I request this in *gentleness and love*, knowing that the cleansing and transmutation process I am about to be a part of is a process of life, of evolution—and not negation.

7. Now, shift your focus and visualize the area to be cleansed.

8. Visualize a thin white sheet of light forming 5 feet *below* the lowest point* of your area. Allow the outside edges of the sheet to extend 5 feet *beyond* the outside boundary of the area.

9. Ask that the light of the christ (evolutionary light) and the light of nature join you as together you *slowly*** move the sheet up and through the area to be cleansed. Allow the sheet to rise 5 feet *above* the highest point of the area you are cleansing, and then stop.

10. State that you now wish to create a bundle with the sheet and visualize you and nature carefully gathering the edges of the sheet forming a bundle of white light that totally encloses the collected energies. To the left of the bundle, see the gold cord from the light of the christ (evolutionary light). Tie the bundle closed with this cord. To the right of the sheet, see the gold cord from the light of nature, and tie it around the top of the bundle along with the first thread.

* If you're not sure where the lowest point is, simply request that this sheet form 5 feet below the area's lowest point, wherever that is. If you're not sure about the location of the highest point, just request that the sheet stop 5 feet above the highest point, wherever that is.

** If the sheet moves too slowly or too quickly, or one side is not rising at the same height, ask that the sheet stop, request any changes and then ask that the sheet continue to be raised. The changes you requested will be in place.

11. State:

> I now release the bundle to the light of the christ (evolutionary light) and the light of nature, so that the energies that have been released can be moved on to their next higher level for transmutation and the continuation of their own evolutionary process.

Watch the bundle lift. *Important:* Just watch. Don't try to determine where the next higher level is.

12. Return your focus to the now-cleansed area. Observe the area and feel, sense or see any changes.

13. Shift your focus to your breathing, focusing on your body as you inhale and exhale 3 or 4 times.

14. Recognize the various energies that assisted during this process: the white light of the christ (evolutionary light), the green light of nature, the white sheet, the 2 gold threads and the energies that were released.

15. Return your focus to the room or environment around you.

16. Balance and stabilize the work that was just completed in this process.* Ask:

> What balancers are needed for this energy cleansing? (Test your soil balancing kit.)

Work with Pan to shift the balancers into the area impacted by the Energy Cleansing Process.
Then ask:

> What stabilizers are needed for this energy cleansing? (Test the flower essences.)

Again, work with Pan to shift the stabilizers into the area impacted by the process.

* Don't panic. This gets explained later in the Soil Balancing and Stabilizing Process section.

17. If you are not doing another energy process now, thank the team, *close the 4-point coning* and test yourself for essences and dosage. If you are going on, keep the same coning activated and simply move on to the next process.

The Energy Cleansing Process Rhythm

Nature suggests that at the present time, in order to keep one's environment balanced, the Energy Cleansing Process should be done on a weekly

** Remember, when determining
when to do the energy processes for the garden, just ask the
deva of the garden for the
rhythm you are to maintain.
If you wish to cleanse the garden and the rest of your property and buildings, you can do
this all at 1 time. Your focus
will be on the larger picture
rather than just on the garden.*

basis.* This will keep the level of emotional pollution constantly moving out and prevent it from building up again. (A professional therapist, counselor, massage therapist, etc., should consider doing the process on a daily basis since that work creates a high release of emotional energy into the environment.) Also, if you or someone else in your environment are going through a particularly difficult time, it may be appropriate to cleanse the area more frequently. The Energy Cleansing Process not only assists the balance of the natural environment, but also assists our ability to maintain equilibrium on all levels by surrounding us with a balanced support environment and allowing us the opportunity to move through personal process without constantly bumping into collected emotional energy which may or may not have anything to do with the present situation. So if the situation is intense, cleanse more frequently.

Making an Energy Cleansing Process Tape

The easiest way to get through the process, especially in the beginning, is by recording the steps on tape, remembering to give yourself plenty of time to complete each step. (In order to maintain the co-creative balance in the process, it's important that no step be eliminated.) It might be helpful to have the tape machine within easy reach so that it can be turned off while the sheet is rising, giving you all the time you need.

If more people want to participate with you, have 1 person read the steps aloud and lead everyone else through the process together. If this is done, it's important that the "leader" try to be sensitive to everyone in the room and keep them moving through the process as a group.

If all else fails and you want another break, I have recorded the process and you can order an Energy Cleansing Process tape from us here at Perelandra. The ordering information is in the back of the book.

THE BATTLE ENERGY RELEASE PROCESS

I stumbled onto this process back in 1984, and it was the final touch that shifted the Perelandra garden to a completely new level of balance. I really can't say enough about the importance of this process regarding its balancing effects on a garden environment (or any environment), and the insights I was given from nature in order for me to make the necessary consciousness shifts in preparation for doing the process itself.

While doing the co-creative gardening research, I observed a level of what appeared to be an antagonistic struggle between insects and plants. I assumed that once I understood and implemented all the steps necessary for creating the balanced garden environment, this antagonism would stop. By 1984, I had all the processes and steps I give you in this book fully implemented, and still there was this level of tension. I asked why. The coning sessions I had with the Deva of Perelandra and Universal Light* in answer to this question are what follows. The result of putting these insights into a workable format is the Battle Energy Release Process, which I include immediately after the sessions.

* Universal Light: An overseeing consciousness connected with the White Brotherhood.

I first did the process at Perelandra. I had been told in 1973, by the previous owner of our land, that Confederate soldiers rested on this location prior to marching to the Battle of Manassas. In 1984 I remembered our conversation. I figured that their thoughts and fears as they prepared for battle had to be intense, and having had experience with seeing the effect of thought on form, it seemed reasonable to me that the battle-related thoughts had to have an impact on Perelandra.

Nature and I set up the process exactly as I have given you, and called for the release of the battle-related energy. Immediately, and I mean *immediately*, I saw white energy shoot out of every bit of natural form in my view. It looked like steam shooting up. This continued for about 20 minutes and created a cloudy layer of white energy about 30-feet thick that hung about 20 feet from the ground. As in the Energy Cleansing Process, I then requested that the released energy move to its next higher level within the universe. The entire cloud disappeared instantaneously.

I was then told to go into the garden, dig up some soil and hold it in my hands. Not more than 2 minutes had passed between the final release of the energy and my holding the soil. Now, from working that garden for 6 years prior, I knew the quality and makeup of my soil very well. Its base is clay.

And even with the soil work I had done co-creatively, it was still of clay character. But now, when I held the soil in my hands, I saw that its character had changed completely. It was now perfectly loamy in texture. I checked the soil in other areas of the garden and found it, too, had changed.

The garden that year also changed in character. The aggressive interaction I had observed between insects and plants for years was no longer present. And it has remained this way ever since.

After completing the process at Perelandra, nature then asked me to go to the Gettysburg Battlefields* and do the same thing. I did, and experienced a similar release of energy from the battlefields. The insights in a series of sessions I had about this process helped me enormously in understanding the relationship between battle energy and the environment. I am including those early sessions for you.

I think it's fair to say that just about every square inch of land on this planet has at some point in history experienced war or battle. Whether the specifics are known or not, just check with the deva of the area you're considering if a Battle Energy Release Process is needed and do the process. Unlike the Energy Cleansing Process that needs to be used on a regular basis for the continuous check of emotional or stressful energy, the Battle Energy Release Process needs to be used only 1 time within a specific land area when dealing with the results of an historic event. However, you will need to check with the deva from time to time about doing this process again because there are present-day events that fall under the category of battle: divorce, certain fights (verbal or physical) within the family, drive-by shootings, gang wars, drug wars, rape, robberies.... By checking with nature 2 or 3 times a year, you let it discern for you whether or not this process is needed.

*I had a right to work in this manner with the Gettysburg Battlefields because they are part of the Federal Park Service—which makes me part owner of the battlefields. Nature would not have requested I walk over to my neighbor's and do this process (or any process, for that matter) because I have no rights to the land. Equally important, this work did not compromise or violate any of the Park Service rules for the battlefields.

UNIVERSAL LIGHT: 1984
1. The Relationship between Nature and War

You, Machaelle, have been correct in that there is a connection between nature and military history. There is a healing role which must be addressed in the area where military presence has touched nature.

Remember the concept of horizontal healing: like healing like, form healing form. When war is waged, it is not simply a matter of moving form, of creating strategy of form against form, man against man, equipment

This session occurred after the first Battle Energy Release Process at Perelandra and prior to my going to the Gettysburg Battlefields.

against equipment. When war is waged, energy is moved on all levels. The many sounds of war (we use "sounds" figuratively and literally) are echoed throughout the universe on all its levels. Up to 1945, the movement of man through the instruments of war (battles, fighting) have been appropriate. It has been one structure in which man can grow, change and move forward. It has not been the only structure in the arena of global government available to man, but surely it has been the most widely used.

If one were to relate the principle of war to a concept with which you are familiar, one would say that war, as a framework of change for man, is conceptually similar to the healing form known as homeopathy, that is, negative creating positive. War, by nature, uses negative tools and disciplines—in this case, negative in that they are designed to negate life and position for the sake of advancing someone else's life, position, land. We do not indulge in the traditional value judgment of this. As a foundation, a framework, we do not see war as wrong; we see it simply as a framework. However, war as a framework for progression, change, growth, is no longer appropriate. The developments in warfare have far unbalanced that relationship of negative creating positive. Now the negative (the tools, the weaponry, the bomb) is so negative, so strong, that it would indeed be difficult for positive to rise out of the rubble. Consequently, we see the traditional war framework as simply inappropriate.

When regarding nature in light of war, one must look at several levels, aspects, functions and roles which nature has played. As you know, nature serves as a buffer for man on the planet in regard to the universal energies that flow to Earth. Were it not for nature, those energies would hit man directly, shattering him. Universal energies, by nature, are more homogenous than the energies of Earth. This, of course, relates to the fact that Earth is of form: energies are in their most differentiated state. Consequently, it is essential that nature serve as the intermediary, as it were, between the souls who reside on Earth in a state of individuation and the larger, more encompassing, homogenous energies of the universe that are available to them.

There is another role that nature plays of which man is not aware: the buffer between man and universal energies in the other direction—war being a particularly prime example of the need for this buffer.

War on Earth is, as a framework, not alien to change and growth processes in the universe. Energy has moved and frameworks have been created in similar ways; however, because of the differentiated form that war takes on Earth, it is, in its impact on the universe, extremely powerful in a most tangible, most intense way. Consequently, it has been important that nature absorb this intensity, and serve as a buffer between Earth and the universe so that the balance of the universe would not be unnecessarily tipped due to the intensity of the individuated warfare.

We speak here of the specific power that is created when one takes the whole, and clearly and fully separates it into all its parts, coordinates it, and moves it as one unit (of its many different parts) in one direction for one cause. World War II is an example of this principle on its broadest level: it was not just one country against another; it was countries against countries—the whole was larger than ever before. There were more individuated parts than ever before, but they were all successfully (albeit not easily) brought together as one unit and moved forward for one purpose.

The impact of this beyond Earth was great. Without the buffer of nature, the universe would have indeed tipped—its balance would have shifted to such a degree that its sense of natural timing would have been thrown off, and it would have needed a period of time to regain its balance. Nature absorbed this intensity and released it to the universe as a less intense and more easily absorbable energy form. Not only was the universe not tipped, but the knowledge, information, and growth experiences occurring within the framework you know as World War II were picked up and used simultaneously in various situations throughout the universe.

One could look at what we have been saying as the vertical role between man and war, nature, and ultimately, the universe. Because man has not understood the principle of energy, he has also not understood the impact of war on an energy level, on the energy around him. Up until now, war may have been an acceptable framework, but (like any framework) that does not mean that it is without implications on an energy level. All action, all intent, moves energy. This is a law man is only beginning to understand. Consequently, he has gone through thousands and thousands of years of functioning within that framework without understanding the implications of the framework except on the basest of levels. We do not use the word "basest" as a value judgment; we mean it in a form context. Reworded, one might say he has not understood the implications of his actions except on the level most "of form."

When war is waged, the coming together and the release of intense, basic emotions occurs. It is the eruption of emotion. Man cannot sustain his life within that intensity, for when the battle is over, the intensity of the battle remains. We are dealing with the very same principle you deal with in the Energy Cleansing Process: how emotions remain within a room after grief, or after a battle between husband and wife. Multiply that by five hundred thousand, and you can imagine the intensity we are dealing with on the war level. In order for man to survive, to continue living, to move out of the framework of battle and continue moving forward, he must be buffered fully from this intensity.

Nature will absorb energies but, on the whole, will not transmute them. Consequently, this enormous body of intense energy created in battle throughout the history of man is being held by nature. It has always been meant to be a temporary assignment, but as one well knows, temporary on one level can mean quite a different thing on another level. Man has the ability to transmute, to change energy from one level to another; however, what you are about to do* is go as the representative of man back into the area or field of battle to join with nature and to release that which has been held for the sake of man—to release these energies from nature, transmute them, release them from Earth, and allow them to take their balanced, healthful position within the context of the universe. Once this is done, this aspect of battle will become useful to and usable by the whole.

* The reference here is to my going to the Gettysburg Battlefields.

*Confronting these intense energies which have been held by nature, you are not acting in the role of the absorber. In fact, you are not acting in the role of the transmuter; you are acting in the role of the conductor, the orchestrator. You will **facilitate** the transmutation process and the release of these energies into their rightful place in the universe. This work will go on **outside you**. You will neither move the energies through you nor serve as the absorber. That has already been done by nature. Consequently, you will be fully protected. Your understanding of the energy dynamics will allow you to facilitate fully the processes that must go on without obstructing them. This is a technical process according to the laws of nature.*

Once these energies have been released from an area of battle, it will then be appropriate to facilitate the rebalancing and healing process within nature by doing a Soil Balancing and Stabilizing Process. We recommend that you remove the energies, test to make sure the area is clear, and then connect with the overlighting deva of that area and the Deva of Soil for the soil balancing and stabilizing. Of course, simply left alone, nature would balance; but by facilitating the process, you once again step into the role of man taking responsibility for his own actions and working co-creatively for the healing of Earth. Not only will these actions actually facilitate the healing process within the realm of nature, but they will also symbolically sound the note of man taking responsibility for the destruction that he has created within nature. So instead of it taking years, possibly, for the rebalancing of nature within the area, you will leave the area of battle having cleansed the energy that has been held within nature all these years, and given back to nature precisely what it needs for its own rebalancing—that is a good day's work.

UNIVERSAL LIGHT
2. Insights on the Battle Energy Release Process

The Battle Energy Release Process you are conducting is not a surprise to nature (in terms of your entering an area and activating this process). Nature is alert, anxious and eager to cooperate with you in releasing these energies. It has been essential that a representative of man work in co-creative partnership with nature in releasing the energies. This is a Pan/Christ* function—nature and man working together in harmony for the purpose of shifting the imbalances within the realm of nature into balance.

*Nature is fully capable of **releasing** these energies (we do not wish to confuse this with the concept of transmuting energies), but nature does not have within it the tool to transmute human energy from one level to another; it can only absorb and release. Consequently, these energies could have been released at any time, but there has been a higher timing involved. Mankind had to change and grow to a level where he could then turn around and take responsibility for the impact he has had on nature (as well as other areas) due to his own actions.*

That growth within man implies his change from Piscean to Aquarian. Since he is entering that period of active change, it is obvious that now is the time he is capable of taking custody of the energies which have been held by nature, and releasing them into the universe so that they may take their rightful place within the universal change from the Piscean to the Aquarian age. The energies that are being released on battlefields are not isolated from this change; timing has been essential in the development of

* "Pan/Christ" is the traditional phrase used for involution/evolution balance.

the Battle Energy Release Process, so as you move into the battlefields themselves, you will find that nature will not be surprised by your presence. It has been waiting for man to return and take custody of that which it has been holding for so long for his benefit.

We warn you that as you move into the battlefield area and do the process, you will experience a greater amount of energy than you experienced at Perelandra. This is one reason the battlefields will have to be approached not as one unit, but as a collection of many different smaller battles all coming together to create a single larger one. If you attempted to release the entire battlefield area at one time, you would truly run the risk of being overwhelmed. That is not a necessary experience for you to have, so we urge you to approach any battlefield as a collection of smaller battles all carried out within one well-defined geographical area, and request from the deva of the battlefield how the area is to be broken down.

Regarding the fact that energies released from nature form appear white rather than war-darkened, these energies have not been transmuted by nature, but over time by history: historical experience, the review and understanding of war; the healing (there have been generations of healing) that has occurred within the families whose husbands and sons experienced that war firsthand; and the healing that has occurred as those who experienced the battles firsthand moved from lifetime to lifetime, dealing with their role and their deaths in that war (they themselves serving in the transmutation process). So as you see, this is not just a collection of energies held by nature untouched since the battle. Those energies have automatically been transmuted because of the continuing evolution of those souls who were a part of the battle and the continuing evolution of the families who were either attached to those surrounding the battle or affected by the battle itself.

If in the future you choose to enter areas of more recent wars where the energies held by nature have not had time to be transmuted by those touched by that war (we think specifically of Vietnam), you will have to alter the process you are using in order to accommodate the untransmuted energies. We suggest, however, that the Battle Energy Release Process not be done for any battlefield, old or new, without prior agreement from the deva of that area. In this way, the various timings known to nature but not necessarily to humans can be maintained.

Recently you have considered the notion that nothing you experience *ever remains forever on the back burner: how, somewhere down the road, you will have to face everything—all emotions, pain, experience—and fully and completely ground those experiences within you, understand their purpose, and transmute them. The transmuted battle-related energies fit within this notion of nothing remaining forever on a back burner. What you are experiencing now by viewing the white, transmuted battle energies is one result of looking at everything on the back burners—bringing it forward, dealing with it, grounding it, and transmuting it. That process within an individual soul does not remain isolated within the soul. As each man who died at the Battle of Gettysburg grounded his own experience, whether in that lifetime or after death, that energy was transmuted.*

This only serves to give you another example of the power which man's actions have, the power man has within himself, and the broad implications of his actions. If man can act in such a way that he can create a huge, massive body of traumatic energy that needs to be held within the realm of nature so that man himself will not self-destruct from its rawness and intensity, then he also has the power to transmute it. It works both ways. Man on Earth has the tendency to see only how destructive he can be; he does not have self-confidence about how constructive he can be.

The question arises: If man has had the ability and has actually transmuted this energy that has been held within nature, then why have these areas remained ecologically unbalanced? The issue here is not primarily the negativity of energy, although the initial impact on nature was this intense negativity: the massive cloud of raw emotional energy released in war and absorbed by nature initially threw off the natural ecological balance. However, the energy of the Battle of Gettysburg has been transmuted, and what remains and continues to throw off the ecological balance in the area is not negativity. The simple fact is that a large body of man-made energy is being held in custody by nature. In essence, nature has been willingly and eagerly performing a service for man at a cost to its own balance and development. While these areas have maintained this service, the ecological balance has never been able to be retained or rediscovered. Once the areas release this body of energy, there will be a strong and evident move toward reestablishing ecological balance.

We emphasize that the role of nature in this area of service has been a willing and cooperative role, not something that was forced on nature.

Nature is an intelligence which can willingly choose its position within the evolutionary process of man on Earth. It could have refused this role; however, had it refused, man would have been in a lot of trouble. He would not have had the healing time he needed in order to evolve to the point where he could then come back and take full custody of these energies. As we have said, nature has buffered man from these energies; it has been an important and necessary service.

ENERGY PROCESSES
FOR THE GARDEN
AND THE PLANET

Regarding the question of nuns praying over battlefields,* they have laid the groundwork upon which you are building. The feeling to which they are responding—the major feeling, as we see it—is from the effect of the energy being held. They are responding to this service. Although they wish to release these energies, this "stigma of war," from these battlefield areas, it has not yet been time, and they have not had the wherewithal to do this. Consequently, the direction of their prayer has been more aligned to the holding pattern and has helped achieve a relative Pan/Christ balance within that pattern. They are, in essence, women who intuitively understand that something within man needs to happen in these areas in order to balance the horror of war. They have responded with prayer, and their response has not gone unheeded nor been ineffectual. If one could see the energy of their prayer, one might visualize it moving from them into the massive energy being held by nature, and that in itself has had a healing effect. However, we repeat: The effort by the nuns has not served to release this energy from the realm of nature, because they have not understood the role of nature in this. Consequently, they have not been able to respond with a process that would release the energies from nature.

* During a discussion I had with someone while working on the Battle Energy Release Process, the question was raised about nuns who spend their lives in service by praying over battlefields. From nature's perspective, does this have any effect on the battlefield?

At this time, we would like to move on to a related matter—to expand on the notion of how an individual soul can affect the impact of history by looking fully and completely at his role within history.

The concept of history has several levels. One level can best be described as simply what happened: A leading to B leading to C creating D. When looked at sequentially, it is quite easy to see how one act in history can affect future acts, movement and changes. However, these things of the future and these acts of the past are not static; their impact is constantly changing. First of all, historians look back at events and judge and re-evaluate them—that alone changes the impact of history. There may have been a specific event which for a number of years carried a particular impact on history. Then suddenly, this event is viewed differently and re-evaluated. From that point on, its impact will indeed change. It may change again and again, depending on how many times it is viewed differently and re-evaluated. Each time it changes, its impact on the present and on the future also changes.

What man does not fully recognize right now is the impact of the souls who were involved in a particular event as they themselves evolve, re-evaluate, change, and look at things they have put on the back burner. As they go through this process, they activate a transmutation process within the event itself.

One might say that history itself goes through an evolutionary process. It is a fluid, moving phenomenon. No one can say of his own life, "Well, I have done that, so now it's over and I never need look at it again." If his personal role in a specific event is incomplete and ungrounded, he will have to look at it again—and again and again. Each time, if he so chooses, he can change his evaluation of the event and his role in it, and thus change the impact, the energy around the event itself.

Another point is that emotions are inherent in every historical event. When individual participants of an historical event place things from that event onto their personal back burners, it is usually in the area of emotions. We would have to say that the principal area preventing or interfering with the forward evolution of history comes from the level of the emotions that participants have placed on back burners. As man evolves within himself, he will have opportunity to recall those emotions.

Now, he often places emotions on the back burner so that he can move forward. One can say that the phenomenon of placing emotional reaction to an historical event on the back burner is very similar indeed to the phenomenon of nature absorbing the emotional energy released during war. If nature did not do this, man would not have the space to evolve and grow in order to get to the point of being able to come back and take full custody of what nature has been holding. Quite often, the emotions experienced during the outplay of historical events are so intense and raw that in order to continue, man must place these emotions on a back burner. But they were never meant to stay there—just as nature was never meant to hold battle energies forever—and must be brought back up when he is ready for those emotions to ground fully through him, to be transmuted and released. When that happens, the body of emotion inherent within the historical event itself will also shift. As each man takes custody of his own emotions within the historical event, the general body of the event will shift.

We do not view placing events on the back burner as an escape, but as survival. There are some experiences within each man's life that must be placed on the back burner until he has the full opportunity and wherewithal to fully ground those experiences through him, transmuting whatever energies need to be transmuted and completing his role on the impact of an historical event (any past event or experience within a person's life, within any lifetime).

The consideration of history as a fluid, evolutionary process is another example of how everything that is, everything that exists on Earth, is an active participant in this change from the Piscean to the Aquarian era. Everything moves, shifts and evolves. Just as separating truth from insanity within the area of war alters the body of information on war available to this universe and beyond, so, too, does the fluid, evolutionary process of history change that body of information available to this universe and beyond. These changes are not just for the benefit of Earth. All of these changes are for the benefit of the whole—this universe and that which is beyond.

UNIVERSAL LIGHT
3. Insights on the Battle Energy Release Process Given After the Gettysburg Battlefield Work

Each battlefield, each battle, each war, is a microcosm reflecting the position of the universe. So often people think war has been an ugly blot on the history of Earth, that it has reflected the ugliness of man on Earth. Well, we do not see it that way, in those judgmental terms. All the wars that have occurred on Earth throughout history have reflected a universal mindset, not a mindset unique to Earth alone. This is another reason how and why the evolution of specific areas of Earth affect the entire universe and beyond. If the effect can flow from planet Earth out through the universe and beyond, then one must consider that the effect also flows the other way—from beyond the universe, into it, and to Earth. This flow is a two-way dynamic involving evolution and effect.

The work accomplished at Gettysburg [Wednesday, March 7, 1984] *has sounded a clear, strong note throughout the universe and beyond; indeed, the mindset of souls, of all that exists, has truly begun to change and is changing. That which has been rippling throughout the universe (this change in terms of problem-solving, this movement from violence to non-violence) was clearly grounded within the arena of form.*

Remember that a battle is a microcosm of the universal mindset that is acted out in the arena of form, and it is not that Earth has acted out universal wars or battles. One must try not to superimpose the form reality of a battle onto other arenas and areas of the universe. What we are suggesting is that man on Earth, in tune with and in touch with the evolution of the universe, taps into the prevailing mindset and interprets that into the arena of form. Up to now, the primary interpretation has been battle, war. Although he is not acting out some universal war that is clashing well beyond his own sense of vision, he is showing very clearly in a form-like manner the implications of the universal mindset were it to be translated into form.

Now, a change takes preparation, and the preparation for the change from Piscean to Aquarian in the arena of war has gone on for some time. There have been many questions arising in people's minds. There has been the realization that since the dropping of the atomic bomb in 1945, war on Earth has been inappropriate. This became the catalyst of an intense period of preparation within the mindset of all souls to move from the old way of doing things to the new. Preparation is not the thing that strikes the tuning fork; it is what gets man to the point where he can strike the tuning fork.

The change from the old to the new, from the Piscean to the Aquarian, begins in the heart. It is a shift in attitude, in how one perceives something. Man has had to go through years of challenge, thought, and struggle in preparation for that shift in attitude, and attitudes have begun to change. But just as a battle is a microcosm of universal thought acted out in the arena of form, it can also serve as a microcosm of a massive change in attitude come together and acted out within its arena (such as a battlefield)—again within the framework of form.

The preparation on Earth up to this point has required that man change his attitude about different realities and events that have occurred around him. For example, his vision about war has expanded so that if one were to break down the components of war and look at just one component—say, death—I think it would be easy to see how man has changed his attitudes. The narrow vision from which he has worked has been that a man dies and that's that; there is nothing more, nothing further. He dies, rots, and goes to earth. Over the years, a large group of humans on Earth have shifted their attitude and understanding of what death is. With that one shift in attitude alone, one can re-enter a battlefield area and view it from a completely different perspective.

Death is just one component of war. There have been many components that have changed, that have gone through a preparation period. What you did when you re-entered Gettysburg was to take the various components that have changed, create a framework called the Battle Energy Release Process using those new attitudes, and therewith release the remnants of the old. You created new form, new structure, and released the remnants of the old which happened to be held within the nature kingdoms. Again, we would like to point out that neither this change in attitude about death nor this collection of attitudes surrounding war is unique to Earth—they are universal. Just as man on Earth is not isolated from the universe, we can also say that this collection of attitudinal changes is a result of man's dance with the universal flow, interpreting that which is within the arena of form. Had there not been a universal transition in progress, and had not man on Earth prepared himself to join in this transition, it would have been impossible for you to effect an efficient framework to accomplish what you did Wednesday. You would have, in essence, superimposed a framework onto the situation and struck an alien note. The Gettysburg battles were fully connected to the universe, so a man-made structure outside that connection simply could not have accomplished any kind of energy move. Again, it would have been an alien structure. Wednesday you tapped into that which is the universe, translated it into structure, and enacted it within the framework of form, thus completing the whole picture. The universal microcosm, acted out within the framework of war, has now changed.

Remember that war is a collection of universal thought patterns come together within the structure of form and acted out in a microcosmic way. At Gettysburg, you took that collection of thought patterns (which had changed since the battle), created new structure, and through the framework of form released the final energy of the old that was being held within the nature kingdoms. Gettysburg was fought within the framework of one understanding. You reflected within yourself the many changes within that framework which have occurred within man on Earth and within the universe. You reflected those changes through the form of the process you performed throughout the battlefields, the result of which was the final release of energy that had been held by nature since the battles.

The principle of horizontal healing plays a strong role in what occurred Wednesday and in what we are saying. The energies of the transition were grounded into a framework of form (The Battle Energy Release Process). Because that intent, attitude, shift, and change were translated and grounded into form, their effect on what was released in battle, in form, was far greater and far more efficient than anything else that could have occurred. This process demonstrates the principle of horizontal healing (form healing form being just one demonstration thereof) and is a fine example of how new attitudes can be translated into the structure of form and used to heal, change, and shift the results of old attitudes.

This brings us to the word "love." What greater love is there than empathy, compassion and understanding. The impetus to all the changes that have occurred, are occurring, and will occur regarding the concept of war lie within the areas of empathy, compassion and understanding—to use one word, love. As the energy of love expands within man, how he views what is around him shifts and changes. At the risk of sounding trite in using that well-worn word, we would say that the basis of what occurred Wednesday rests within the area of love.

The preparation for what occurred lies within the area of man's growth in understanding love. The changes in man's attitudes toward history, death, decision-making, nature, his connection to the universe, the universe's connection to him, the dynamic of man's and nature's reality (known as energy)—all those attitudinal changes center around his shift in empathy, compassion and understanding; his growth in love; his ability to open himself to something greater, wider and broader.

If one were to see Wednesday's result as a fully vibrating tuning fork, one would also have to see that what struck the tuning fork to make it vibrate fully were attitudinal changes brought about by empathy, compassion and understanding—that is, love. At the same time the tuning fork began to vibrate fully and completely, the universe was infused with an enormous rush of energy that also can best be described as the energy of love—that is, empathy, compassion and understanding. It is no wonder that what may have appeared to you to be a small act (when compared to the universe) had such an impact on the whole.

UNIVERSAL LIGHT
4. The Battle Energy Release Process
From the Vantage Point of Nature

The role of nature in battlefield areas such as Gettysburg has been to hold a vast energy while man has consciously and unconsciously worked to transform that dynamic into something less traumatic until the change has reached the point where he may return to an area such as Gettysburg and reclaim the energy. We will talk about the effects of releasing such energy. To hold the energy is a voluntary decision on nature's part, in its service to mankind. But there has been a cost to both nature and man.

When nature holds such a vast body of energy as at a battlefield, its own perfect balance is tipped. When nature places its balance to one side, its entire physical makeup reflects this shift in intent. Nature voluntarily has shifted its intent—from existing within the laws of spirit flowing fully and perfectly through form—to existing off-balance. When that occurred in Gettysburg, for example, the entire physical makeup of nature changed there. It was an all-encompassing ecological shift of every cell and molecule. Everything within the environment of the Gettysburg battlefield shifted its makeup, function and purpose to a position that was slightly at odds with the surrounding environment. It created an environment of stress, an environment of slight abrasion. We say slight because had nature reflected a dramatic change on all levels, in proportion to what it had absorbed, the nature kingdom itself would have been destroyed there. The environment would have been destroyed.

Imagine the entire environment of Gettysburg to be a set of gears. Each gear went slightly out of alignment in relation to the other gears and this created a slightly abrasive situation with an immediate physical change in the environment. The soil shifted, the health of the trees changed, the basic overall health of the environment went from a position of strength to a position of vulnerability, very much like a human body under stress. As the years progressed and nature in the area continued to function off-balance, its physical form continued to deteriorate. The makeup of Gettysburg shifted as the town grew, more people came and technology changed, and the environment did not enfold these changes into a balanced ecology. Very much like the domino effect, an increasingly more complicated and complex imbalance occurred, one imbalance building on another imbalance and so on. The co-creative relationship between man and nature simply could not exist.

In a co-creative relationship man and nature work in partnership and when there is a change, for example in appropriate technology, nature has the agility and the ability to incorporate that change into its own environment with balance. We are assuming that the changes are used appropriately, and that man is working in partnership with nature and not with manipulation. When the environment itself is off-balance, a co-creative relationship in technology between man and nature simply cannot exist. In the area of Gettysburg the changes in the town, the farms and the technology reflected in an imbalanced way in nature there.

Many people feel that in order for man to be responsive to nature, he must live what you call the simple life—a life devoid of advancement, technology and change. That simply is not true. Technology is one of the areas where man and nature most clearly come together in partnership. Man acts on his ideas and from the elements of nature invents a new form, thus he creates technology. Nature has always been an eager and full participant in the development of form through the art form of technology. The key is to work in technology co-creatively with nature. An ecological balance in technology must also be maintained. The laws of ecological balance are not excluded from the arena of technology. As man enters an environment bringing with him development and growth, the nature of that environment is designed to envelop and cooperate with those changes.

When nature absorbed the energies released from the intensity of battle, its balance tipped. Added to that, man has not understood his co-creative relationship with nature. These two factors are holding nature back in its evolution on Earth.

The battlefield of Gettysburg instantaneously changed in response to the work you did there. The most dramatic and important change was the shift in the flow of nature energy in the area from imbalance into balance. It is as if the dominos dropping were falling to the right. That was the direction of imbalance, shall we say. What you did was go back to the first domino, set it up, and tip it to the left. That is the familiar direction of a balanced evolutionary flow. This is a dramatic change, and although there were many instantaneous shifts within each cell of nature in that area, there was not a complete restoration to full balance. It had taken a long time for the battlefield area of Gettysburg to establish its complex, difficult position of imbalance. Now that the energy is moving in the proper direction, balance will more quickly be restored. But certain aspects there will need more time.

When nature is moving in imbalance, although there is an irritation, a grinding of the gears so to speak, people become very used to it, they acclimate themselves to that environment. The attitude of the people flows in the direction of imbalance. Now nature has shifted into a flow of balance. But little has been done to attain support for that shift from the people in the environment. Nature will continue to flow in the direction of regaining its balance, but balance will take longer to achieve because of the lack of support from the people there.

If people were to shift their attitude towards nature, the environment could shift into perfect balance instantaneously. That is the power of man's relationship to nature. When he takes responsibility as co-creator, the evolutionary flow of nature responds. Just as man develops far more quickly and fully when his environment supports him lovingly, so does nature.

There is always the possibility for physical change to occur instantaneously, according to the attitude of the people involved. The Battle Energy Release Process is timely now because people are beginning to change their attitudes toward the environment. Your work in the battlefield areas will be received, albeit on an unconscious level, by a less alien society. The changes in man's general attitude toward ecology over the past ten to fifteen years have not gone unnoticed. As the people in the Gettysburg area continue to grow, the environment which has already shifted into the direction of balance will move more quickly.

The Battle Energy Release Process

1. If you do not have a coning already activated, open a 4-point coning. The deva to be connected with in the coning will be the overlighting deva of the land you are working with. Balance and stabilize the coning. Check yourself for essences.

2. State that you come to nature in the spirit of care, concern, love and co-creativity to help release any battle energies held by nature, and to facilitate that process.

3. *The release:* Ask nature to now release all the battle energies *with gentleness and ease*,* and request that the released energy gather as an energy cloud above the land area.

Watch or feel the release. Or just wait quietly while the release is going on. This will take anywhere from a few minutes to a half-hour. When you sense that the release is complete, kinesiology test to verify.

4. When the release is complete, request that the released energy that has gathered as an energy cloud over the land now move to its next higher level within the universe. (Do not try to determine where that might be.)

5. Spend a moment noticing the changes and sensations you might be feeling from the land. This serves to fully ground the completed process for you.

6. Balance and stabilize the work you have just completed. Use the same steps you used when balancing and stabilizing in the Energy Cleansing Process. (See step 16.)**

7. *Close the coning* after thanking the team, and check yourself for essences and dosage, unless you are going on immediately to the next process.

.꧁❀꧂.

* If, at any time, you are uncomfortable while an energy release is going on, simply ask that the release occur a little more slowly or gently—or whatever is needed for you to feel comfortable. Nature will immediately comply with your request.

** Energy Cleansing Process: step 16. Balance and stabilize the work that was just completed in this process. Ask: What balancers are needed for this energy cleansing? (Test your soil balancing kit.) Work with Pan to shift the balancers into the area impacted by the Energy Cleansing Process. Then ask: What stabilizers are needed for this energy cleansing? (Test the flower essences.) Again, work with Pan to shift the stabilizers into the area impacted by the process.

THE SOIL BALANCING AND STABILIZING PROCESS*

Since introducing this process, I have found that its use is greatly expanded from what I originally anticipated. In the beginning, I used it as a process by itself. Then nature and I found that it was advantageous to use the Energy Cleansing Process, the Battle Energy Release Process and the Soil Balancing and Stabilizing Process together as a unit.

With this, the Soil Balancing Process expanded in 2 more ways. 1) The flower essences were added to the process and used to *stabilize* the balancing already accomplished in the process. Consequently, the name of the process changed to the Soil Balancing and Stabilizing Process. 2) We discovered that by balancing and stabilizing *every* energy process, we greatly strengthened, protected and enhanced the work done in the process. To do this, once the energy process was completed, I would balance the area I was working with, using the soil balancers in the kit (lime, greensand, rock phosphate, etc.**), and stabilize that area using the flower essences.

To fully appreciate the importance of the Soil Balancing and Stabilizing Process, it is helpful to understand something about form and nature's relationship to form. To help with this, I include excerpts from the Co-Creative Definitions to clarify what nature means when it refers to form, nature and life vitality.

FORM: *We consider reality to be in the form state when there is organization, order and life vitality combined with a state of consciousness.*

NATURE: *Nature comprises all form on all levels and dimensions, and is responsible for and creates all of form's order, organization and life vitality. Nature is the conscious reality that supplies order, organization and life vitality for moving soul-oriented consciousness into any dimension or level of form. Nature **is** form's order, organization and life vitality.*

LIFE VITALITY: *To understand life vitality, it is best to see it in relationship to order and organization. Order and organization are the physical structures that create form framework. In short, they define the walls. But we have included the dynamic of life vitality that initiates and creates action. Nothing in form is stagnant. It is life vitality that gives to form its action. If the framework that is created from order and organization is incomplete, ineffective, deteriorating or being dismantled in an untimely manner, the dynamic of life vitality decreases within the overall form*

* In the first edition of the Workbook, this process was called "Soil Balancing." This Soil Balancing and Stabilizing Process is the new and improved version.

** The list of soil balancers is included in this section.

reality, thus causing life movement to decrease accordingly. There is a movement towards a state of stagnation. It is the dynamic of vitality that gives life—movement—to any individual or object. Organization and order alone cannot do this. However, vitality without corresponding organization and order has no sense of purpose to its motion. It cannot function without organization and order. The three must be present and in balance with one another in order for there to be quality form expression. Nature, on the devic level, creates organization, order and life vitality in perfect balance. Nature, on the nature spirit level, maintains that balanced relationship as individual life units move through their evolutionary paces.

We would like to illustrate what we are saying by focusing your attention on the soil balancing process that improves and enhances the level of soil vitality. This process does not work directly with the soil's vitality level. Instead, it works with those elements of the soil that comprise its order and organization. The process shores up the physical structure of its order and organization. As a direct result, the soil begins its shift back to its original form balance among organization, order and life vitality, and as a consequence of this shift, the soil vitality level (the soil's life vitality) automatically increases to its new state of balance. When this occurs, there is a comparable shift in the interaction and movement among all the different elements that comprise soil. This is why when someone observes change in a field that has had its soil balanced through the soil balancing process, he sees greater efficiency in the interaction between the soil and the plants. The dynamic of action and movement in the soil has been raised by returning the soil's order and organizational structures back to the state (or nearer to the state) of the original devic order, organization and life vitality balance.

Now to fill you in on some of its history since this process was introduced.

In December, 1988, I received a letter from a Canadian soil scientist requesting that I send him a soil sample from the Perelandra garden and another (control) sample from the field surrounding the garden so that he could get an idea of the condition of the soil my garden started with. He was involved with soil testing using radionics, and he suspected that the Perelandra garden soil sample might provide him with some interesting information. I sent him the sample, and on February 5, 1989, I received a letter from him saying that (using radionics) the control sample (field soil) vitality measured 220, and the Perelandra garden soil vitality measured 470. He then went on to explain: "The analysis that I undertook using my radionic machine is enclosed. Basically what was found was that the Perelandra soil has the highest energy readings of any soil sample that I have tested to date. To explain what the numbers on the sheet mean, the vitality is the overall energy level of the soil. . . . an average for most soils is 200 to 300." He further explained that prior to getting the *Workbook*, he had been using the radionics method to raise soil vitality, which took 3 to 4 days to accomplish. With the Soil Balancing Process, he was able to raise the vitality level of the soil in 2 to 3 hours.

Regarding the wisdom of working with nature in these matters, he said in another letter: "I have been doing research on the effect of flower essence combinations that are chosen according to the methods explained in your book [the *Workbook*]. The flower essences chosen by the devas always raise the general vitality reading to the highest of any possible combination."

The soil scientist and I continued working with understanding soil vitality and its relationship to the energy processes for a year and a half. We discovered that soil vitality has an annual rhythm that reaches its peak in the summer at the summer solstice and hits its lowest point in the fall at the fall equinox. It then levels off throughout the winter, and begins to rise again in late winter to the spring equinox.

In the spring of 1989, the soil scientist began a new garden in a new location he had just moved to. He wrote me a letter just after doing the Perelandra vitality readings for the summer solstice, saying that the Perelandra garden was now at a level of 530 to 540. Then he said:

> My garden soil started this spring with a vitality reading of 220 and currently is 530. During this time [May to July] there have been 2 soil balancings on the garden as well as 1 atmospheric balancing. Also there have been several physical treatments on the soil using the best that I as a soil scientist and the Deva of Soil can muster. . . . One thing that I have noticed is the almost ethereal quality of our vegetables compared to the store-bought ones. Watching the garden unfold this year has been a real adventure since the majority of activities of the garden given by

the devas were different than I normally would have expected based on my experience. . . .

One of the things that impressed and excited me about what this scientist was saying was that by using the processes set up by nature, he was able to shift the vitality level of his soil from 220 to 530 in just *2 months*.

So, the Soil Balancing and Stabilizing Process is now used in 3 ways: (a) to balance and stabilize a coning, (b) to raise the vitality level of any given area or object,* and (c) to balance and stabilize any area or object right after it has been shifted and changed due to any of the energy processes.

* This gets explained later.

During this research, we were working with soil to a depth of at least 5 feet. It would be impossible, short of destroying the soil structure, to add balancers and stabilizers to that depth. (When we fertilize, we work only with the top 6 to 8 inches of soil, which is far more accessible.) So, within the process, we rely on nature spirits—Pan, in this case—to assist us in distributing the balancers and stabilizers appropriately. We supply a seed amount (about 1/8 teaspoon) of the balancers and a drop of each of the stabilizers. Pan expands the seed amounts of the energies to whatever amounts are needed by the soil, and transfers those energies to appropriate depths in the soil. Once the energies are seated in the soil, Pan shifts them back to appropriate form (not solid matter), and thereby makes them accessible to and a part of the total soil environment.

IMPORTANT: This process does not replace the fertilizing processes described in Chapter 9 of this book, nor does it replace the need for fertilizing in general. The Soil Balancing and Stabilizing Process impacts the soil's order and organization on a molecular level which, in turn, enhances the soil's life vitality and not its physical fertilizer levels. However, when you use the Soil Balancing and Stabilizing Process, you will find that the soil will test for fewer fertilizer needs. This is because the soil balancing and stabilizing have improved the soil vitality, which has then allowed for more efficient interaction between plants and their surrounding soil. Hence, the need for fewer fertilizers.

DEVA OF THE PERELANDRA GARDEN

ENERGY PROCESSES FOR THE GARDEN AND THE PLANET

You have found that the energy balancing of an area in most cases must be coupled with the balancing and stabilizing of the area's soil. Without the latter, the weakened soil environment will be susceptible to attracting new but similar traumatic vibrations. Form conforms to the makeup of the energy it contains. The land where these traumatic emotions have been held for so long physically reflects that imbalance. Once the energies have been released, the land, if left on its own, will go through an evolutionary process leading to the point where it will reflect the clearer energy state. However, while the land is in this time of transition, it will be vulnerable— not yet removed from the old, not yet stabilized in the new. When important and where necessary, we can eliminate the transition period by using the nature spirit level to balance and stabilize the land.

The intent of this process should be the complete and full stabilization of the five-foot-deep soil base of the garden or any land area you wish to work with. The soil's interaction with man's environment is primarily held within this five-foot-deep layer. This is why the Energy Cleansing Process sheet of light should be formed five feet below the land's surface. Below five feet, the interaction rate is minimal and can safely be left to evolve only in "form time." From five feet and above, the evolution can occur at what we may call "energy time," which is why the nature spirit level is utilized. They know how to transcend relative time in an evolutionary process. So, not only are they assisting you by shifting form into energy, then after application, back to form again, they are also changing the relative time aspect of the evolutionary process.

By completing the Soil Balancing and Stabilizing Process, you have stopped any influx of traumatic emotional energy from outside Perelandra that was being drawn to the Perelandra environment because of the principle of like attracting like. Another way of saying this is "imbalance attracting similar imbalance." We should say here, however, that because of your extensive work with us on the nature levels, that influx to Perelandra was minimal. This last step has fully closed that door.

PERELANDRA GARDEN WORKBOOK 275

Tools for the Process

You will need to make available to the nature spirits small amounts of organic amendments which together as a set create a balancing unit. For convenience, I made a kit using 1/2-ounce bottles which hold:

Bone Meal	Cottonseed Meal
Rock Phosphate	Dolomite Lime
Nitro-10 (nitrogen)	Kelp
Greensand	Comfrey Flower Essence*

* I'll explain this later.

Except for the Comfrey Flower Essence, these are the nutrients I add to my garden. If you use different organic fertilizers, that's perfectly fine—as long as you make available something for phosphorus, nitrogen, potassium, and the acid/alkaline balance.

If you are planning to do the process at sites away from your garden, you may wish to make a small kit also. Stopper bottles (with the glass stopper removed) are convenient; small envelopes or zip-lock bags can be used as well. You only need to have the equivalent of about 2 tablespoons of each amendment. This should last you through 20 to 25 tests.

For those of you who use animal manures only: the natural earth amendments are preferred for this process because of the depth of the work. One normally does not find cow manure five feet below the surface of the ground. But greensand, rock phosphate and bone meal can be integrated into that level without changing the character of the soil.

** I work with this expanded soil kit because the more detailed testing provides me with valuable input about the soil balancing I do. It also allows nature to work with more precision. Nature said it "can assemble more complex and effective combinations of elements for the Soil Balancing and Stabilizing Process if given more to work with." But, nature also tells me that the basic soil balancing needs are present in the original list of 8 balancers. So, if you want to just stick with the original 8, you'll do fine. However, if you wish more detailed work with nature, I suggest the expanded kit.

THE EXPANDED SOIL BALANCING KIT**: I work with the 3 sets of the Perelandra Essences. I also make available the trace minerals found in the soil. I bought small, inexpensive bottles of each at a health food store. They are:

Alfalfa	Magnesium
Boron	Manganese
Calcium	Molybdenum
Chromium	Potassium
Copper	Salt
Iron	Sulfur
Liquid Seaweed	Zinc

In 1992, per nature's instructions, I also added the following vitamins:

Vitamin A	Vitamin E
Vitamin C	Niacin
Vitamin D	B-Complex

Other Tools*: Paper, pen, a spoon and a paper towel or 2. You are now ready.

To give you additional information about the soil balancing kit, the following is a session I did with nature in December 1990 on the amendments and Comfrey Essence used in the Perelandra Soil Balancing Kit as well as whether folks should expand their kits, as I have done, to include a full set of essences and a wider range of soil nutrients, vitamins and minerals.

COMBINED NATURE SESSION

*We understand that you have questioned whether the soil balancers in the kit need individual definitions similar to those given with the flower essences.** They do not. Soil balancers do not work through healing patterns like flower essences do. The soil balancers address the molecular structure, strength and building needs of form or, in other words, the order and organization within form. They do this specifically on the molecular level.*

There is no change in nitrogen, phosphorus and potash levels because soil balancing does not alter or add elements (solid matter) to a soil. The balancers are energetically applied within the molecular level specifically for the benefit of that level's structure, strength and building.

*When the balancers*** are tested, each balancer offered is instantaneously fused with the form's molecular makeup to see which balancer or combination of balancers is needed to improve structure, strength and building. There is no definition-type patterning occurring here. We of nature will indicate which balancers do the best job within the molecular level.*

The seven balancers in the Soil Balancing Kit were chosen by nature for the range of what they offer for strengthening and building the molecular structure of the soil form. Because of the overall environmental impact on the form being balanced, each balancer does not always interact the same way within the molecular level of the soil. Consequently, one cannot say that rock phosphate, for example, will always be needed for one specific,

* *There's one other balancer I've recently added. It's called "Factor-X" and is nothing more than a labelled, empty bottle in my kit. Nature suggested I provide this bottle for those times when a mystery balancer is needed. When the Factor-X bottle tests positive, I know that nature is adding something to the balancer mix that I don't know exists. Now, I know this is going to sound real goofy, but I actually go through the exercise of opening the Factor-X bottle and "pouring" the mystery ingredient into the spoon. This act coordinates between human and nature the adding of Factor-X to the balancer mixture. Factor-X has only tested positive 2 or 3 times.*

** *I had questioned if the individual balancers functioned in a way similar to flower essences, thus needing definitions of specific patterns like flower essences.*

*** *Balancers: The nutrients, vitamins and minerals that make up the kit.*

* Such as Niacin and B-Complex, which contains Niacin.

** That is, expand the kit to include the Perelandra Rose, Rose II and Garden Essences.

*** Sometimes a flower essence or two are needed as balancers. Whenever I test for balancers, I always ask if any flower essences are needed. If so, test the essences and add a drop of the needed essence(s) to the mix of other balancers testing positive.

defined set of conditions because the impact of the environment surrounding the form changes the makeup and quality of the conditions within that form.

Regarding the question about why kelp **and** liquid seaweed may be needed as balancers for the same form at the same time: Kelp and liquid seaweed (and other balancers that are similar to one another)* may have similar properties but, from our perspective, they have a very different impact on form within the molecular level. It is the quality of impact that will differentiate between the two and tell us whether one or both are needed for the same form. It is not the similarity in their basic form properties but rather the quality of their impact upon the molecular level that determines what is needed.

Comfrey was added to the Perelandra Soil Balancing Kit to serve as an "all-purpose" stabilizer. It is one flower essence that has within its properties the widest range of impact that covers the broadest range of needs within most form. If one is to expand his soil kit, we suggest that he first expand it with the flower essence stabilizers.** The stabilizing part of the soil balancing/stabilizing process is what links that process to human intent, direction and purpose. When man balances and stabilizes form, he physically balances the nature elements, and then shifts the human intent, direction and purpose that have been fused with that form from one level to another. The use of a wide range of flower essences facilitates the stabilization process and enables the person doing the process to understand what is needed for stabilization to take place. It is in this area of the process that a person can discover patterning for learning purposes. Therefore, it is appropriate to have the benefit of the definitions.***

Regarding the expansion of the basic soil balancing kit to include a wider range of soil amendments, vitamins and minerals: We can work with the basic kit as it is offered at Perelandra. However, when we are given more balancers with which to work, we can assemble more complex and effective combinations of elements to impact the molecular level in a more sophisticated manner. From our point of view, it is strictly up to the person as to whether he will feel more comfortable working with the basic soil balancing kit during the process or using an expanded kit that includes more soil amendments and minerals.

We'd like to add another point: The name "Soil Balancing and Stabilizing Process" was given for this process because it was originally set up to *balance and then stabilize **soil**. But any form can be balanced and stabilized using the same process, whether the form is soil or not. It can be "natural form" such as trees, rocks, land and sky. It can also be inanimate form such as machinery, furniture, equipment, tools. . . . This process, therefore, is not limited to soil and, as we have seen with the Perelandra research, it can be used successfully to balance and stabilize any and all physical form because all physical form contains molecules. As we have said, the balancing and stabilizing process addresses the molecular level directly. It thus affects the form's order and organization, and also impacts the life vitality of that form. The result is that a new level of life vitality is reached that is in balance with the new level of order and organization.*

Soil Balancing and Stabilizing Process

To do this process, you will need your soil balancing kit (basic or expanded), the Perelandra Flower Essences (if you're working with an expanded kit), a spoon,* paper towel, paper and pen.

1. Open a regular 4-point coning, if one is not already activated. You'll be working with the deva of the area to be balanced and stabilized. *Add to it the Deva of Soil, if working with land.* Verify your connections. Balance and stabilize the coning. Check yourself for essences.

2. State your intent to do the Soil Balancing and Stabilizing Process for this specific area. Clearly describe the area, such as your garden, your full property, the south field, the woods, or physically be present at the site you wish to balance.

3. Ask:
   What balancers are needed?
Then test all of the balancers included in your soil balancing kit. Ask:
   Do I need _____?
 Whatever gets a positive response is what is needed for that section.

4. Now ask Pan to assist you. (Pan is already in the coning. You are focusing on Pan in a special way for this part of the process.)

5. Pour a small amount (about 1/8 teaspoon) of each balancer needed into a spoon or onto your hand. Hold the spoon or your hand out in front of you. State:

* A good-size spoon, like a soup spoon, is optional. You can pour the balancers onto your hand, but a spoon makes life a little easier. The paper towel will be needed to wipe your hand or spoon clean.

I ask Pan to receive the energies from these balancers and shift them in the appropriate amount and to the appropriate depth for the section we are working with.

Continue holding out your hand for about 10 seconds, giving ample time for the shift. Once completed, verify that the shift has occurred (ask if the shift has occurred, then test), and drop the balancers on the ground. Don't try to save them because they are now form without energy and are no longer useful.

6. Turn your attention to the stabilizers—the flower essences. (If you do not have a set of flower essences, but you do have the Perelandra Soil Balancing Kit, you will be able to test for Comfrey Flower Essence, which is included in the kit for stabilization. It is not as strong a stabilization as one gets when using the full sets of essences, but it is better than doing no stabilizing at all.) Ask:

What flower essences are needed for stabilization?

Test all of the essences you have available. Whatever tests positive is what is needed.

7. Place *1 drop* of each needed essence onto your hand or spoon and hold it out in front of you. State:

I ask Pan to receive the energies from these stabilizers and shift them in the appropriate amount and to the appropriate depth for the section we are working with.

Wait 10 seconds for the shift to occur. Verify that the shift has occurred. Dry the essences from your hand or the spoon.

8. Spend a moment sensing the land or area you have just balanced and stabilized.

9. After thanking the team, close the coning by disconnecting from each member of the 4-point coning and the Deva of Soil.

10. Test yourself for flower essences. Take those that are needed and test for dosage.

NOTE: You can use the Soil Balancing and Stabilizing Process for larger, more general areas such as a field, meadow, garden, farm, woods, etc. And you can use this process to work with more precision in small areas such as a specific plant or row that seems to be in trouble, or for strengthening and balancing individual perennial plantings. In these cases, the soil being balanced and stabilized is that which is impacted by the specific plant or row. And, as nature has said, you can also use this process to balance and stabilize machines, equipment or other such objects.* To work with the process, simply define what you intend to focus on, and proceed through the Soil Balancing and Stabilizing Process for this smaller area or object, exactly as you would for a larger area.

At first glance, it would seem that this process involves a little magic. But it is based on solid principles of energy and matter. Remember that the nature spirits are true masters of working with energy and form. At will, they can shift energy out of form, move it to another form, and even make the form itself disappear. It all has to do with the universal principles of energy and matter. And this is what is utilized during the Soil Balancing and Stabilizing Process which you will be directly participating in.

* To avoid confusion, you can refer to this process as the Balancing and Stabilizing Process when using it for something other than soil. It's the same process.

COMBINED NATURE SESSION

The sense of celebration you feel on both the devic and nature spirit levels when you do the Soil Balancing and Stabilizing Process is most accurate. We now have a spot of land on Earth where human and nature have come together to create deep, inner balance. We keep referring to this balance as deep and inner because what occurs is not a surface shift in the soil. We would like to refer to it as a "soul shift" within nature. It is a shift so deep within all the levels of form that one might say its impact is "of the soul." When we refer to the stabilizing effect, we mean a stabilization of such depth that again, one could sense it to be of the soul.

From this point on, there will be a strong vibrational rippling effect that will flow to every corner of Earth. Now, this may sound a bit dramatic to you, perhaps even over-blown or exaggerated, but believe us, we do not exaggerate about this. We celebrate and rejoice, but our exuberance does not lead us to exaggeration. The positive flow that radiates will affect the entire planet. The higher realms of nature are now alert to the shift. Your action serves notice that man and nature are coming together in new partnership. That fact alone will do much to begin to heal the battered soul of the planet. This soil work will act as a salve to that soul.

Mankind wishes to shift his awareness, his life, his intent from Piscean

ENERGY PROCESSES
FOR THE GARDEN
AND THE PLANET

*SPECIAL NOTE: It is not appropriate to do the energy processes on land that you do not own or are not renting. It is also not appropriate to do the energy processes on public land or battlefields open to the general public and supported by public funds **unless** nature gives you the go-ahead.*

to Aquarian. Those on Earth cannot do this unless they reestablish their relationship to nature on all levels. The Soil Balancing and Stabilizing Process touches into another aspect of this area of relationship. In order for man to be physically, emotionally, mentally and spiritually supported as he evolves into the Aquarian era, he must, in partnership with nature, work toward full ecological balance. Nature has corresponding levels which relate to the human physical, emotional, mental and spiritual levels. Now, some understand nature supporting human form, the physical. The other support relationships are not understood very well at all. What we wish to get across to you now is that the quality of this work creates such deep stability within nature that the quality of support and nurturing from nature to mankind on the levels beyond the physical has increased dramatically. Mankind's shift, change, and evolution can now be supported in kind by the nature energy radiating from the balanced and stabilized areas.

We thank you. As has been suggested, it's been a long time coming. We are overjoyed and we rejoice.

MORE HELP FROM
THE "GIVE ME A BREAK" DEPARTMENT

For those of you who:

1. live in the city and have no access to organic amendments but wish to work with the Soil Balancing and Stabilizing Process in conjunction with the other 2 energy processes in your environment;

2. live anywhere, but have no garden and don't plan to have one (What are you doing with this book?), and also don't have easy access to the amendments but wish to work with the process;

3. have a garden or farm and are firm believers of using animal manures only, but would like to incorporate the Soil Balancing and Stabilizing Process which requires different organic amendments and don't wish to purchase bags of it just to make a little kit;

4. want to do this process, could make the kit but, what with everything else you have to learn and make and obtain because of this book, just don't want to deal with this, too . . .

I am offering the Soil Balancing Kit with the 8 basic amendments.*

The 8 amendments in the Soil Balancing Kit are: bone meal, rock phosphate, Nitro-10, greensand, cottonseed meal, dolomite lime, kelp, and Comfrey Flower Essence. There are eight 1/2-ounce bottles in an easy-to-haul-around box. This should give you enough for 25 to 30 tests. Ordering information is in the back of the book.

19

CO-CREATIVE PARTNERSHIPS: FROM POTTED PLANTS TO FARMS

I have presented this co-creative gardening process for 1 individual working in a garden. Primarily, this is my experience. Over the years since the *Workbook* was first published, garden groups, communities and farmers have instituted co-creative gardening. Landscape architects, greenhouse keepers, potted plant enthusiasts, pond designers, tree nurserymen and forestry managers have also incorporated these co-creative principles into their particular areas. It is not difficult to apply the *Workbook* to different situations. The setup with the nature intelligences is the same. All you need to do is modify the lists, charts and processes by inserting words that apply to your different situation. Use what I've given you in this book as your foundation. Then, think about what in your situation is equivalent to what I am presenting in the *Workbook*. For example, instead of using garden fertilizers in a pond, you would work with the fertilizing approach that is unique to a pond situation. Or, if you are a landscape architect, you would not care about what broccoli is to be interplanted with. You would be concerned with placement of trees, bushes and shrubs. And *your* garden doesn't have rows.

FARMING

It is easy to apply co-creative principles to farming. Instead of dealing with sections and rows within a garden, the farmer is focused on a collection of fields. Instead of a garden chart, there would be a farm chart that would show the layout of the fields. The farmer works with the devic level in much the same manner as the gardener. Only now, instead of asking what gets planted in each row, when, and with what fertilizer, that same information will be requested for each field. The devic level would indicate the best field placement for each crop, the best planting time, the fertilizers needed, and the annual rotation of those crops. There is new information regarding field management and animal herd management. In essence, all the questions and considerations that applied to the garden may be expanded to apply to all farm issues. Instead of moving the garden toward a level of balance, the farmer would be balancing the farm as a whole.

The starting point for getting information is the overlighting deva of the specific farm. That's where the primary, overall blueprint is created once the farmer defines the focus of the farm—livestock, crops, orchards, etc. Once individual sections or fields are identified, then one can work with the deva of each field much as was done with the deva of each vegetable in the garden. The Deva of Soil would have the fertilizer and soil management information for all the fields. And kinesiology would still be the tool used for translating the devic information.

Practically speaking, if you are a farmer just starting out with the co-creative approach and are faced with a hundred acres or a thousand acres, it is best to choose just 1 field in the beginning for learning the co-creative processes. You'll see that field, when managed according to devic information and worked with in cooperation with the nature spirit levels, will demonstrate change from what it had been before. And you'll be able to compare its condition and productivity with the other fields. Also, working with one field first will make the task of changing and integrating the process more manageable.

I think it's important, if you are someone whose livelihood is dependent on your farm, not to feel pressure to scrap every practice you've been using for the co-creative approach. My reason for this is simple. If you suddenly throw everything out the window in favor of the co-creative approaches, you will be trying to learn new things while at the same time carrying a terrific additional burden—the financial welfare of your farm and family. It'll be impossible to learn under these conditions and, with this kind of stress, your kinesiology could be shakey. Picking 1 area or 1 field on which to concentrate the co-creative method assists in substantial heart-attack reduction and gives you that all-important sense of avoiding self-destruction. In short, it buys you time as you go through the inevitable learning curve.

I suggest the "small area approach" to anyone who wants to learn and practice the co-creative method but feels uncomfortable about throwing all caution to the wind, as they say. "Small" is relative to the person defining it. So just pick an area you feel comfortable about using as a classroom—however large or small that may be. As you learn and as you experience success and change, you'll automatically begin to incorporate the practices into the other areas. Before you know it, you'll be doing the whole operation co-creatively.

A NOTE ON GREENHOUSES, NURSERIES AND LANDSCAPING

Keep in mind that the goal is to create a balanced environment. The overall health may require that the traditional way of arranging plants, shrubs and trees will need to be modified or abandoned altogether in order to achieve a level of balance. All the information you need can be obtained by using the co-creative garden setup, working with the nature intelligences involved, and applying their information to the situation.

A SPECIAL NOTE FOR LANDSCAPE ARCHITECTS: Landscapers must deal with an additional element: the owner contracting the job. I think it will save a landscaper a lot of aggravation if it is remembered that ultimately the landowner is the one responsible for the evolution and healing of the land. He is, after all, the recognized custodian of that piece of land. Nature recognizes this, as well. If you sense or devically receive that a bush should be placed at spot X, but the landowner wants it at spot Y no matter what you say, the bush goes at spot Y. You may suggest and recommend, as is your responsibility as the professional, but you can't override the landowner's position regarding that land's development. Nature doesn't look to us to come charging in from outside and taking over.

To be honest, this kind of conflict is not a major issue with those landscapers who have developed and incorporated co-creative methods. They find that they draw to them customers who are open to a different approach to the land and have similar concerns regarding health and balance. Like attracts like. Don't be surprised if the landowner already intuitively knows that a specific bush is to be planted at spot X.

Another point: When a landscape architect consciously incorporates the co-creative methods into his practice, the processes are as much a part of his approach to landscaping as what equipment he uses. When someone contracts him for work, it is implied in the contract that the owner is giving permission to the landscaper to accomplish the agreed upon work utilizing all the skills he has. In this case, that includes the co-creative processes. In short, you don't have to embarrass yourself professionally by openly discussing this part of your practice. Just work with nature co-creatively and let the results speak for themselves.

GROUP PROCESS

By group process, I mean a number of gardeners seeking to function with group consensus, rather than 1 head gardener taking the full responsibility of planning the garden and organizing helpers to assist.

In the group process, there are 3 approaches using kinesiology to translate information from the nature intelligences.

Approach Number One: As a group, ask to be connected with the specific deva or nature spirit. That intelligence will open to everyone there. Pick 1 person who does kinesiology well as the tester. As everyone asks yes/no questions, that person will test the answer. Because everyone is connected, there will be a great deal of common intuitive verification. A faulty test will clank with someone—or everyone. The thrust of this setup is the special dynamic that can occur as everyone participates in the questions. Option and direction will come through everyone and be verified by the tester. Proceed through the charts and information gathering as presented in this book, but with this group setup.

Approach Number Two: As a group, ask to be connected with the specific nature intelligence. This time, after each question is asked, *everyone* can test kinesiologically at the same time. This works. I have done it in a group context. Its advantage is that there is instant verification of the answer. Its disadvantage is that everyone must understand each question precisely. A question that is asked aloud by 1 person is immediately translated in the minds of everyone hearing that question. So you can end up with 5 people testing positive and 1 person testing negative. At this point, the question needs to be reviewed so that all 6 people truly understand exactly what is being asked and have the same definition for all the words being used. (You'll learn a lot about communication with this!) Then retest.

Approach Number Three: Do the major garden chart as a group using one of the above methods, then break down the garden into areas with 1 person being responsible for a specific assignment or area. For example, 1 person gets all of the pertinent information on the broccoli row. Or 1 person works only with the Deva of Soil and gets the soil information for the entire garden. Then come back together as a group once the information has been gotten and weave all the threads into place. This exercise will go a long way to verify the accuracy of everyone's work. It has to weave together without knotting up into a big ball. Questions that come up may be asked using either of the first 2 approaches or having the individual originally responsible for this area of information function again as the tester.

Whatever setup is used, always be sure everyone involved is connected with the nature intelligence and verify that connection. When each session is over, be sure everyone has disconnected with the nature intelligence they were working with.

GARDENING WITH YOUR PARTNER WHO THINKS THIS CO-CREATIVE BUSINESS IS CRAZY AND SO ARE YOU

From the responses I've gotten since the *Workbook* was first published, a lot of people fall into this category! Longstanding marriages ride on my answer to this dilemma. One of you thinks co-creative gardening is the wave of the future. The other is casually leafing through newly acquired brochures from local mental institutions. You have worked the garden together for years and neither one of you wants to stop. For both, it's a matter of principle.

Neither of you can continue working in the garden under these conditions. For one thing, the garden itself will suffer. The situation between you and your partner has literally set up an energy battle zone in the garden. If you want the marriage to continue, you'll need to call a cease-fire and acknowledge that you have these differences between you now. (And it's okay and all that stuff.)

The best solution I've found to this situation, regarding clashing ideas and rights in a garden, is to divide the garden. One area for your partner, the other area for you. Then agree that each of you will not impose his/her ideas and methods on to the other's part of the garden. Also agree that each of you will not make comments about anything the other is doing in his/her part of the garden. In short, you solve the battle problem by freeing one another.

As the co-creative gardener, you will be working with nature just for your part of the garden. It will operate as a smaller but still a complete garden in itself and nature will take into consideration that it is attached to your partner's part of the garden. So, whatever your partner does, nature will automatically include this as a variable when addressing the layout, pattern and rhythm of your part of the garden.

HINT: You might need to do a Battle Energy Release Process for your part of the garden. Check with nature.

20

OVERLIGHTING DEVA
OF PLANET EARTH

I have looked forward to this moment, to the opportunity to add to the effort being made through the vehicle of this book. I am the overlighting consciousness of the planet upon which you live. I have been referred to as "Gaia" by many. I would like to give you insight into the physical evolution of the planet as seen from my perspective.*

All that exists in the solar system of which planet Earth is a part, and in the countless realms and dimensions beyond, is presently moving through a major shift. This you refer to as the movement from the Piscean era to the Aquarian era. Earth is not an out-of-step planet struggling within an in-step universe to reach the level of perfection that surrounds it. It is quite a common thing for the humans on Earth to perceive themselves as lesser, behind in development, and out of step. This very notion is what one may call "Piscean" in its dynamic. It sets up this planet and those souls who are choosing to experience the lessons of form in a parent/child situation— the universe being the parent, the planet and its inhabitants being the child. This continuous sense of the child striving and moving forward toward the all-knowing parent was an important dynamic of the Piscean era, and a dynamic which was played out in one way or another on every level of

* I did not have this session until I reached this part of the book. Most of the sessions were done especially for the Workbook, and occurred right with the rhythm and timing of the book's writing. The opening remarks of the Overlighting Deva of Planet Earth refer to this rhythm and timing.

289

interaction on Earth. The notion of the parent served as the impetus to keep the child moving forward in the hope that one day, after much work and growth, the child would attain the peer position with the parent.

The parent/child concept has not been exclusive to Earth. It is a dynamic that has been part of reality on all other dimensions and levels. And as already stated, has been an important dynamic of the Piscean era for souls on all levels to come to grips with in whatever manner needed. I point this out to emphasize that Earth is an acknowledged and respected part of an ever-evolving whole and not the bastard child of that whole.

The important lesson to be integrated into the picture of reality from the parent/child dynamic was the conscious, personal dedication of the individual to move forward. The parent dynamic stood before the child within all, and encouraged those vital steps toward the perceived notion of perfection represented by the parent. It served to weave into the individual's fabric of life that continuous sense of constant forward motion and the knowing that its resulting change led to better and greater.

Now, although the parent/child dynamic has been a tangible force that has permeated the levels of reality during the Piscean era, the actual notion of all being the child seeking to move toward a parent has been illusion. It is how a Piscean dynamic was translated into a workable reality. An impulse was released within all levels of reality some two thousand years ago, and each individual receiving the impulse translated it into an understandable, tangible concept. The main thrust of the overall translation on planet Earth has been the parent/child dynamic. There has been, in fact, no parent outside or beyond who has enticed and encouraged the children forward. Just as the child is within all, so, too, is the parent. But in order to develop the tools one needs to move forward in confidence, individuals needed to establish that sense of the all-knowing parent standing before them in the unknown, ready to catch, comfort and receive them as they take those shaky steps forward.

I have not forgotten to address the planet Earth. I needed to lay the foundation for you to understand how the principles presented in this book fit into the larger picture—and that includes Earth.

When the impulse of what I have referred to as "the parent/child dynamic" was released throughout reality, it was received not only by individual human souls, but by the planet itself. I have stated that the impulse was sounded on all levels of reality. In order for there to be harmonious evolution, there must be a sense of movement in concert within the whole. The impulse was received and seated within planet Earth, which in turn, stabilized the seating of the impulse within individuals. Now, as human souls translated that impulse into the workable parent/child dynamic, that translation itself seated into the planet and its various natural forms, thus modifying the original impulse to conform to the translation. This is natural law. Form conforming to the energy within. It is a necessary part of the support system between spirit and matter. One cannot have the spirit reflecting one reality seated within a form energized by another reality. It would be as if two horses were hitched to one another but pulling in opposite directions. There would be no chance of forward movement. So, form must conform in order for there to be mutual support and evolution between matter and spirit.

To broaden this picture even more, let me say that the impulse and the translation of the impulse, as with all the Piscean impulses and their translations, placed the individuals and the planet squarely and solidly into the evolutionary picture of its universe as a whole—not out of step from it. As already stated, the planet has been an active participant in understanding and working with what we might call "contemporary issues," for the issues have been the same throughout reality, only the translations have differed. It has been vital that the specific parent/child translation, for example, be fully explored and understood by those on Earth so that the resulting knowledge could be made accessible to the whole. Likewise, other translations of the very same impulse have been made accessible to the whole and have been received at various times throughout the Piscean era by individuals and the intelligences of nature on Earth.

Now a new set of impulses has been sounded throughout reality, and they are the impulses commonly referred to as "Aquarian." All of reality has moved into a period of transition. The impulses are in the process of being fully seated in and translated everywhere. On Earth, we have full reception of the initial Aquarian impulses. They are seated well within the planet and are now serving the shift of those living on the planet from Piscean to Aquarian.

If you have followed my train of thought, you will realize that with the planet itself holding the Aquarian impulses, all that exists on the planet and all its individuals are not only receiving the similar impulses but the impetus and support from the planet to change as well. This means that those translations and the resulting systems and procedures from the old simply will not function as smoothly in the present. The soul energy of the planet has shifted and no longer correlates with the old form translations which exist on its surface. You will see a rapid deterioration of all that has worked so well in the past. New translations are required. New systems and procedures. The planet is already holding the new impulses.

The co-creative gardening technique as presented in this book is a translation of the new. It works because it once again aligns spirit and matter with parallel intent and purpose. In this case, one could say we have a double alignment. We have the human spirit translating impulse into new form and action, and we have the reconnection of the human spirit with the new impulses contained within the planet around him. As you incorporate these translations into thought and action, you will see evidence of effortless change all around you. As already stated, this is because the intent of spirit and the intent of matter are realigning and once again moving in concert.

This brings me back to the parent/child notion of the Piscean era. One of the translations of this dynamic by humans has been in the arena of nature. That is, humans have tended to look at nature either as the parent looking at a child in need of discipline, or the child seeking beneficial aid and assistance from the powerful and all-knowing parent. In essence, humans have translated the parent/child dynamic in nature as either manipulation or worship. Both translations were working, viable frameworks for learning, but they are now no longer workable. For humans to continue attempting to respond and act within these two old mindsets is wrecking havoc on the planet itself.

With the Aquarian dynamic, the parent/child is uniting as one balanced, integrated force within the individual. It is the uniting of the universal wisdom contained within all and the absolute knowledge that in order to have full conscious access to that universal wisdom, one must continue to move forward in the learning and changing mode. The parent and child come together in balanced, equal partnership.

The co-creative garden translates this fundamental Aquarian dynamic into the arena of nature. Human and nature come together in conscious, equal partnership, both functioning from a position of wisdom and change. Wherever such a garden is initiated, it will immediately sound a note outward into the universe and inward into the core of the planet, the very soul of the planet, that the shift from Piscean to Aquarian dynamics within the nature arena is in the process of change. And immediately, the evolving intent of the garden will be aligned with the prevailing universal flow and the corresponding planetary impulses, one buttressing from above, the other buttressing from below within the planet. The result will be forward motion in tandem—the gardener in tandem with his planet and his universe. With this massive support, it is no wonder the co-creative garden works.

Allow me to give you another insight. The Aquarian impulses are already seated within the planet. Visualize, if you will, the planet as a container of these impulses. Energy held beneath the Earth's surface. This energy is seated within the very soul of the planet, seated within its heart. It is there to be released and integrated into all levels of life on the planet. Now, picture one small co-creative garden on the planet's surface. See it as a window into the interior of the planet, into its soul. As the gardener works to align this garden to the new dynamics, watch the window open and the energy contained within the core of the planet gently gravitate to and release through the window. Feel the sense of relief and freedom within the Earth's core as the energy moves outward and up. And watch the actions and the form living on the Earth's surface suddenly shift to reflect the impact of the heart energy which has now surfaced. That which exists on the surface has begun to connect to and integrate with the heart and soul of the planet, which, in turn, is fully aligned with the heart and soul force of the universe. As with the experience the human receives when he consciously shifts his perceptions in such a way that the heart energy he holds deep within is suddenly released and allowed to surface, so, too, will Earth as each person opens the window through the framework of the co-creative garden to the heart and soul energy of the planet.

It is not enough to move about the planet in a state of benevolent love for it. The human state alone will not create the passageways through which the heart energy of the planet is allowed to release. It must be accomplished through the state of the human mind, his consciousness, combined with parallel and appropriate action. Once released, this heart energy from the planet will permeate all living reality upon its surface and support the evolutionary process of the planet and its inhabitants in tandem movement with the universe into the Aquarian era.

I fully understand that I am aligning deep planetary change and universal movement with the actions of one gardener tending one small garden. This is precisely what I mean to do. One need not wait for group consensus in such matters. One need only move forward, sound the note for change, and follow that intonation with parallel action. Each gardener, in the role of the Knower, shall hold the seed to his heart and shall plant this seed in the earth. The fruit of this plant shall be the winged and shafted Sun above his head, and a new kingdom shall be grounded on Earth. This I can promise you. This is what awaits you.

APPENDICES

Appendix A
GLOSSARY

ACID SOIL: See pH

ALKALINE SOIL: See pH

ANNUAL: A plant that completes its life cycle in a single growing season.

AQUARIAN (AQUARIAN AGE/ERA): The term used to describe the coming phase of evolution facing not only those on planet Earth, but all souls and all life forms within the universe as well. Although it is termed "Aquarian" because of its loose connection to the astronomical alignment of Aquarius, it is more importantly a term that connotes an emphasized pattern and rhythm in life behavior. The Age of Aquarius will see the coming to the fore of the concepts of balance, teamwork and partnership played out on all levels of life.

ARAGONITE: A grainy, sand-like, high-calcium lime mined from the ocean floor near Bermuda.

BONE MEAL: Finely ground, steamed animal bone used for fertilizer. Contains 20 to 25 percent phosphoric acid and 1 to 2 percent nitrogen.

CLAY: Soil composed of fine particles that tend to compact. It is rubbery when wet but hard when dry. It takes water slowly, holds it tightly, drains slowly, and generally inhibits water and air circulation.

CO-CREATIVE GARDENING: A method of gardening in partnership with the nature intelligences which emphasizes balance and teamwork. The balance is a result of concentrating on the laws of the life energy behind form. The teamwork is established between the individual and the intelligent levels inherent in nature.

297

COLLOIDAL PHOSPHATE: A mixture of fine particles of phosphate suspended in a clay base. Contains 18 percent phosphorus and 15 percent calcium.

COMPANION PLANTS: Plants that when planted close together influence each other, either beneficially or detrimentally.

COMPOST: Mixture of manure, loose vegetation, or other once-living wastes that is left to decay through bacterial action. Used for fertilizing and soil conditioning.

CONING/4-POINT CONING: An energy vortex created when an individual "calls together" or connects with a deva, a nature spirit, the White Brotherhood level and the higher self of the individual for the purpose of receiving more complex input and insight. An advantage of working with a coning is that it has inherent in it both clarity and protection. The 4-point coning has built into it the involutionary/evolutionary balance.

COTTONSEED MEAL: Ground cottonseeds, used for fertilizer. Contains 6 to 9 percent nitrogen, 2 to 3 percent phosphorus and 2 percent potassium.

CROP ROTATION: Growing different crops in a plot or field in successive years for the purpose of balancing the drain on soil nutrients and inhibiting the growth of certain plant diseases.

DEVA: An intelligent level of consciousness within nature that functions as the architects within all of form. Devas are universal in dynamic. (Also see "Co-Creative Definitions.")

DOLOMITE LIME: A limestone rich in magnesium. Neutralizes soil acidity.

DRIED BLOOD: Dried animal blood used for fertilizer. Contains 9 to 15 percent nitrogen.

EARTH: The planet upon which most of us reading this book reside. The word "Earth" can also refer to a specific level of reality—i.e., form.

ENERGY: Form that cannot be perceived by the average 5 human senses.

FISH EMULSION: A liquid mixture containing discarded soluble fish parts, used as fertilizer. Contains 5 to 10 percent nitrogen and lesser amounts of phosphorus and potassium.

FLAT: A shallow box in which seeds are planted to produce seedlings, generally indoors.

FORM: That which can be perceived by any or all of the 5 human senses.

GENESA CRYSTAL: An energy device which looks like a ball formed by 4 precisely positioned bands. It functions as an antenna. The genesa crystal draws to it life energy, then cleanses it, shifts it up "a spiral," and shoots it back out into the environment. A two-foot-diameter genesa crystal affects the life form within a two-mile radius. The odd-looking wire ball in the middle of the Perelandra garden and pictured on the cover of this book is a genesa crystal. (See Appendix B.)

GERMINATION: Sprouting of a new plant from seed.

GRANITE MEAL OR DUST: Finely ground granite, used as a fertilizer. Contains about 8 percent potassium and a number of trace elements.

GREEN MANURE: Crops which are commonly cultivated to be later plowed or tilled into the soil, adding soil nutrients. Also, as a cover, they protect topsoil from soil and wind erosion.

GREENSAND: Sea deposit containing silicates of iron, potassium and other trace elements. Usually mixed with clay or sand. Contains 6 to 8 percent potassium and is used for fertilizer.

GROUNDED ENERGY: Energy that has moved through its complete involutionary process and is fully accessible to the form level. When an individual is grounded, the life and movement of that person is "of form" and accessible to others through the 5 human senses. That person is functioning within the involution/evolution balance. A distinction of grounded action or energy is clarity.

GYPSUM: Mineral containing the soil nutrients calcium and sulfur, and often used as a soil conditioner.

HIGH CALCIUM LIMESTONE: Contains 72 percent calcium carbonate. Especially useful where the magnesium level is already high.

HILLS: Mounded soil containing 2 to 3 plants that generally need room to spread—such as watermelon, cucumber, zucchini, squash.

INTERPLANTING: Planting 2 vegetables close together, usually in the same row or space. Often one is quick-maturing and the other slow-growing. The quick-maturing vegetable is harvested first, giving more room for the continued growth of the other.

KELP: A loosely defined group of large brown seaweeds, used as a fertilizer and soil conditioner. Contains 2 to 6 percent potash, 1 to 2 percent nitrogen.

KINESIOLOGY: A method of discerning the strength or weakness of an individual body's electrical system through the use of muscle testing.

LOAM: Soil containing a fertile and well-textured mixture of clay, sand and humus.

MANURE: Livestock dung used as fertilizer.

MULCH: Protective covering placed over the soil between plants in order to reduce evaporation, maintain even soil temperature, reduce erosion, and inhibit weed sprouting.

MULCH GARDENING: A gardening method originated by Ruth Stout in which 6 to 8 inches of mulch is left on the garden year-round.

NATURE SPIRITS: An intelligent level of consciousness within nature that works in partnership with the devic level, and is responsible for the fusing and maintaining of energy/spirit to appropriate form. Nature spirits are regional and attached to specific land areas.

NITROGEN: One of the 3 most important plant nutrients, the others being phosphorus and potassium. Particularly essential in production of leaves and stems. An excess of nitrogen can produce abundant foliage and few flowers and fruit.

NUTRIENT: Any of the 16 elements that in usable form are absorbed by plants as nourishment. Plants obtain carbon, hydrogen and oxygen from water and air, and the other elements from the soil. The main soil elements are nitrogen, phosphorus and potassium; the trace elements are boron, calcium, chlorine, copper, iron, manganese, magnesium, molybdenum, sulfur and zinc.

ORGANIC: Deriving from living organisms—that is, either plants, animals or minerals.

ORGANIC GARDENING: Grown with fertilizers and mulches consisting only of animal, mineral or vegetable matter, with no use of chemical fertilizers or pesticides.

OVERLIGHTING DEVA: A deva who oversees a larger reality such as a large land area like a battlefield, farm or country. Within this broader area are individual devas working as a team with the specific smaller areas that make up the larger picture. In essence, the overlighting deva would "oversee the whole operation."

OYSTER SHELLS: Ground oyster shells, used as an amendment to composts and as a liming material. Contain 31 to 36 percent calcium.

PAN: A specific nature spirit who functions as the organizing force among the nature spirits and the nature spirit level. Although a nature spirit, Pan has devic qualities in that he is universal and will often represent the nature spirits as "spokesman." The nature spirit CEO.

PERELANDRA: Of the heart. The word "Perelandra" comes from the science-fiction novel *Perelandra* by C. S. Lewis.

PERENNIAL: A plant that continues living over a number of years.

pH: Index of the acidity or alkalinity of a soil. Technically, it refers to the relative concentration of hydrogen ions in the soil. The index ranges from 0 for extreme acidity to 7 for neutral, to 14 for extreme alkalinity. The extremes are rarely reached. A pH of 4.0 would be considered strongly acid; 9.0, strongly alkaline. Adding peat moss, sawdust, or rotted bark to the soil increases acidity; adding lime increases alkalinity.

PHOSPHORUS: One of the 3 most important plant nutrients, the others being nitrogen and potassium. Especially associated with the production of seeds and fruits and with the development of good roots.

PISCEAN (PISCEAN AGE/ERA): That period of time, roughly 2000 years long, out of which the planet Earth and the universe are presently passing, and during which specific universal laws were grounded on the planet. In a broad and loose sense, one may say that the Piscean era explored, developed and worked with the dynamic of the parent/child, higher/lower, and masculine-energy-dominate relationship, and expressed this dynamic in both action and structure throughout all levels of form.

POTASH: Any potassium or potassium compound used for fertilizer.

POTASSIUM: One of the 3 most important plant nutrients, the others being nitrogen and phosphorus. Promotes the general vigor of a plant and increases its resistance to disease and cold. Also promotes sturdy roots.

RING-PASS-NOT: The boundary of limitations we each have which separates our working knowledge and reality from the rest of all knowledge and reality. As we evolve, the ring-pass-not shifts appropriately so that we have access to what we need but are not overwhelmed by all that there is.

ROCK PHOSPHATE: Finely ground rock powder containing calcium phosphate. Contains up to 30 percent phosphoric acid.

SAND: Tiny, water-worn particles of silicon and other rocks, each usually less than 2 millimeters in diameter. The granules allow free water and air movement; so free, however, that water readily flows out and leaches nutrients quickly.

SOIL AERATION: Flow of oxygen and carbon dioxide within the soil, between the ground surface and plant roots and soil microorganisms.

SUBSOIL: Bed of earthy soil immediately beneath the topsoil. The size of the soil particles may be larger than that of topsoil, sometimes approaching gravel size.

SUCCESSION PLANTING: Planting a new crop as soon as the first one is harvested within the same growing season.

SUGAR BEET WASTE: A compost readily available in sugar beet growing regions. Contains 1 to 4 percent nitrogen.

SULFUR: A nonmetallic natural trace element which has a major importance to plant growth.

SUL-PO-MAG: Sulphur (22 percent), potash (22 percent), magnesium (22 percent). A soluble fertilizer derived from the mineral langbeinite.

THINNING: Pulling up young plants from a group so that the ones that are left in the soil have more room to develop.

TOPSOIL: Surface layer of soil, containing fine rock particles and decayed or decaying organic matter. Its thickness varies from 1 to 2 inches to several feet, depending on the geographic region and past treatment of the soil.

UNIVERSAL LIGHT: An overseeing consciousness connected with the White Brotherhood.

UNIVERSE: All existing things, including Earth, the heavens, the galaxies, and all therein, regarded as a whole.

WHITE BROTHERHOOD: An organization of higher souls who are keenly and deeply involved in the evolution of planet Earth and, to this end, function with us and in us in various capacities.

❧

CO-CREATIVE DEFINITIONS DEALING WITH NATURE, LIFE, SCIENCE, THE UNIVERSE AND ALL ELSE
by
Nature and Friends

Let us give you the basic understanding of these terms. We feel that these definitions, kept short and simple, will be more helpful than lengthy, detailed ones. Consider these definitions to be starting points.

FORM: *We consider reality to be in the form state when there is organization, order and life vitality combined with a state of consciousness. For the purpose of understanding form in a constructive and workable manner, let us say that we consider consciousness to be soul-initiated and, therefore, quite capable of function beyond what we would term "form." There are dimensions of reality in which the interaction of life reality is maintained on the level of consciousness only. There is no surrounding organization, order or life vitality as we know it. There is only consciousness.*

We do not consider form to be only that which is perceptible to the five senses. In fact, we see form from this perspective to be most limited, both in its life reality and in its ability to function. We see form from the perspective of the five senses to be useful only for the most basic and

The "Co-Creative Definitions" were written in 1990 and introduced in Workbook II. I have included them in this book because they lay the foundation of the work going on at Perelandra and co-creative gardening.

fundamental level of identification. From this perspective, there is very little relationship to the full understanding and knowledge of how a unit or form system functions.

*All energy contains order, organization and life vitality; therefore, **all energy is form**. If one were to use the term "form" to identify that which can be perceived by the basic senses and the word "energy" to refer to that aspect of an animal, human, plant or object's reality that cannot be readily perceived by the basic senses, then one would be accurate in the use of these two words. However, if one were to use the word "form" to refer to that which can be perceived by the basic five senses and assume form to be a complete unit of reality unto itself, and use the word "energy" to refer to a level beyond form, one would then be using these two words inaccurately.*

On the planet Earth, the personality, character, emotional makeup, intellectual capacity, strong points and gifts of a human are all form. They are that which gives order, organization and life vitality to consciousness.

Order and organization are the physical structures that create a framework for form. In short, they define the walls. But we have included the dynamic of life vitality when we refer to form because one of the elements of form is action, and it is the life vitality that initiates and creates action.

NATURE: *In the larger universe and beyond, on its many levels and dimensions, there are a number of groups of consciousness which, although equal in importance, are quite different in expression and function. Do not misunderstand us by thinking that we are saying that all reality is human soul-oriented but that there are some aspects of this reality that function and express differently. We are not saying this. We are saying that there are different groups of consciousness that are equal in importance but express and function very differently. Together, they comprise the full expression of the larger, total life picture. No one piece, no one expression, can be missing or the larger life picture on all its levels and dimensions will cease to exist. One such consciousness has been universally termed "nature." Because of what we are saying about the larger picture not existing without all of its parts, you may assume that nature as both a reality and a consciousness exists on all dimensions and all levels. It cannot be excluded.*

Each group of consciousness has what can be termed an area of expertise. As we said, all groups are equal in importance but express and function differently from one another. These different expressions and functions are vital to the overall balance of reality. A truly symbiotic relationship exists among the groups and is based on balance—universal balance. You are absolutely correct to characterize the human soul-oriented dynamic as evolution in scope and function. And you are correct in identifying the nature dynamic as being involution in scope and function. Nature is a massive, intelligent consciousness group that expresses and functions within the many areas of involution, that is, moving soul-oriented consciousness into any dimension or level of form.

*Nature **is** the conscious reality that supplies order, organization and life vitality for this shift. Nature is the consciousness that is, for your working understanding, intimately linked with form. Nature is the consciousness that comprises all form on all levels and dimensions. It is form's order, organization and life vitality. Nature is first and foremost a consciousness of equal importance with all other consciousness in the largest scheme of reality. It expresses and functions uniquely in that it comprises all form on all levels and dimensions and is responsible for and creates all of form's order, organization and life vitality.*

DEVAS AND NATURE SPIRITS: *"Devas" and "nature spirits" are names used to identify two different expressions and functions within the nature consciousness. They are the two groups within the larger nature consciousness that interface with the human soul while in form. There are other groups, and they are differentiated from one another primarily by specific expression and function.*

*To expand from our definition of form, it is the devic expression that fuses with consciousness to create order, organization and life vitality. The devic expression is the architect who designs the complex order, organization and life vitality that will be needed by the soul consciousness while functioning within the scope or band of form. If the consciousness chooses to shift from one point of form to another point, thereby changing form function, it is the devic expression of nature that alters the organization, order and life vitality accordingly. The devic expression designs and **is** the creation of the order, organization and life vitality of form.*

The nature spirit expression infuses the devic order, organization and life vitality and adds to this the dynamic of function and working balance. To order, organization and life vitality it brings movement and the bond that maintains the alignment of the devic form unit to the universal principles of balance while the consciousness is in form.

*To say that nature is the expert in areas of form and form principles barely scratches the surface of the true nature (pardon the pun) of nature's role in form. It is the expert of form and it is form itself. A soul-oriented consciousness cannot exist on any level or dimension of form in any way without an **equal**, intimate, symbiotic relationship with the nature consciousness.*

CONSCIOUSNESS: *The concept of consciousness has been vastly misunderstood. To put it simply, consciousness is the working state of the soul. In human expression, as one sees it demonstrated on the planet Earth, the personality, character, emotional makeup, intellectual capacity, strong points and gifts of a human are all form. They are that which gives order, organization and life vitality to consciousness.*

We say "working state of the soul" because there are levels of soul existence that are different than the working state and can best be described as a simple and complete state of being. The closest that souls on Earth come to this notion is the state of unconsciousness. But this is to give you a glimpse of what we mean by "state of being." We urge you not to assume that what you know as unconsciousness is equal to the soul state of being.

Humans tend to think of the soul as being something that exists far away from them because they are in form. This is an illusion. The core of any life is the soul. It cannot exist apart from itself. Like the heart in the human body, it is an essential part of the life unit. A human in form is, by definition, a soul fused with nature. Personality and character are a part of the nature/form package that allows the soul to function and to express itself in form. They are not the soul; they are the order and organization of that soul.

Consciousness physically fuses into the body system first through the electrical system, and then through the central nervous system and the brain. This is another aspect of nature supplying order, organization and life vitality. Consciousness itself cannot be measured or monitored as a reality. But what can be measured and monitored is the order, organization and life vitality of consciousness. Consciousness is the working state of the soul and is not form. It is nature, not consciousness, that supplies form.

We wish to add a thought here so that there will be no confusion about the relationship between nature and the soul. The devic level of nature does not, with its own power, superimpose its interpretation of form onto a soul. We have said that nature and soul are intimately and symbiotically related. This implies a give and take. No one consciousness group operates in isolation of the whole or of all other parts of the whole. When a soul chooses to move within the vast band of form, it communicates its intent and purpose to nature. It is from this that nature, on the devic level, derives the specifics that will be needed for the soul to function in form. It is a perfect marriage of purpose with the order, organization and life vitality that is needed for the fulfillment of that purpose. Nature, therefore, does not define purpose and impose it on a soul. It orders, organizes and gives life vitality to purpose for expression of form.

SOUL: *We perceive that most likely the question of soul will arise for anyone reading these definitions. This will be most difficult to define since the soul is, at its point of central essence, beyond form. Consequently, it is beyond words. However, it is not beyond any specific life form. As we have said, an individual is not separate or distant from his or her soul. Souls, as individuated life forces, were created in form at the moment known as the "Big Bang." Beyond form, souls are also beyond the notion of creation. So we refer to the moment of the Big Bang regarding the soul, since this gives you a description of soul that will be most meaningful to you.*

The Big Bang was the nature-designed order, organization and life force used to differentiate soul into sparks of individuated light energy. The power of the Big Bang was created by intent. And that intent originated from the massive collective soul reality beyond form.

It is reasonable to look at the Big Bang as the soul's gateway to the immense band of form. To perceive the soul and how it functions exclusively from the perspective of human form on Earth is akin to seeing that planet from the perspective of one grain of sand. The soul's options of function and expression in form are endless. What we see occurring more frequently now on Earth is the shift from the individual soul unknowingly functioning in an array of options, all chosen only because they are compatible to the immediate purpose of the soul, to the individual beginning to function with discrimination and intent in more expanded ways. Using the words in their more limited, parochial definitions, we can say that we see the beginning of a shift from soul function in which an individuated personality remains unaware of many of its options to soul function in which the personality begins to take on conscious awareness of all its options.

ENERGY: *For those experiencing life on Earth, energy is form that is perceived by an individual beyond the scope of the basic five senses. All energy contains order, organization and life vitality; therefore, **all energy is form**. The makeup and design of the specific order, organization and life vitality within that which can be perceived by the basic five senses is identical to and therefore harmonious with its broader reality, which cannot be perceived by the basic five senses. If one is to use the term "form" to identify that which can be perceived by the basic senses and the word "energy" to refer to that aspect of an animal, human, plant or object's reality that cannot be readily perceived by the basic senses, then one would be accurate in the use of these two words. However, if one is to use the word "form" to refer to that which can be perceived by the basic five senses and assume form to be a complete unit of reality unto itself, and use the word "energy" to refer to a level beyond form, one would then be using these two words inaccurately. From our perspective, form and energy create one unit of reality and are differentiated from one another solely by the individual's ability to perceive them with his or her sensory system. In short, the differentiation between that which is form and that which is energy within any given object, plant, animal or human lies with the observer.*

BASIC SENSORY SYSTEM PERCEPTION: *We define basic sensory system perception as being that which the vast majority of individuals on Earth experience. The acts of seeing, hearing, touching, tasting and smelling fall within what we acknowledge as a basic, fundamental range of sensory development that is predominant on the Earth level. What is referred to as an "expansion experience" is, in fact, an act or experience that is perceived by an individual because of an expansion of the range in which his sensory system operates. Expansion experiences are not perceived outside or beyond an individual's electrical system, central nervous system and sensory system. These three systems are interrelated, and an accurate perception of an expansion experience requires that the three systems operate in concert. Therefore, it is quite possible for something to occur in an individual's life that registers in the person's electrical system and central nervous system but then short-circuits, is altered or is blocked* *simply because the person's present sensory system does not have the ability to process, due to its present range of operation, what has registered in the other two systems. People say that "these kinds of strange things never happen to me." This is inaccurate. "Strange" things, experiences and moments beyond the present state of their sensory systems, are continuously happening around them and to them. They are simply not at the point where their sensory systems are capable of clear, useful processing. They waste time by directing their will and focus to "make things happen." That is useless since things are happening all the time around them. Instead they should relax, and continue through an organic developmental process that is already in effect and which will gradually allow them to accurately perceive what is happening around them. In some cases, where events or experiences are vaguely perceived or processed in outrageous, useless ways, their sensory system is expanding but still not operating within the range where events can be usefully processed.*

REALITY: *From our perspective, reality refers to all levels and dimensions of life experience within form and beyond form. Reality does not depend on an individual's perception of it in order to exist. We call an individual's perception of reality his "perceived reality." Any life system that was created in form (which occurred at the moment of the Big Bang) has inherent in it all dimensions and levels that exist both within form and beyond. How we relate to an individual or object depends on our present ability to enfold and envelop an individual's many levels. The scope within which one exists, the reality of one's existence, is truly beyond form, beyond description. If one understands that the evolutionary force which moves all life systems forward is endless—beyond time—then one must also consider that it is the continuous discovery of these vast levels inherent in all life systems that creates that evolutionary momentum. Since that dynamic is beyond time as expressed on any form level or dimension, it is endless.*

PERCEIVED REALITY: *This is the combination of elements that make up an individual's full system of reality and are perceived, embraced and enfolded by him or by another individual at any given time. From this, an individual "knows" himself or another individual only from the perspective of the specific combination of elements he or she is able to perceive, embrace and enfold. Any one element can be considered a window to the* *larger whole. When in form, these elements take on the dynamics of order, organization and life vitality, and are demonstrated through these specific form frameworks. The extent to which perceived reality corresponds to the larger, all-encompassing reality depends on the ability of an individual to accurately demonstrate these elements within form frameworks, and the ability of that or another individual to accurately perceive what is being demonstrated.*

BALANCE: *Balance is relative and measured, shall we say, by an individual's ability to faithfully demonstrate the various elements comprising his larger reality through the specific frameworks of form in which one has chosen to develop. When what one is demonstrating is faithful in intent and clarity to these elements and the larger reality, one experiences balance. And those interacting with this individual will experience his balance. One experiences imbalance when there is distortion between what one demonstrates through the form framework, and the intent and clarity of the elements comprising the larger reality as well as the larger reality itself.*

If you truly look at what we are saying here, you will see that balance as a phenomenon is not an elusive state that only an exultant few can achieve. Balance is, in fact, inherent in all reality, in all life systems. Balance is defined by the many elements within any individual's reality. And it is the dominant state of being within any reality and any form system. It is also the state of being that links individual life systems to one another and to the larger whole. When one says that he is a child of the universe, what one is acknowledging is the relationship and link of his higher state of balance to the universe's state of balance. Whether one feels linked to or distant from this relationship depends on the closeness or distance he creates within himself with respect to his larger personal state of balance— that dynamic which is part of his overall reality.

LIFE VITALITY: *We have used this term frequently in these definitions and feel it would be useful to clarify what we mean. To understand life vitality, it is best to see it in relationship to order and organization. Order and organization are the physical structures that create the framework for form. In short, they define the walls. But we have included the dynamic of life vitality when we refer to form because one element of form is action, and it is life vitality that initiates and creates action. Nothing in form is* *stagnant. It is life vitality that gives to form its action. If the framework that is created from order and organization is incomplete, ineffective, deteriorating or being dismantled in an untimely manner, the dynamic of life vitality decreases within the overall form reality. This causes life movement to decrease accordingly, and is a movement towards a state of stagnation. It is the dynamic of vitality that gives life—movement—to any individual or object. Organization and order alone cannot do that. However, vitality without organization and order has no sense of purpose to its motion. It cannot function without organization and order. The three must be present and in balance with one another for there to be quality form expression. Nature, on the devic level, creates organization, order and life vitality in perfect balance. Nature, on the nature spirit level, maintains that balanced relationship as individual life units move through their evolutionary paces.*

We would like to illustrate what we are saying by focusing your attention on the soil balancing process that improves and enhances the level of soil vitality. This process does not work directly with the soil's vitality level. Instead, it works with those elements of the soil that comprise its order and organization. The process shores up the physical structure of its order and organization. As a direct result, the soil begins to shift its form back to the original balance among organization, order and life vitality. As a consequence of this shift, the soil vitality level (the soil's life vitality) increases to its new state of balance. Those changes involve a comparable shift in the interaction and movement among all the different elements that comprise soil. This is why when someone observes change in a field that has had its soil balanced through the soil balancing process, he sees greater efficiency in how the soil and plants interact. The action and movement in the soil have raised the soil's order and organizational structures back to the state (or nearer to the state) of the original devic balance of order, organization and life vitality.

GROUNDING: *Quite simply, the word "grounded" is used to acknowledge full body/soul fusion or full matter/soul fusion. Grounding refers to what must be accomplished or activated in order to both assure and stabilize body or matter/soul fusion. To be grounded refers to the state of being a fused body (matter)/soul unit. To achieve this unit fusion and to function fully as a fused unit is the primary goal one accepts when choosing to* *experience life within form. Functioning as a grounded body (matter)/soul unit is a goal on all levels and dimensions of form, whether the form can or cannot be perceived by the five senses.*

Nature plays two key roles in grounding. First, it is through and with nature that the grounding occurs. Nature, which organizes, orders and adds life vitality to create form, is what creates and maintains grounding. Secondly, the levels of nature know what is required to fuse the soul dynamic within form. Nature itself provides the best examples of body (matter)/soul fusion. Humans have recognized the form or matter existence of nature on the planet, but have only recently begun to understand that within all form there are fully functioning soul dynamics. On the other hand, humans acknowledge or concentrate on their personal soul dynamics but have little understanding as to how they, in order to be functional within form, must allow the soul to fuse with and operate through their form body. Humans do not see the examples and learn the lessons of the master teachers of body (matter)/soul fusion that surround them in all the kingdoms of nature. Humans also deny the fusion within themselves. The relative extent of this denial interferes proportionately with the quality and stabilization of the fusion.

INTENT: *Intent refers to the conscious dynamic within all life that links life vitality with soul purpose and direction. When an individual uses free will to manipulate what he or she willfully desires instead of what is within the scope of higher soul purpose, then intent is combined with the manipulative power of free will and this combination is linked with life vitality. If you will recall, it is life vitality that adds action to order and organization. It both initiates and creates action. To maintain harmonious movement with soul purpose and direction, life vitality must be linked with the soul dynamic. This linkage occurs on two levels. One is unconscious, allowing for a natural patterning and rhythm of action through form that is consistent with soul purpose. As the body/soul fusion moves through its own evolutionary process as a functioning unit, it takes on a greater level of consciousness and an expanded level of awareness and knowing. As a result, the unconscious link between soul dynamic and life vitality takes on a new level of operation, thus shifting it into a state of consciousness. The shift is a gradual, step-by-step evolutionary process in itself. Intent is conscious awareness of soul purpose, what is required within the scope of* *form to achieve soul purpose, and how the two function as a unit. Consequently, when one wishes to express soul purpose, one need only consciously fuse this purpose with appropriate form and action. This act is what is referred to when one speaks of intent.*

Intent as a dynamic is an evolutionary process in itself and, as we have said, does not suddenly envelop one's entire life fully and completely. Intent is only gradually incorporated into one's everyday life. Therefore, one does not suddenly and immediately function within the full scope of the intent dynamic in those areas of life where intent is present. Intent as a dynamic is as broad a learning arena as life itself. And in the beginning, intent can often be confused with or intermingled with free will. However, as it is developed, it becomes the cutting edge of the body/soul unit and how it operates. Intent is the key to unlimited life within the scope of form.

INTUITION: *Intuition as it is popularly defined relates to a sixth sense of operation. This is false. This is not a sixth sense. When individuals experience a phenomenon that they consider to be beyond their five senses, they tend to attribute this experience to another category, the sixth sense, and call it intuition. The fact is that these expanded experiences are processed through their five senses in an expanded manner.*

Intuition, in fact, is related to and linked with intent. It is the bridge between an individual's conscious body/soul fusion—that state in which he knows and understands about the body/soul fusion and how it functions— and the individual's unconscious body/soul fusion. The intuition bridges the unconscious and the conscious. This enables what is known on the level of the unconscious body/soul fusion to be incorporated with and become a part of the conscious body/soul fusion. Intuition is the communication bridge between the two which makes it possible for the conscious body/soul unit to benefit from those aspects of the unconscious body/soul unit. This benefit results when the conscious unit opens to and moves through the lessons surrounding intent. Where intent is functioning fully, these two levels, the unconscious and the conscious, are no longer separate but have become one—the expanded conscious level. Consequently, there is then no need for the bridge known as intuition.

However, lest you think otherwise, intent is not considered greater than intuition; rather, they are two excellent tools utilized equally by the highest developed souls functioning within form. We say this to caution those who read this not to think intent is "greater" than intuition and to be aimed for at the exclusion of intuition. Evolution as seen from the highest perspective is endless. Therefore, discovery of all there is to know about both intuition and intent is endless. For all practical purposes, an individual can safely consider that there will never be a time in which the development of intent will be such that the need for and development of intuition will be unnecessary. As we have said, the highest souls who function to the fullest within the scope of form do so with an equal development and expansion of both intent and intuition.

Appendix B
THE GENESA CRYSTAL AND ITS CONSTRUCTION

by Clarence N. Wright, Jr.

Dr. Derald Langham developed the Genesa® concept while he was working in plant genetics in South America in the 1940s. (The word is derived from "gene" plus "S. A." for South America. *Genesa* is a registered trademark of the Genesa Foundation. See p. 318 for address.) He discovered certain shapes that represent natural growth patterns through which energy flows. We have used one of these shapes, the Genesa crystal,[*] in the Perelandra garden for a number of years, as an energy "air conditioner." It draws in energy from within a radius of 2 miles, cleanses and balances it, and then sends it back out. We have also used Genesa crystals in our house, with a similar energy cleansing and balancing effect.

The Genesa crystal is very easy to construct. It can be made any size. The larger it is, the further out its influence can be felt[**] It can be made from any material that is strong enough to support the shape. However, you should ask nature, using kinesiology testing, which material is appropriate for your particular garden or other site in which the crystal will be placed.

The instructions for making a Genesa crystal are as follows: Make *4 equal size hoops*. Using a marker, divide each hoop into *6 equal divisions*.

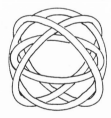

[*] ***The Genesa Crystal***

[**] *Check with nature (the deva of your garden) for the appropriate size you should construct or purchase.*

Insert 1 hoop inside a second, so that they intersect only at division marks.[*] Then, insert the first 2 hoops inside a third, again making sure they *only intersect on the division marks.*[**] Finally, insert the 3 hoops inside the fourth hoop the same way.[***] When you are done, you will have a Genesa crystal—4 hoops meeting only at common division points.

You have to fasten the hoops to each other where they intersect to keep the crystal together. If you are using cardboard or stiff paper, glue works well. Our main garden crystal is made from copper refrigeration tubing, so we used solder at the joints. Your method of fastening will depend on the material you are using.

It's important to use materials that are relatively thin compared to the diameter of the hoops. This insures that the circular shape won't be distorted when the hoops overlap. Our main garden crystal is 24 inches in diameter, made of 3/8-inch tubing. To maintain the shape of the circles, we flattened each hoop at the intersecting points by crimping with strong pliers. This also gave us good surfaces to solder. If you use PVC plastic tubing, you can bolt them together (we recommend using a circular rasp to file notches in the tubing) where they meet. The notch of 1 hoop will rest

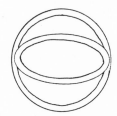

* Two Hoops Together

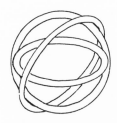

** Three Hoops Together

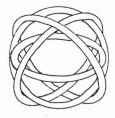

*** Four Hoops Together

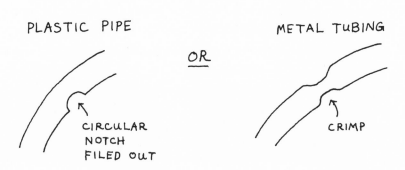

PLASTIC PIPE   OR   METAL TUBING

CIRCULAR NOTCH FILED OUT   CRIMP

Fig. 1. Detail of Intersection Points

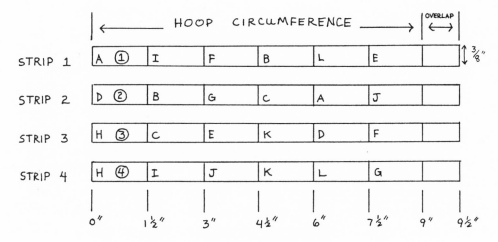

Fig. 2. Layout of Strips for Paper Hoops

in the notch of the other 1, again maintaining the circular shape (see Fig. 1).

You can make a simple cardboard or paper crystal before getting into stronger materials. You will need stiff paper or posterboard, scissors, pencil, ruler, glue, 12 small straight pins and a thimble (to keep from sticking the pins into your finger!).

Cut 4 strips to the same length. For an easy first crystal, make your strips 9 1/2-inches long and 3/8-inches wide. The width should be narrow compared to the length, but wide enough that the strip will not be flimsy. Experiment to find the best width for your paper.

Now, using Fig. 2 as a guide, mark the 1/2-inch *overlap* on each strip. Mark the remaining length in 1 1/2-inch increments, using lines *across* the width so that you have *6 equal divisions*. Then, number each strip, and mark the letters on each strip, exactly as in Fig. 2. This will make it easy to assemble the crystal properly. Next, put some glue on each strip's overlap area and join the ends to make the hoops. Leave the division marks facing *out*. You now have 4 hoops, marked into 6 equal segments.

To assemble the hoops, start by inserting hoop 1 inside hoop 2, matching point A of one to point A of the other, and point B to the point B. Carefully stick a pin into each joint. Next, insert the first 2 hoops inside hoop 3, matching points C, D, E and F. Insert pins into these intersections.

Here's a hint we find helpful when assembling the hoops: hoops 1 and 2 meet at 2 points; hoop 3 meets the first 2 at 4 points; and hoop 4 meets the

The length of the strip depends on the diameter you want the crystal to have. Use the formula:

Length of strip = 3.14 times the diameter plus the overlap.

All the measurements should be in the same units, such as inches or centimeters.

Genesa crystal artwork by Sandra Hirth.

THE GENESA CRYSTAL

For further information on the principles of the Genesa crystal, contact:
The Genesa Foundation
4702 San Jacinto Terrace
Fallbrook, CA 92028

For handcrafted copper Genesa crystals and more information about their construction, contact:
Young Design
HC 31, Box 30
Bath, Maine 04530
Tele. & Fax: 207-386-0089

first 3 at 6 points. Also, if 2 points match when you add either hoop 3 or 4, but not the others, reverse the hoop. If you have done everything right, there will be 2 and only 2 hoops crossing at each intersection, and all the letters will match. (Pat yourself on the back!)

When you are sure everything lines up, carefully remove 1 pin at a time and place a drop of glue or some double-sided tape between the hoops at each intersection. Let dry and, voilà! You have a Genesa crystal.

NOTE: When looking at the Genesa crystal, you will notice that the intersecting hoops create square and triangle spaces. You can set the crystal down on a square or a triangle. When the major thrust of the Perelandra garden is on research, nature tells Machaelle to set the crystal on a square. When the emphasis is on outreach, she is told to set the crystal on a triangle. She's not exactly sure why, she just does it. Ask nature how you should place your Genesa crystal, and periodically check with nature to make sure the placement hasn't changed. If so, change it! Chances are, the reasons for the specific position will be different from person to person.

Appendix C
PERELANDRA
FLOWER ESSENCES

If you are intrigued, interested or curious about flower essences and wish to investigate them further, I offer some suggestions on how you might proceed without feeling overwhelmed.

❖ For those who would like to try essences and experience how they work, read through the Perelandra Essences definitions. Then think about some physical, emotional, mental or spiritual problem you would like to address. Think of it clearly or even write it out. Then say to yourself, "What essence(s) do I need to help me with this problem?" Read through the definitions again and note which one(s) *intuitively* pop out to you. (Of course, if you know kinesiology, you can simply test the list of essences, choosing the ones which test positive for you.) Order the essences that stand out when you read the definitions. (Try to keep your rational mind out of the process!) Take the essence(s) per the instructions in Chapter 16. Then see how you feel. Also, get the book *Flower Essences* so that you can understand more clearly when and how they are to be used.

❖ For those, like myself, who are immediately struck between the eyes by these things called "flower essences" and *know* they belong in your life, I strongly suggest that you get the **Basic Set** of Perelandra Essences—that is, the **Rose Essences (set I)** and the **Garden Essences**. This is an excellent starter combination for day-to-day process and issues. Now, to be honest with you, I've been reluctant to suggest this to people. I'm sensitive to the fact that we're talking about money here and, as the producer and developer of the Perelandra Essences, there is an obvious conflict of interest

This section on flower essences has been modified specially for the Workbook *from our 1997–98 catalog. Please understand that future price changes may not be reflected in this book. If you wish to order the essences and you think these prices may be old, just go ahead and mail or call in your order. We will notify you of any significant difference in pricing. You could also either request our current catalog or go to the Perelandra web site:* http://www.perelandra-ltd.com

in my suggestion. But now I feel urged to come out of the closet with this suggestion for three reasons:

1. These two sets often work in *combination* with one another. The Rose Essences address and support the various steps of the transition process we move through as we face daily challenge and change. The Garden Essences address specific issues on the physical, emotional, mental and spiritual levels that either trigger transition or arise because of it. In my work as an essence practitioner, I have found that often a person needs support for both the daily transition process itself and the specific issues coming up due to the process.

2. The Basic Set of Perelandra Essences covers a wide range of transition and specific issues. What is needed this week will often be different from what is needed next week or next month or next year. The essences are used one or two drops at a time and have an indefinite shelf life. In short, you'll be keeping and using the set for many years. It's fair to assume that you or someone close to you will be needing each of the essences at some point. It's more convenient to have them on hand when needed rather than have to order those specific bottles and wait for them to arrive in the mail before using them.

3. I've noticed over the past years that a fair number of people initially ordering single bottles or partial sets end up ordering the Basic Set. After using them, they came to the conclusion that to use the essences with the greatest agility and accuracy, one needs to have on hand the wide range provided by the Basic Set of Perelandra Essences.

I also suggest that when ordering the Basic Set of Perelandra Essences, you include *Flower Essences* along with your order. I know I am suggesting this book a lot. But I feel strongly that it will help you to organize and integrate the essences into your life in a precise and extremely effective manner.

Expanded Set of Perelandra Essences: In 1992 we developed a third set of flower essences: **Perelandra Rose Essences II**. This set of eight essences balances and stabilizes the body's central nervous system. They also address the balancing needs of our central nervous system that are activated and/or impacted during a deep expansion experience. These experiences, by their nature, require that we address and integrate something completely new and, as a result, we change our personal and world view. Here, one is not processing ordinary, everyday occurrences. Rather, one is faced with an experience that challenges the central nervous system's capability to balance and function. From the response we had from flower essences folks to this set, it seems that nearly everyone is testing for Rose II a lot. If you are interested in incorporating flower essences in your life, I suggest that you purchase the Expanded Set—that is, the Perelandra Rose and Garden Essences plus Rose Essences II.

Additional Essence Developments: The Perelandra Nature Program Essences were developed in 1993, and the Perelandra Soul Ray Essences were developed in 1994. For full descriptions of these two extraordinary essence sets, please see the Perelandra catalog. The Nature Program and Soul Ray Essences sets combined with the Expanded Set cover a full range of an individual's essence needs.*

With each purchase of Perelandra Essences—individual bottles or sets— you get the beginner's Guide, which gives the step-by-step basic processes for testing yourself for the essences you need and the correct dosage— i.e., how many drops of the essences are needed for how many days. Also included in the Guide are long definitions for each of the essences. Reading them will give you a clearer idea of what the essences address.

* I have also found that, in using the essences with Workbook *processes, bottles from all five sets (Garden, Rose, Rose II, Nature Program and Soul Ray) will test positive and need to be used in combination.*

Perelandra Rose Essences

The Perelandra Rose Essences are a set of eight flower essences. Made from roses in the Perelandra garden, these eight essences function with one another to support and balance an individual as he proceeds in day-to-day evolutionary process. As we move forward in daily process, there are mechanisms within us that are set in motion to facilitate our periods of growth. The Perelandra Rose Essences help stabilize and balance us and our process mechanisms.

To help clarify, the following are short definitions of the Perelandra Rose Essences. The name of each essence is the same as the rose from which it is made.

GRUSS AN AACHEN: Stability. Balances and stabilizes the body/soul unit on all PEMS levels (physical, emotional, mental, spiritual) as it moves forward in its evolutionary process.

PEACE: Courage. Opens the individual to the inner dynamic of courage that is aligned to universal courage.

ECLIPSE: Acceptance and insight. Enhances the individual's appreciation of his own inner knowing. Supports the mechanism which allows the body to receive the soul's input and insight.

ORANGE RUFFLES: Receptivity. Stabilizes the individual during the expansion of his sensory system.

AMBASSADOR: Pattern. Aids the individual in seeing the relationship of the part to the whole, in perceiving his pattern and purpose.

NYMPHENBURG: Strength. Supports and holds the strength created by the balance of the body/soul fusion and facilitates the ability to regain that balance.

WHITE LIGHTNIN': Synchronized movement. Stabilizes the inner timing of all PEMS levels moving in concert and enhances the body/soul fusion.

ROYAL HIGHNESS: Final stabilization. The mop-up essence that helps to insulate, protect and stabilize the individual and to stabilize the shift during its final stages while the individual is vulnerable.

Perelandra Rose Essences II

This set of Perelandra flower essences was developed in 1992. The eight essences are made from roses growing in the Perelandra garden and address the specific balancing and stabilizing needs of the body's central nervous system. They also address the functions within the central nervous system that are activated and/or impacted during a *deep expansion experience*. Here, one is not simply processing ordinary, everyday occurrences. Rather, one is faced with an experience that is new and challenging to the present balance and functioning of the body. When faced with this kind of expansion, the central nervous system is required to function in new ways, and with patterns and rhythms yet to be experienced. The Rose Essences II address this phenomenon by balancing and stabilizing this system's functions that have been impacted by the expansion.

I wish I could list specific experiences that would identify deep expansion situations for you, but a deep expansion for some is an everyday life process for others. The only thing I can say is that if you are interested in Perelandra and incorporating flower essences in your life, you are the kind of person who doesn't shy away from deep expansion. I think it would be good to have this set handy.

The following are the short definitions for Rose Essences II. The name of each essence is the same as the name of the rose from which it is made.

BLAZE IMPROVED CLIMBING ROSE: Softens and relaxes first the central nervous system and then the body as a whole, thus allowing the input from an expansion experience to be appropriately sorted, shifted and integrated within the body.

MAYBELLE STEARNS: Stabilizes and supports the sacrum during an expansion experience.

MR. LINCOLN: Balances and stabilizes the cerebrospinal fluid (CSF) pulse while it alters its rhythm and patterning to accommodate the expansion.

SONIA: Stabilizes and supports the CSF pulse after it has completed its shift to accommodate the expansion.

CHICAGO PEACE: Stabilizes movement of and interaction among the cranial bones, CSF and sacrum during an expansion experience.

BETTY PRIOR: Stabilizes and balances the delicate rhythm of expansion and contraction of the cranial bones during the expansion.

TIFFANY: Stabilizes the cranials as they shift their alignment appropriately to accommodate the input and impulses of expansion.

OREGOLD: Stabilizes and balances the cranials, central nervous system, CSF and sacrum after an expansion process is complete.

Perelandra Essences Prices

Just keep breathing! This price list may look complicated, but it's really not. What we're trying to do is give you as many options as possible for purchasing the flower essences you want with as much of a price break as we can give for each option.

BASIC SET: The Perelandra Rose (set I only) & Garden Essences: Both full sets purchased together. Available in 1/8-oz. (dram) and 1/2-oz. bottles. Perhaps it might help you decide which size set is better for you if I point out a couple of things.

1. Obviously, the 1/2-oz. set is more economical. The 1/2-oz. bottles are four times larger than those in a dram set. It consists of the 26 Perelandra Rose & Garden Essences in three boxes. It also includes the beginner's Guide with full definitions, plus instructions on how to test for the essences you need and how to do kinesiology. And you get a short-definitions card to tape on the inside of the box lid for quick reference.

Basic Set: 26 1/2-oz. bottles **E-301 . . . . $102**

2. The Basic Dram Set contains the 26 Perelandra Rose & Garden Essences, the Guide, 1 empty dram solution bottle and the short-definitions card in *one box* that measures 6-by-8 inches. This is convenient if you take the essences on trips or shift them between home and office.

Basic Dram Set: 26 dram bottles **E-204 . . . . $74**

EXPANDED SET: Includes the Basic Set (Perelandra Rose & Garden Essences) plus the Perelandra Rose Essences II Set. This combination is the most economical way to purchase all three flower essences sets.

Expanded Set: 34 1/2-oz. bottles **E-307 . . . . $136**

Expanded Dram Set: 34 dram bottles **E-309 . . . . $95**

ALL ESSENCES 1: The Perelandra Expanded Dram Set (Rose, Garden and Rose II Essences in 34 1/8-oz. bottles), plus the 17 Nature Program and Soul Ray Essences in the 1/2-oz. bottles. Each set is boxed (total of three boxes) and includes the beginner's Guide with full definitions, plus instructions on how to test the essences for yourself and others in your family. You also get a short-definitions card with each box to tape on the inside of the lid for quick reference.

All Essences 1: 34 dram bottles, 17 1/2-oz. bottles **E-601 . . . . $173**

ALL ESSENCES 2: All five sets of Perelandra Essences (51 bottles) in the larger 1/2-oz. bottles. Each set is boxed (total of six boxes) and includes the beginner's Guide and a short-definitions card with each box. The 1/2-oz. sets are more economical because the bottles are four times larger than those in the dram set.

All Essences 2: 51 1/2-oz. bottles **E-602 . . . . $214**

PERELANDRA ROSE ESSENCES SET: (set I) Includes a box with 8 dropper bottles (1/2-oz. bottles only), the Guide and the short-definitions card.

Rose Essences Set: 8 1/2-oz. bottles **E-201 . . . . $40**

PERELANDRA ROSE ESSENCES II SET: Includes a box with 8 dropper bottles (1/2-oz. bottles only), the Guide and the short-definitions card.

Rose Essences II Set: 8 1/2-oz. bottles only **E-202 . . . . $40**

PERELANDRA GARDEN ESSENCES SET: Two boxes containing a total of 18 dropper bottles (1/2-oz. bottles only), the Guide and two short-definitions cards to be taped to the inside of each box lid for quick reference.

Garden Essences Set: 18 1/2-oz. bottles only **E-203 . . . . $78**

PERELANDRA NATURE PROGRAM ESSENCES SET: A boxed set of 9 dropper bottles (1/2-oz. bottles only), the Guide and a short-definitions card.

Nature Program Essences Set: 9 1/2-oz. bottles only **E-205 . . . . $47**

PERELANDRA SOUL RAY ESSENCES SET: A boxed set of 8 dropper bottles (1/2-oz. bottles only), the Guide and a short-definitions card.

Soul Ray Essences Set: 8 1/2-oz. bottles only **E-206 . . . . $42**

INDIVIDUAL FLOWER ESSENCES: 1/2-oz. dropper bottles, plus the Guide. NOTE: We offer only 1/2-oz. bottles for refilling the dram set. One bottle will give you 4 dram refills.

Individual Bottles: List essences on order form. **E-101 . . . . $6.50 ea.**

NOTE: If you are sensitive to brandy, you may special order your essences preserved in distilled white vinegar. The prices are the same. Please note your request for vinegar on the order form.

Also, the Perelandra Essences are natural and will not interfere with any medications you may be taking. However, essences are not a substitute for needed medical care.

AND FINALLY: We guarantee the integrity and potency of the Perelandra Essences. They have an indefinite shelf life and we preserve them in a brandy or vinegar base to ensure that shelf life. Of course, we can't guarantee against mishaps that occur due to "user carelessness," such as replacing a dropper before washing it off after it has touched your mouth or having several bottles open at one time and forgetting which dropper went into which bottle. But we certainly back the integrity of the essences in the areas that we here at Perelandra can control.

FLOWER ESSENCES:
*Reordering Our Understanding
and Approach to Illness and Health*

Flower Essences is a complete and practical manual that describes the essences in a moving, down-to-earth and often humorous style. (Clarence told me to say all that.) I detail their extraordinarily beneficial effects on our health and balance. Also, I give easy, step-by-step procedures that help you discern which essences you need at specific times so that you can use them with precision and pinpoint accuracy. As with the *Workbook*, these are all procedures that have been worked out with nature and used successfully by me and others since 1979. Using personal examples, I explain how flower essences can improve our health and overall quality of life, and how the various procedures can dramatically change our approach to illness and health.

Included throughout is pertinent information from nature on the new direction of human health and how flower essences are a vital part of achieving this direction.

Flower Essences includes:

When to use flower essences
How the Perelandra flower essences are made
Techniques for determining which essences are needed
How to use them for colds, flu, asthma, allergies, etc.
Using them during serious illness and surgery
How to surrogate test
Using flower essences with therapeutic processes
When and how to test and treat children
Using flower essences during the death process
Using flower essences with animals and plants
Hints on buying flower essences

Appendix D
SUPPLIES AND RESOURCES

W. Atlee Burpee & Company
300 Park Ave.
Warminster, PA 18974
800/888-1447

Park Seed Company, Inc.
1 Parkton Ave.
Greenwood, SC 29647-0001
800/845-3369

Seed Savers Exchange
3076 N. Winn Rd.
Decorah, IA 52101
319/382-5990

For organic fertilizers:
Mellinger's Inc.
2310 W. South Range Rd.
North Lima, OH 44452-9731
800/321-7444

For the garden nets:
Gardener's Supply Company
128 Intervale Rd.
Burlington, VT 05401
800/863-1700

The Gruber Almanack Company
P.O. Box 609
Hagerstown, MD 21741-0609
301/733-2530

If you would like an international list of companies who produce flower essences, please send a self-addressed, stamped envelope to:
Perelandra, Ltd.
P.O. Box 3603
Warrenton, VA 20188

Lorusso & Glick. *Healing Stoned: The Therapeutic Use of Gems and Minerals.*
Brotherhood of Life
110 Dartmouth Dr., SE
Albuquerque, NM 87106
505/873-2179

For more information on our relationship with devas:
Dorothy Maclean. *To Hear the Angels Sing: An Odyssey of Co-Creation with the Devic Kingdom*
Lindisfarne Press (1990)
R.R. 4, Box 94A1
Hudson, NY 12534

The layout of pages 327 and 328 is dedicated to Elizabeth McHale!